BIG MONEY, BEAUTIFUL GAME

'They should get a reality check.'

Celtic chairman Fergus McCann, August 1998

BIG MONEY, BEAUTIFUL GAME

SAVING FOOTBALL FROM ITSELF

PAUL DEMPSEY
& KEVAN REILLY

NICHOLAS BREALEY
PUBLISHING

LONDON

To Samantha, Macarena and Gabriela

First published by
Nicholas Brealey Publishing Limited in 1998

36 John Street
London
WC1A 2AT, UK
Tel: +44 (0)171 430 0224
Fax: +44 (0)171 404 8311

1163 E. Ogden Avenue, Suite 705-229
Naperville
IL 60563-8535, USA
Tel: (888) BREALEY
Fax: (630) 428 3442

http://www.nbrealey-books.com

ISBN 1-85788-215-6

British Library Cataloguing in Publication Data
A catalogue record for this book is available from the
British Library.

Printed in Finland by Werner Söderström Oy.

CONTENTS

ACKNOWLEDGEMENTS

TWO OF US COLLABORATED TO PRODUCE THIS BOOK, BUT THERE is a sizeable group of others without whom it would never have been possible.

In particular, we would like to extend a Skinner and Baddiel-esque 'hello!' to – in a sort of chronological order – Ian Shuttleworth, Clinton Manning, Leslie Gardner, Alastair McLellan, Nick Brealey, Sally Lansdell and Andy Duffy. There are, to our knowledge, at least two Arsenal fans in that list, but we thank you all nevertheless.

This being a football book, a couple of pubs must also merit a mention, specifically The Redan in Bayswater, where this book was born, and The Park Tavern in Southfields, where Mick Reed and the rest of the staff had to endure numerous 'editorial conferences'. Mick's phlegmatic support for Spurs no doubt explains his extraordinary patience.

Then, on a more serious note, there are those figures from across the game and the financial world who agreed to be interviewed. We would like to thank them all – both those mentioned by name and those who preferred anonymity – for their openness and the frequent subtlety of their insights. As the saying goes, the good bits mostly started with these people, whereas the mistakes are all our own.

Almost finally, our love and thanks go out to our wives, Samantha Findjan and Macarena Vidal, and all our families. Living with two thirtysomething sports fans is bad enough, but enduring a pair who can legitimize their absence every Saturday afternoon because 'sorry, this is work, you know' can be trying.

Oh, and yes, before we go, a very, very big thank you to those former 'Boro superstars Fabrizio Ravanelli and Emerson. If it had not been for the startling impact you chaps made in the North East, we honestly would never have had the conversation that led to this book taking flight in the first place.

INTRODUCTION

A FINANCIAL REVOLUTION IS SWEEPING THROUGH FOOTBALL which threatens to destroy the game just as it has again rightfully claimed its role at the centre of British life. Throughout the 1970s and 1980s the game was in the grip of hooliganism and was seen as a social problem to be avoided by all right-thinking people. Now it is rich and fashionable and beloved by all right-on people.

Much of the froth and talk about the new riches in football is harmless. Supporters can see that the game has improved. There are much better stadia with world-class foreign players performing in them. Fans of English clubs can boast about having World Cup winners in their squad again all these years after 1966.

But the transformation has been bought at a price and it is a price that will shortly become much, much higher. And that price will be paid by the fans. Supporters can already complain that they pay through the nose for tickets, TV subscriptions and merchandising. They may be worried that multimillionaire footballers are becoming too big for their boots. But at the moment they can console themselves with the fact that there is still a game to watch. Once the revolution reaches its inevitable conclusion, they will not be able to watch the game they know and love.

Big money now rules the beautiful game. 'New Football' has changed enormously and it is all down to money. The game has wads of the stuff and is not afraid of boasting about it. Indeed, it is good at boasting but bad at communicating and worse at listening. It is worst of all at looking into the future and deciding what sort of game it wants to be.

The rules have been changed by the money, to the extent that nobody now really knows what the rules are. The FAs and UEFAs and FIFAs, which ought to be in complete control, are not. Super-clubs, media moguls and even players have taken over their role. The European Union is more powerful than any administrator, capable of destroying the transfer system and threatening to do the same to the way in which the leagues sell rights to watch their games on television. But the European Union is not in control – because nobody is.

Nature abhors a vacuum and football has had a sight of what will fill the space, as this book will show. Multinational companies have already come close to buying leading English clubs with the specific intention of using them to turn the game into a shadow of US sports. It is almost inevitable that we will have clubs as super-powers unfettered by national leagues and superstar players totally removed from the censure of their clubs. The prospect of the same few clubs winning everything forever is a grim one, but it looms large.

Multinationals are being attracted by the fortunes made by British club owners. They recognize that the game is seen, in the jargon of the City of London, as being 'all about brands and media rights'. That translates as merchandising and TV. Fans are fed a diet of multimillion transfer deals, multimillion pay deals and multi-million business deals. Games are routinely referred to as £10 million or £20 million or even £50 million matches, because of the riches on offer to the winners and the financial damage done to the losers.

The clearest illustration of football's descent into a corporate mire is the proposed European Super League. This mooted replacement for the Champions' League (which has itself ousted the European Cup) would offer a diet of at least eight games on each midweek evening throughout the traditional season and would feature the continent's most glamorous – but not necessarily most successful – sides pitting their wits against one another. Teams involved in the talks make it seem a mouthwatering prospect: Manchester United, Arsenal and Liverpool have been invited to the party, as have Real Madrid, Barcelona, AC and Inter Milan, Ajax and Paris St Germain, among others. The idea is that this would be a great draw both at the turnstiles and on television. But what about that old-fashioned sporting notion of competition?

The Super League is a worrying development because it is a concept based not on sport but on profitability. The bigger members should not initially need to suffer the indignity of relegation, under one of the more popular blueprints, thereby guaranteeing that they will spend the first six years of its existence earning millions regardless of their on-pitch performance. The fact that others will be given 'a chance' later on is hardly mitigated by the fact that those seasons of free money for the founders will emphasize still further their muscle in the international transfer market and on their balance sheets.

And who is behind this idea? A media titan, of course. Former Italian Prime Minister Silvio Berlusconi still dominates Italian commercial TV and owns AC Milan. His vision is of the best of the best competing on his networks (or one should perhaps say 'his vision of the best'). What this means for those beyond Berlusconi's horizon, and indeed his idea of what these sunset clubs have contributed and continue to contribute to football, are topics for lively debate.

All for one?

The big money takeover of the beautiful game means that the old ethos of all clubs together will finally be dumped. Until now, football has roughly held to the view that the big clubs need the smaller teams if the game is to prosper. After all, Manchester United has to have other clubs to play and has to be seen to lose every now and then to keep the game exciting. And who would have thought that most fans would welcome the often equally loathed Arsenal pipping United to the 1997–8 title?

But inside the game this community view is now seen as sentimental claptrap fit only for the knacker's yard. That this Old Football nostrum has persisted is surprising in any case. In the UK, the foundation of the English Premiership and its Scottish counterpart means that the game is only paying lip service to the idea that the big and the small live and die together.

New Football, with its talk of European Super Leagues, is having none of it. The men who run the English and Scottish Premierships want to take more control over their finances and are having none of it either.

Football faces a fight between two alternative and uniformly bleak visions of the future. Some inside the game believe that now is the time for football to cut the number of clubs so that those that are left can divide the spoils more fairly. Others simply believe that football is a branch of the entertainment sector and has to put on the best show for television.

Both views mean a cull of clubs. This might sound reasonable to some fans. After all, if a club does not have enough supporters and enough money to survive, what is wrong with it shutting down? Plenty have gone bust in the past, as the supporters of Aldershot, Accrington Stanley and Third Lanark can testify.

But the slaughter will not be well organized and will not be a case of only the lowly. English football could be reduced to 40 of its current 92 and Scottish football to 20 of its current 40 clubs. It would not just be the obscure and unloved who would be out of business. Big-name clubs with large and dedicated followings would go bust. And once a club goes bust it is banished from the professional football world.

The damage will spread wider because football, for all its new-found riches, is not playing the business game at all well. The game has always been a business but never really a properly run one, as the finances of smaller clubs show. Many of these minnows are already close to collapse and prone to rely on ridiculous ways out, as this book will show.

Where the money goes

The game in the 1990s may claim that throughout Europe it is run by shrewder businesspeople than ever before, it may be earning more money than ever before and it may be more fashionable than ever before. Yet its business plan is in a mess and it is managing to lose more money than ever before, while also annoying its supporters more than ever before.

Fans are angry, and rightly so. Fear and loathing abound about £1000-plus season-ticket prices, £40 replica kits and multimillion pound television deals. Ticket prices are pushing supporters out of the game and TV subscription charges are alienating stay-at-home fans.

Communication from directors to club followers is at best per-functory and at worst contemptuous. They are not able to shake people's widespread feeling that the game is being milked dry by owners and shareholders on a 'get-rich-quick' campaign.

On top of its inability to talk to its fans, the game is incapable of doing much with its riches. In the past decade the money coming into the game has risen twentyfold. Yet the cash still floods out and the majority of clubs are reporting loss after loss after loss.

It is the players who are bathing in the flood of money. A 1998 report by consultants Deloitte & Touche showed that average wage rises in the English Premier League are running at 35 per cent, compared with the 5 per cent average increases that British workers are getting. The money paid to top players climbs and climbs, with each season bringing a new landmark. The £42,000-a-week players? We've now gone past that to £50,000.

When clubs were run by wealthy men, either as playthings or as contributions to the local community, this kind of thing did not matter too much. If they wanted to waste it, it was their money.

But now the role of big money means that clubs are playing a different version of financial football with much higher stakes. Almost 30 European clubs – from Preston North End and Millwall to Manchester United, Ajax and Bayern Munich - have floated or are about to float on the stock markets. Many others have had to bring in institutional shareholders or venture capitalists or even raise cash on bond markets.

The banks providing the money are not in football for fun. They want dividends and profits off the back of the game's riches and they are already running scared. The City of London's ardour has cooled dramatically as the moneymen wake up to just what is going on. Since mid-1997, most clubs have seen their share prices fall because of the financiers' concerns.

Clubs and the City all bought into the idea that digital television was the way ahead, based on breathless reports about the value of pay-per-view match broadcasts. Everyone thought that supporters would happily pay to watch the English game of their choice rather than stump up each month to watch what BSkyB chose to show.

Consultants vied to come up with even bigger estimates of the value of pay-per-view. Bids started at £1 billion, then hit £2 billion and kept on going before the cracks started to appear. In 1998, England's Premier League voted against its introduction, supposedly because it did not want to anger supporters any further.

That explanation ignored the fact that Sports Minister Tony Banks was threatening clubs with the prospect of government regulation and that there had been pay-per-view experiments in Spain, Italy and France which had drawn smaller than predicted audiences.

The continental experience shows that only a country's top two or three sides draw enough viewers, leaving the Premiership's smaller clubs worrying whether this goldmine would only benefit Arsenal, Newcastle United, Liverpool and, of course, Manchester United.

Other parts of football's wealth dream are turning into nightmares. The merchandising boom is slowing and will get worse. Clubs such as Spurs and even Man United have already admitted that kit sales have fallen. A major sportswear group, Pentland, is gradually pulling its Pony brand out of kit sponsorship. The beautiful game is heading for an ugly reckoning.

But it's not over yet

This book looks at the debate about the game's future by examining it as a business but from a fan's viewpoint. Football needs to change and change in a way that benefits not just the owners but the supporters as well.

Our aim is to set out in plain English how the football economy works and how it has reached the position it now faces. But more importantly, we want to get the message across that it is not yet too late for the game to overcome its difficulties. Football might be 2–1 down, but it is still only half-time.

CHAPTER ONE

IT'S MORE IMPORTANT THAN THAT

They think the goose is going to keep on laying the golden eggs. That it'll never stop. Well, I don't buy into that. It could so easily all go very wrong. I don't think that football has fully digested or understood many of the big money changes that have been going on recently.

Tony Banks, Minister for Sport, Football Task Force meeting, London, June 1998

IN THE LAST 10 YEARS, BRITISH FOOTBALL HAS BEEN transformed, some would even say reinvented. Growing numbers of supporters watch the game in state-of-the-art stadia and at some point every weekend a host of World Cup stars (plus Paul Gascoigne) seeks to entertain them. As in the UK, so now in Europe, as continental clubs adapt the same, chiefly financial techniques that have reinvigorated the British sport and pulled it back from the very brink of extinction.

But there is serious and growing disquiet among both supporters and football professionals and it goes beyond the dour gruffness typically associated with both communities. The game has undergone many necessary changes, yet there is a strong feeling that it has forgotten its roots in the process, roots that are not merely cultural but also economic. In a sport where passion and pride play such important roles, any revolution that renders clubs

– the vital brands of the industry – faceless and sterile and leaves many of the customers disillusioned and disaffected is bound eventually to provoke another uprising.

The rush of British clubs to the Stock Exchange has led many supporters to believe that directors, who are supposed to have a custodial role, have begun to indulge in the naked and destructive exploitation of what defines a club in itself and of its followers. For passion read profit, for glory read income streams and revenue projections. The day is coming when share options mean more than England caps and Goal of the Season is judged not on the most spectacular moment of skill but on the penalty that wins a play-off shootout or European Cup and brings millions of pounds to the victors. However, the changes afoot are about more than greed.

City of London-backed bonanzas may be only the beginning of a more dangerous process that sees football's cultural and regional strengths swallowed up within the ambitions of conglomerates and multinationals. It may surprise you, but so far most, although, importantly, not all of the game's loyal fans have found that they can live with high ticket prices, overpriced souvenirs and monthly direct debits to pay-TV companies. They shouldn't have to put up with this, but they do.

Would they still be so phlegmatic if the game were shrunk to about half its current size and decisions about buying players and charging supporters were taken not in the stadium's boardroom, but a glass-clad edifice in London's Docklands, New York or even Atlanta, Georgia? And these decisions would be based on some very strange criteria.

More than a club?

An English Premiership club should already have its headquarters in Atlanta, alongside Coca-Cola and the global news network CNN. This historic city is the base of media mogul Ted Turner, and Mr Turner is very keen to buy a football club. In fact, he is so keen that he was once within days of getting himself one and achieving this is still very much on his agenda.

Fans worried by the financial revolution that has hit European football have often joked about the Walt Disney Company buying their clubs and making the players dress up as Mickey Mouse. Sometimes they would see this as an appropriate punishment for their highly paid idols when they play badly. But these have only really been jokes about how far the financial takeover of the game would go. Nobody has ever appreciated just how close the game came to domination by seriously big money.

The fully fledged corporate takeover did very nearly become reality. In a series of secret meetings during the Spring of 1995, Ted Turner's executives scouted England looking for a club to buy. They had a specific shopping list and looked closely at a number of teams. Inevitably Manchester United was the top choice, but Arsenal and Leeds United also figured in their calculations.

Turner, who founded CNN and is married to Jane Fonda, currently sits as vice-president of Time Warner, the world's largest media company. One source close to the original talks comments:

> *Buying a Manchester United or an Arsenal or some team like that was a key component in a strategy to create an English-language entertainment channel. One which could boast a guaranteed audience from Day One, not only in competition with Sky but also the BBC and ITV networks.*

He adds that there were 'plenty of takers' and that the 'numbers really worked for us'.

Another senior footballing figure says:

> *Ted's lawyers could see that Brussels was likely to interpret EU competition law to make teams auction their TV rights individually rather than through leagues and associations. So that would cancel out the Premier League's deal with Sky, and piss Murdoch off.*

A takeover by Turner might not seem that terrible. It is entirely possible to construct a benign and attractive picture of football life under Ted. After all, whatever angry fans may have to say about Rupert Murdoch and BSkyB's control of the British game, the so-called Mouth from the South can come up with something much more abusive. Given the two men's business rivalry, Ted knows how you feel – because he feels the same.

He is a genuine sports fan, although his enthusiasm is for American sports. Anyone who thinks they could do a better job of managing their team can sympathize with him: Mr Turner, who already owns Major League Baseball's Atlanta Braves and the National Basketball Association's Atlanta Hawks, once briefly stepped in to coach the Braves when he reckoned his players were not performing well enough.

He would bring even more glamour to the English Premiership. With all due respect to pop divas Louise and Posh Spice, Jane Fonda is in a different class. She would undeniably be only the second Oscar winner to enter a director's box by right (the first was Elton John!).

There would be no problem with money for Turner's team. Cash would definitely be available for players and there would be none of this tight-fisted moaning about maintaining salary ceilings. Zidane? *Pas de problème*. Del Piero? *Non c'e problema*. Ronaldo? Don't wet the bed over it. And rest assured, he would bring players like that to the English game.

However, the arrival of Turner or someone like him in an English football boardroom would be the beginning of the end for what remains of the traditional game. He views ownership of European sporting sides almost entirely in terms of the rights they hold, for TV and elsewhere.

It is a tactic he pioneered in the US during the early 1980s with the Hawks and the Braves. He used those teams to guarantee exclusive coverage of games on his national cable TV network, the TNT SuperStation. Turner has long wanted to have a similarly broad-based channel up and running in Europe, particularly Britain, to compete with and weaken his archrival Murdoch. At the moment, his specialist networks – CNN plus The Cartoon Network and TNT with its classic movies – lag some way behind BSkyB in the European ratings, but Premiership football would make a big difference.

The original 1995 bid plan was scuppered when Turner merged his then independent Turner Broadcasting System with Time Warner and the terms of the deal forced him to put all capital acquisitions on hold. But those moles close to Turner suggest that he is ready to come back for a second bite. One remarked:

> *Only the block on capital acquisitions stopped them but, believe me, a lot of the Turner people who've moved to Time Warner want to put this kind of deal together soon, even if the price tags on the big English clubs have gone up in the last few years.*

That someone like Turner is interested in British football demonstrates perfectly the way in which European sporting teams are now viewed by their current and, more importantly, future owners.

This is no longer simply about acknowledging football as a big business. Not that long ago, even Britain's biggest club, Manchester United, was predominantly a regional rather than an international club. It was, like other sides, a reflection of the hopes and dreams of a very specific, geographic community. Its ownership was local and its purpose was to deliver a very glamorous variant of the football drug to its slice of the North West. It was, to borrow Spanish giant Barcelona's famous motto, 'more than a club'.

United's image today is different. It is still fair to say that it is more than a club, but as City analyst Nigel Hawkins of brokers Williams De Broe explains, the meaning behind that phrase has changed:

> *If you look at what makes up United's perceived market value, it starts with the football and its tremendous success in the Premier League, but then it goes some way beyond that. United is a collection of media and merchandising rights, it is a global brand, it is seen as a very wide-ranging series of possibilities. As such, that doesn't make it attractive to only a typical club owner, the ambitious or egotistical local tycoon, but to any firm – and it need not just be a media firm – that can see ways of tapping into those opportunities.*

As the moneymen in the City of London have recognized the change, so has Turner. He cannot even really be described as a European pioneer in his attempts to buy into Premier League football, although his ambitions and financial muscle are way beyond other contenders. Even by 1995, two major continental clubs – AC Milan and Paris St Germain – had been in the hands of broadcasters for some time. Former Italian Prime Minister and European Super League exponent Silvio Berlusconi bought AC to add to his ReteItalia TV empire in 1986, and France's leading pay-TV firm Canal Plus acquired Paris St Germain in 1991. There were restrictions on what they could do with the TV rights. Berlusconi initially had to watch Italy's state broadcaster Rai retain exclusive coverage of Serie A, including AC, Milan, although he could show friendly matches and his side's at one point all-conquering European outings. Canal Plus, meanwhile, primarily saw Paris St Germain as a way to make sure that it was included in French league TV negotiations rather than as a route to exclusivity in itself. However, both groups had got themselves an important seat at the table.

But in 1996, two court judgments based on European Union law made those seats look a lot more comfortable and began a review of the traditional relationship between football and television which has yet to be settled.

Judges in both Germany and the Netherlands concluded that certain deals between national European leagues and broadcasters breached competition law, because leagues, in these instances, were acting as cartels. Instead, the courts ruled that each individual club should have the right to strike its own separate rights deals for home games. Because of its basis in EU competition law, these rulings suggest that deals such as that between BSkyB, the BBC and the English Premier League could soon be broken and that the remainder of the UK's footie-starved channels then also be allowed to bid for what they consider to be the most attractive games. This opens up the prospect of more media firms actually buying clubs.

According to the Turner insider, his TBS operation had seen such a change on the horizon even in 1995 and wanted to buy into the English game before a formal judgment in a UK court sent valuations on the top sides skyrocketing. Nobody doubts that under these circumstances Murdoch and others would want to do the same. One ex-BSkyB executive says:

The big kicker will be if the leagues are forced to unpick all their domestic TV rights deals. If each club has to do its own sales, all hell will break loose. Never mind Ted Turner, Murdoch will be in there like a shot. He'll just have lost the one thing – control of live Premier League games – that really delivers Sky subscriptions. Martin Edwards at Manchester United could probably think of a number, triple it, and still have Rupert begging to sign the cheque.

But today in the eyes of the media moguls, there is more to the football business than TV. The TBS–Time Warner merger also opened Turner's eyes to markets such as merchandising. Time makes movies, music, TV and books and then exploits its brands with considerable skill. Its Warner Bros Studio Stores have mushroomed across the globe throughout the 1990s, with their range of Bugs Bunny, Friends and Batman-emblazoned clothes and knick-knacks. Following the Turner deal, Warner added 'properties' from his library including Scooby Doo, the Flintstones and the original Wizard of Oz, and they have done very nicely, much to Mr Turner's satisfaction. If this side of the company were also to move into football, the opportunities would be obvious.

In an intriguing deal, Warner announced in March 1998 that it was effectively franchising control of these shops to an outfit called the English National Investment Company. ENIC is an investment trust which has itself developed a football portfolio involving shares in four European clubs with controlling interests in three – Rangers (ENIC's minority stake), AEK Athens, Slavia Prague and Vicenza. The published agreement with Time Warner does not mention any sporting deals, but the possibilities must have occurred to someone.

Among the really big entertainment players, any high-budget film or TV proposal is not examined today just on the basis of the quality of the script, but also on its merchandising opportunities. Once you see the film you are expected to buy the T-shirt and eat the pizza. Warner's own surprise flop in 1997, its fourth Bat-movie *Batman and Robin*, was dismissed by critics and public alike for being no more than a long toy advertisement. Football or any sport is no different in the minds of media moguls.

And it is not just Time Warner and ENIC that are promoting a new, more all-encompassing view of the football club as, to lapse into the patois of international commerce, a multitiered business opportunity. IMG, the company run by *überagent* Mark McCormack, has considerable experience not just in broadcasting but wider marketing and merchandising agreements and sales. It was appointed to drum up sponsorship for London's Millennium Dome, for example. IMG is also looking to build up a number of 'well-priced' club holdings.

It all adds up to a vision of the future which is light years away from the very recent past.

'There used to be a football club here'

Keith Burkinshaw's famous parting shot on quitting as Tottenham Hotspur's manager in 1984, shortly after its Stock Exchange flotation, has become a motto for all those who believe that big money has already destroyed much of what was good about football. Burkinshaw had been the club's most successful boss since the legendary double-winning Bill Nicholson and the team he built won the 1984 UEFA Cup under his successor Peter Shreeves. However, he had no time for the recently installed Irving Scholar-led plc regime. Too many bean counters, too many marketing men, too much emphasis on profit and nowhere near enough football. 'Glory, glory, Tottenham Hotspur' – not any more, thought Keith.

Over a decade later, resistance to any further corporate moves into football would continue to focus on perceived damage to the character of the game and mounting complaints about poor relations with, and shoddy treatment of, supporters. If Chelsea chairman Ken Bates believed he could get away with a top-of-the-range £1250 season ticket in 1998 and yet still claim to have the good of the club at heart, what might a pinstriped, profits-hungry Wall Street executive think he could levy?

However, a longer-term analysis of the potential consequences of opening football up to the Turners and IMGs of this world gives Burkinshaw's comment an even more chilling force. If big owners move in, many clubs will die not figuratively but in reality. When Deloitte & Touche partner and football consultancy guru Gerry Boon introduced his firm's 1996–7 *Annual Review of Football*

Finance, he made two observations: there will be growing corporate investment in the game and there will be more club financial crises. 'As the market develops, it will become clear that it cannot support as many teams as we have today,' he added.

The financial environment in British football has loaded the pressures facing many smaller clubs to near breaking point. The game's problems with the distribution of income are widely recognized. Teams in the FA Premier League earn at least £6 million a season from TV alone, and this is five times as much as their rivals in the competition immediately below them, Football League Division One. At the same time, the cost differentials between the two divisions are far narrower, particularly for wage bills. In 1997–8, at least three First Division clubs – Nottingham Forest, Middlesbrough and Sunderland – had salary costs that were equal to those of many sides in the Premiership and many more were not that far behind. With the riches on offer in the top flight tending to set the going rates, Football League clubs are therefore already in crisis – meeting the bills essentially means taking on ever-growing mountains of debt or, equally dangerous, slumping back and accepting that the team will never have the resources to meet the ambitions and demands of its supporters.

Already, First Division clubs are showing the strain over aspects of their finances that will affect their long-term viability. Less TV money and increasing wage costs have meant higher ticket prices. The cheapest seat at Selhurst Park to watch Terry Venables' Crystal Palace in Division One during the 1998–9 season was £16, compared with £21 at Tottenham Hotspur and £22 at Chelsea. There is, therefore, roughly a 25 per cent differential, reflecting the lower level of competition. But Palace's prices were still at a level where some fans complained that either they could not go themselves or, more worrying for the club if it is to have a fan base five or ten years hence, that they could no longer afford to take their children, even if they would continue to support the team.

Allowing for some child reductions (as rare as a hen's molar at many grounds anyway), tickets for a family of two together with food, parking and everything else needed for a 'day out' could see a dad run up a final bill in the region of £100, just for the First Division. And that is a level of expenditure supposedly to be made every other Saturday during the season, rather than once in a while at, say, the Chessington, Alton Towers or Legoland theme parks.

This is just one part of what many clubs and supporters' organizations are already calling the 'little acorns' problem. Another concerns a lower-division club's ability to develop talent. In the traditional football economy, clubs outside the elite have survived by selling players to bigger teams. To some extent, the Bosman ruling giving footballers total freedom of movement at the end of their contracts (see Chapter 4) has made this much more difficult – poorer clubs cannot afford to give nascent talent long-term contracts, so they run the risk of developing future superstars who can leave their first clubs without the people who initially trained them receiving any financial reward whatsoever. However, the drain on resources that a Football League side endures merely to maintain its first-team wage budget adds still further to its difficulties.

Youth policies are proving increasingly difficult to maintain as Premier League and a handful of richer First Division clubs establish fully equipped training 'academies' with state-of-the-art facilities, while their lesser brethren struggle merely to replace a shower head or a set of hand weights. It really is getting that bad in many cases, as clubs are driven to deal with their most immediate priorities and, in effect, damn the future.

This all adds up to higher costs, a battle to recruit supporters, a dearth of youngsters and a squeeze on the bottom line at the most basic level.

More corporate ownership would tip many smaller clubs over the edge. Many of the likely buyers would spend heavily and have the resources comfortably to outstrip anything seen in the game so far. Manchester United is undoubtedly a wealthy club with millions of pounds in the bank, but it simply does not compare with Time Warner, which boasts worldwide revenues in excess of $20 billion.

A Turner or a Murdoch as club owner would invest vast sums, because it would be a prerequisite that the teams they controlled were always successful. They would have to be to deliver the ratings and sell the merchandising that would be the most absolute requirements of the business plan. By whatever means necessary, they would seek out the best players, thereby inflating transfer fees and wages across the board, pour millions more into marketing, and continually seek a holy grail where only a handful of clubs dominated all competitions in perpetuity. To reduce the risks, they would point across the Atlantic. In the US, they already have considerable sporting interests; there is often no relegation or promotion from the most elite leagues – membership is elective; there are strict controls on how many teams can operate in a single area; and there are options to move clubs to regions that are not represented in major competitions.

In this scenario, even if the lower leagues continued to exist, they would be scrambling for attention with megaclubs that received ever more wall-to-wall promotion on TV, in newspapers and through all other major media outlets. With this kind of muscle being applied, the door would be shut for ever more to those outside a small elite.

This may sound like a nightmare. But it is not that far from the point which football has already reached. A club such as Hull City has a large catchment area – 265,000 people in the metropolitan area – and no competing teams nearby. Yet it recently came close to collapse and still struggles to fill its 13,000 capacity stadium. Its biggest competition comes not, as you might expect, from the North's 'other' national game, rugby league, but from football on TV, particularly Premier League coverage. As a club spokeswoman commented:

> *Premier League clubs do not just have the money, they have the image. Sky sells those 20 teams hard. It says: 'This is what's worth watching, forget everything else.'*

Take a walk around Hull's shopping centres and the implications become clear. In sports shop after sports shop, window displays are dominated not by kits for local teams, but by those from Manchester United, Arsenal, Liverpool and Leeds United – and that list includes two Lancashire clubs getting a big push on the 'wrong' side of the Pennines. Hull may even be lucky. In other regions, lots of close neighbours compete for their slice of the pie. Even when they have successful seasons, teams like Bury, Rochdale, Stockport County, Bolton Wanderers and the beleaguered Manchester City are attempting to build for the future in the immediate shadow of Man United, while in London and its immediate surroundings 18 teams fight for supporters' attention, with typically a third of these in the Premier League at any one time.

Bill New, author of a report on New Football's relationship with TV published by the DEMOS think tank, says:

> *I suppose that there has always been the scope in English football for a few club sides becoming national rather than regional teams. Big clubs, usually the most successful as well, have sometimes achieved national profiles with nationwide support. This is not necessarily a bad thing, if the overall economy of the game is kept in balance. You saw it happen with Liverpool in the 1970s, but it didn't mean that they started to gobble up so much of the available spending that the other clubs were driven to the wall. That was because the game's income was more evenly divided up. The difference now is because of the way the money is shared out, with the big clubs getting so much more than everyone else because of the Premier League. When the Man Uniteds, the Arsenals and the Liverpools sell more merchandising and get the big TV audiences, the extent to which that eats into what the smaller clubs can earn becomes much more noticeable and much more dangerous.*

A big conglomerate would want any team it controlled to be a 'national' side. This would, as noted before, be essential in developing spinoffs and building TV audiences. It would be the only way to justify the expenditure that would initially be involved.

In the Premier League itself, serious difficulties are already being created by a distinct gap between the riches at the summit and those even at the middle of the top flight. TV deals favour the biggest sides with large merit components for appearances on the air and league position, but the income goes up higher still for those who get into European competitions. That bastard son of the European Cup, the Champions' League, is a licence to print money, with millions of Swiss francs on offer even to sides that do poorly during the group stage. The UEFA and Cup Winners' Cups also carry major financial benefits, as in these cases British clubs are already free to strike individual TV deals. The proposed European Super League can only exacerbate the situation.

This disparity is forcing some clubs to spend almost as much as they earn just to stay in the top division, as the greater resources of the richer clubs above continue to drive up wages and transfer costs. Alan Sugar, Spurs' ebullient and abrasive chairman, has characterized this as the 'prune juice' effect. The financial balance in a supposed wonderland of riches is therefore very delicate, and a sequence of events that could take a club from apparent comfort to desperation is not beyond the bounds of possibility. As Bill New says:

You do see some examples in the Premier League of not so much day-by-day as season-by-season existence. Every year, what comes in is just about balanced by what is going out and the team ploughs on without ever really banking that much for a rainy day. So if the price of competing were to get considerably higher, if the top teams really inflated the costs, then even some apparently wealthy sides would find themselves in serious trouble. Basically, you're looking at any club from about tenth or eleventh downwards.

Further corporate investment, therefore, could deliver the killer blow to many more clubs than even some pessimists have suggested. The clubs at risk would not just be the halt and the lame, the teams which historically have had little support or are simply badly run. After all, there are only so many big firms out there likely to shop for major clubs. There are certainly not enough to support all 132 teams that play in the main English and Scottish competitions. The effect would be no more or less than that which supermarket chains like Tesco and Sainsbury's have had on the corner shop. One former Second Division director commented:

Once upon a time, small clubs had a role. They fed players through to the major divisions and they served their communities. That has all changed in the last 10 years. The money now going around in the Premier League means that clubs shop more widely for talent. On one side of the question, the leading teams want to buy the international superstars, on the other, they argue that the standard young English player has become overpriced, so they go to Eastern Europe instead. The stars are there to help Mr Murdoch sell his subscriptions. At the same time, lower-league English talent may look expensive, but that again is a reflection of overall inflation in the game caused by, and it's a bitter irony, the spendthrifts at the top of the game. Either way, a smallish club is now like a fringe supplier or retailer in a big market sector, and that means he is going to get squeezed and squeezed and squeezed.

In traditional industrial parlance, this is called consolidation. Many gung-ho free marketeers will tell you that it is simply an inevitability of the marketplace – a sector shrinks to the number of players that it can properly support. But given football's history, is this desirable either socially or economically? Almost certainly not, but this is the inexorable direction in which the game is headed.

And the greatest irony of all is that, while some experts may believe that this makes perfect economic sense even if it could be a social catastrophe, it could ultimately leave the whole game – big and small, rich and poor – in ruins. Big teams depend on there being a wider community of sides. They need competition and they also need some kind of ranking to justify their own positions at the head of the pack.

All sporting economies are unarguably interdependent. In football's case this was well expressed by one Inverness Caledonian Thistle fan on Channel 4's magazine show *Under The Moon*:

Football is a hierarchical meritocracy, and in a hierarchical meritocracy, somebody needs to be Rangers and somebody needs to be shite! Caley fulfils that second role.

The problem for football is that its long-established meritocracy faces the danger that it could become an invincible oligarchy with a small clique of clubs dominating everything for ever. That would not merely ruin the game, it would be an example of self-destructive economics.

Together we stand, together we fall

The idea that football should reduce and consolidate has wider implications for the game's future. Economist S. Rottenberg wrote the following about American baseball over 40 years ago in a classic analysis of the sports business that still applies today to football or any other team game:

> *Two teams opposed to each other in play are like two firms producing a single product. The product is the game, weighted by the revenues derived from its play. With game admission prices given, the product is the game weighted by the number of paying customers who attend. When 30,000 attend, the output is twice as large as when 15,000 attend. In one sense the teams compete; in another, they combine in a single firm in which the success of each branch requires that it be not 'too much' more efficient than the other. If it is, output falls.*

In all team sports, even individual sports like golf, tennis and athletics, there has to be what economists call uncertainty of outcome and what most fans would recognize as Man United being dumped out of the FA Cup by Barnsley. 'Anything can happen over the next 90 minutes', 'It only takes a second to score a goal' and 'It ain't over till it's over' – all good clichés and yet all sporting essentials.

As Rottenberg observes, the issue is not that no team can be better than another can, it is that one team becomes 'too much' better. In the football economy this can as easily apply to a group of teams, an elite, if that group is never properly challenged from outside. Corporate football, however, wants it that way. Even before large owners have arrived on the scene, the Premier League's chairmen have, on three separate occasions since 1996, tried to reduce the number of teams promoted and, more importantly for them, relegated each season. When various disputes between them and the Football League have arisen, there have even been dark mutterings about abandoning relegation altogether – nobody is wrenched from the cash cow, but nobody new gets to attach themselves either. The European Super League goes further in being initially established on a 'no relegation' basis.

In their initial phases, periods of domination by one, two or three clubs in foreign leagues have seen overall attendances fall although the most successful clubs have continued to prosper. However, in the longer term, even the sides at the top see fans stay away. The best example of this occurring recently was in Spain, where Barcelona and Real Madrid dominated the championship during the late 1980s up until 1996. The deadly rivals both control 100,000-plus capacity stadia and, when playing one another or in European competition, these were not difficult to fill. But with only a handful of exceptions – particularly their local derbies against Espanyol and Atletico Madrid respectively – they found it difficult to get anywhere near these levels the rest of the time.

Spanish fans are even more passionate than their English rivals, but these supporters could not be bothered if they felt that the opposition was not up to much, and attendances of 60,000, only a fraction above the season-ticket audience at both clubs, were common. Year-on-year declines in average gate were a factor throughout that decade. In the mid-1990s, a sudden influx of – surprise, surprise – TV money has reinvigorated Spanish competition, with clubs like Real Betis emerging to challenge the duopoly, but the figures are still some way from what they could look like. It is one of the great ironies of Spanish football that for all but the very biggest games you go to a ticket tout in Madrid to buy a seat for *less* than its face value.

This should be an instructive lesson for all other Premier Leagues and their counterparts, and there are some signs that a few clubs have taken it on board. But the general trend remains towards exclusivity and strictly defined tiers of competition. The fact that, as the Scottish fan said, it is largely the Caleys of this world that make the Rangers and Celtics look as good as they do is being lost. In essence, it is as though the changes to football now underway have allowed a new breed of owners to forget completely what the game is all about. Competition is not just about winning – it is about having someone to compete with. And it is about giving fans something they will pay for.

For the good of the game

By mid-1998, sports minister Tony Banks was hinting that he would like to introduce some kind of formal regulation for British football. However, at the time of writing, it seems more likely that this would involve an ombudsman-type figure to control the prices charged to supporters, rather than an individual who would regulate financial competition in the sport and the distribution of income. Nevertheless, Banks told a public meeting of the Football Task Force in London that he recognized that patterns of club ownership, stock market flotations and various other financial developments were reshaping the football landscape and needed to be watched closely. He even suggested that much of the problem may stem from the fact that not merely were fans being blatantly exploited, but football's major investors still had not fully digested the implications of the changes taking place and understood how their economy works.

As New Labour met New Football, a game like the political creed reinvigorated by a drive towards the middle classes, Banks was careful not to raise too many social or woolly liberal concerns about football's conduct, preferring to draw direct economic comparisons between the game's business practices and those of utilities like water, electricity and gas. In each case, this passionate Chelsea fan said that there were forms of monopoly at work:

> *If I don't like the product on offer at Chelsea, I can't ditch that and go down to West Ham instead. Football doesn't work like that. As I keep saying, it's more like a drug. You end up with an addiction to a particular team.*

All this is perfectly good consumer protection stuff, up to a point. But, as such, it only skirts around some of the key issues as corporate power advances.

Professor David Weir was formerly director of the business school at the University of Bradford, a job that kept him well situated for trips to see his beloved Leeds United at Elland Road. Unfortunately, he is now making a longer trip from Newcastle University. The dapper Yorkshireman is an unusual combination, a passionate fan who has also made a dispassionate study of the sports market, advising organizations such as the England & Wales Cricket Board. If there is a genuine threat that clubs are going to be culled, implicitly or explicitly, he does believe that social issues should be brought into the debate:

You are talking about the fulfilment of dreams, a very rich form of escapism. Now, that's good for the individual, but it is also demonstrably good for the community, both socially and economically. Most of us have seen these stories about productivity going up in local factories when the local team is doing well. It's an exercise that's been done many times, but I think it is instructive. Recently, you had the case where Nissan in Sunderland had one massive leap in performance when the club won the First Division and were promoted one year and then that fell back when they were relegated from the Premier League the following season, but it did not fall back as far as it had advanced. There was also mass absenteeism in Newcastle when its manager Kevin Keegan quit, but I think it's also interesting that Scottish & Newcastle, the brewers and club sponsors, gave hundreds of their staff the morning off when the club signed Alan Shearer.

As much as Tony Banks talks about the football addiction, Weir rightly notes that 'for many people, football provides something they cannot get anywhere else'. The fan pledges allegiance to his or her club for many reasons – for its expression of community and to be part of a community, for the adrenalin rush, for the escape from the workaday and so on. A club that delivers or even just tries to satisfy its part of this bargain is in turn rewarded by a loyalty that translates into expenditure and thereby into both profitability and survival. Weir continues:

If you are an administrator or an owner or anyone involved with football on a professional level, you tamper with that equation at your peril. What you should be doing, in fact, is to extract as much real benefit by bolstering that feeling of attachment and commitment. At the end of the day, football's social role is what has brought people to the game in the past and continues to bring them to the game today. It is what makes them spend their money. Watching team sports is not like any other form of entertainment. It is not like a film or a concert or a play or anything like that. Once you sign up for a football club, you sign up for life, regardless of whether what's happening on the pitch is bloody brilliant or bloody awful.

The economics at work here are powerful because they are so emotional; a factor that also makes it easy to misunderstand them. Abdul Rashid is one of the youngest senior executives with a Premier League football club. As commercial manager of Aston Villa, he believes that the game is only part of the way along a learning curve that it should have mastered long ago:

> *The club–fans relationship is the start of the business. The more passionate the fan is, the more likely he is to commit to buying a season ticket and to spending in the ground and the club shop. That passion is something the club has to nurture, it is not something that it can take for granted. The facilities have to be good, the ticket prices have to stretch across the right range and the products you sell have to be of a high quality. But, most of all, the team on the pitch has to be something that the fan can believe in. That's the hierarchy. That's the business. Write it on your mission statement or whatever.*
>
> *Yet, maybe some clubs do take fans for granted, they do not invest in the team in the right way, the prices are too high and the products are crap. So the fans go away, they stop coming and what a lot of people have not yet woken up to is the reality that once they have gone, it is nearly impossible to get them back. Whatever the passion was, whatever the commitment was, you can only very, very rarely recreate it. For the fan, they feel as though they have been spurned by a lover. Now, how often do you see those kinds of relationships get patched up?*

Echoing Tony Banks's feelings, Rashid notes that once a fan is lost to one club, he or she is lost to all. Supporters do not typically transfer their allegiances to another team, an argument also put forward by Rashid's colleague, Villa financial director Mark Ansell:

> *When we were first presenting to the City institutions, one or two asked that as the only one of Birmingham's clubs in the Premier League, how did we see the opportunities to grow the business by taking supporters away from Birmingham City or West Bromwich Albion? You had to sit down and explain that football does not work like that. Yes, you do want to catch supporters young when they are still settling on which is going to be their team and being in the*

Premiership does help you do that. But there is this idea out there that the Premiership teams can tap into more long-standing supporters. Frankly, I think that's rubbish. If the idea is that we will take 20 or 30 teams and dump them and then everybody else will share up their supporters, somebody needs their head examining.

Corporate football, controlled by conglomerates and executives with media and merchandising targets, and with its emphasis on national audiences fed predominantly by television, would appear to have its very foundations in this last belief at the expense of the more traditional relationship. It is about selecting a small number of super-elite teams and telling everyone that they have to pick one in the same way that they choose a supermarket. But will they come, will they buy, will they even be remotely interested? The chances are that the game could be about to destroy a whole generation of supporters.

People do not transfer their emotions about football; indeed, those emotions affect their judgements in surprising ways. David Weir admitted as much when the conversation came round inevitably to the financial powerhouse that is Manchester United:

Some things definitely do short circuit when it comes to football. Manchester United is without a doubt the best-run club in English, possibly European, football, but, as a Leeds fan, I'll wince if you put me saying that into print. Leeds hate all things Man U – end of story. A friend is bound to call up and say 'What were you praising them for?' and I'll probably end up apologizing. It defies logic, but there it is. That is the attitude of the football fan.

Masters of their own misfortune

If a corporate takeover is the threat on the horizon, then what is already happening in football offers little comfort. The game is showing all the classic signs of a bubble economy, which might well end up needing some very financially powerful white knights to save it.

The most pressing threat to football is the game's inability to control costs, which basically means players' wages. That is followed by the lack of a serious, coherent long-term vision; a dependency on volatile or unproven sources of income to fund its expansion; genuine difficulties in growing the market; and weak central regulation and administration.

As soon as money comes into football, even at its summit, it seems to leave just as quickly. A Deloitte & Touche analysis of just the Premier League found that the total wage bill had risen from £54 million in 1993–4 to a mind-blowing £135 million in 1996–7. Football saw tremendous growth in its income over that period, but the report noted that 'players' wages have increased at 25.7% compound annual growth over the life of the Premiership compared to 22.7% compound annual growth in turnover'. The average player is now earning about £190,000 a year and got a 35 per cent rise in 1997.

Nigel Hawkins of Williams de Broe is quick to point out that this is not merely an English problem, however:

> *Data from the Continent is less reliable, but the signs are that wage growth has been comparable in Italy, Spain and Germany. Only France has really tackled the issue, but there, most of the star players have now moved abroad to get the best salaries, and attendances have suffered as a result. Dutch clubs have been forced to keep wages under control also, but there has never been that much money in the market. There again, there is the interesting comparison that even at Ajax, the market's biggest team, top players stay for no more than three years and then typically move outside domestic competition altogether.*

Clubs therefore appear to be caught in a classic dilemma. If they pay big wages, the business will suffer, but if they don't, the business will still suffer because they will not win any trophies.

Long-term visions are absent. That view is backed even by one of the men behind the new breed of stock-market-quoted clubs, Chris Akers, former chief executive of Leeds Sporting, owners of Leeds United:

> *There is no unifying blueprint for football, although I know the English FA has a document called something like that. Leeds has a five-year business plan, but that was largely part of the flotation*

process. If you are going to the City for money, you have to do the
exercise. However, apart from the other plc clubs and ourselves there
are not that many people even looking beyond the millennium.

As football's income has doubled, tripled and quadrupled over the
last few years, fuelled largely by TV's appetite for rights to games,
there has also been genuine concern over the sport's revenue
streams and their ability to grow. Hawkins comments:

Pay-per-view is still an unproven force. It has been tried on the Con-
tinent, but the results in Italy and France have been very ordinary.
There is also a suggestion that it just redivides the cake, so that ordi-
nary pay-TV games are seen as having less value by viewers when
PPV is brought in. The result is that your gross revenues can appear
almost static.

He is sceptical about the clubs' ability to continue delivering heavy
income from merchandising and other ancillary activities:

For the first time ever, in the 1997–8 season we saw some clubs
admit that they do not expect the replica kit boom to go on for ever.
The idea is that this is a fashion item, and fashions change.

Already, the rumour is that Manchester United has seen disappointing sales on its new design, the latest version of its classic red
top.

Then there is the idea that football may not be growing any
more, but merely cannibalizing its own audience. Bill New of
DEMOS says:

On paper, attendances still look very good, but as the rate of growth
slows you need to look at where the new people, the source of those
attendances, are coming from. What is problematic is that there does
seem to be a slowing down among the younger audience. At 25 and
over, the figures are still going up, but below that, they are static,
particularly among children. Children 'go' on TV, if their parents can
afford it.

His fear was echoed in a recent report from the FA itself, which was produced by the Sir Norman Chester Centre for Football Research. It found that parents were not taking their children to games because, while they could attend themselves, they could not afford to take their kids as well.

The City's Nigel Hawkins did the sums:

Quite a few grounds are all season ticket, so a parent is being asked for £600, £700, £800 or, in some cases, over £1000 for himself and two children, and that is an outlay he is expected to make in summer, just after having spent several thousand pounds on the family holiday. Even for someone on a good income, that's quite a hole in the finances. And there are all the extras – the shop, food, parking or travel and so on. For the more casual family spectator, who can get one-off tickets, the whole day is still going to work out at well over £100. So, ask yourself, are there still as many children going to football as before? These parents might be passionate fans but they will draw the line somewhere, and, if those 'little acorns' are not being planted, where are the clubs going to get their consumers from in five, 10 or 15 years' time?

Hawkins extends his argument to cover TV fans:

OK, you can say that lots of these families have Sky – and yes, people with children represent a far higher proportion of cable and satellite homes than the national average – but Sky is about delivering the top teams that play the best football to encourage the armchair viewer to keep subscribing. In other words, this family might live in Brighton but the teams the children grow up with are Manchester United, Arsenal, Newcastle United and Liverpool. That is accentuated by terrestrial television, as ITV and the BBC only get the big clubs live because they only secure live rights for the major European competitions. Indeed, your seven-year-old might see Italy's Juventus on Channel 4 more often than the local side just half a mile down the road.

Even Newcastle United's *eminence grise* and former chairman Sir John Hall, who until recently presided over a stadium that locked out most of its young fans, is worried, as he said in an interview before his first two farewells from the St James' Park boardroom:

> *As things are at the moment, we've got huge waiting lists for season tickets. So unless we build a new stadium or do something to allevi-ate the situation, we're going to kill off the next generation of fans. It's something that we've really got to look at carefully if we want to fulfil our mission of becoming one of the top three clubs in the UK and one of the top ten in Europe.*

At the root of the problem may be the administration or, more appropriately, regulation of the game. Bill New's DEMOS report concluded that football has transformed itself into a big business without operating within the typical constraints that would apply to any other sector:

> *Football is what an economist would term a natural monopoly. Because of the league structure and the obstacles that presents to potentially new competitors, and because it necessarily graduates performance, it is a monopoly, but one that needs to exist to deliver the competition that is at its heart.*
>
> *The answer in any other sector would be to impose some tier of statutory regulation, in the sense that one has bodies overseeing public utilities, for example. That could lead you into areas such as wage capping and price fixing, which clubs do resist, but in economic terms such regulation has to exist in some form. The alternative is that you see what is happening now, massive internal inflation, some companies – or in this case, clubs – handicapped to the degree where they may never be able to compete in the long term, and so on.*

Ultimately, football is playing a dangerous game. Rickety finances are chasing a market that might be about to dry up while being pursued by vengeful supporters, and the government has woken up to the fact that the game is popular and there are votes in them there grounds.

Many people, Sports Minister Tony Banks among them, now believe that the beautiful game needs saving from itself and that the process must begin soon. He has said:

It's spend, spend, spend because they all think that the goose will never stop laying the golden eggs. Well, I just don't believe that. I just can't believe that. My feeling is that the government might have to take the initiative, do something now before it all gets out of control. Because if we get to the point where the game comes running along saying, 'Look, we are in the most awful bloody mess', then it will already be too late. You will already have clubs going bust or going into irreversible decline.

Thankfully, it is not too late to head off the threat of a mass cull with the remainder turned into obedient corporate zombies. However, the game does need to take a long, hard look at where it stands and maybe even relearn a few old lessons. After all, the irony remains that the financial changes came about in order to restore the sport following years of decline. Perhaps remembering all that is a good place to start.

CHAPTER TWO

A WHOLE NEW BALL GAME

Suddenly a policeman ran on to the pitch and talked to the referee, Ray Lewis, who stopped the game. Lewis sent the teams back into the dressing rooms and told us to wait for news. Nobody knew the scale of the disaster. I ordered the players to stay inside and went out into the corridor. A few fans had gathered there. They called out to me 'Kenny, Kenny, there are people dying out there.'

Kenny Dalglish, *Dalglish: My Autobiography*,
Hodder & Stoughton, 1996

AS TONY FRAHER OF MERCHANT BANK SINGER & FRIEDLANDER and head of the Football Fund investment trust points out, the wealth dream began with a nightmare-turned-reality:

What has happened in football in general came out of a disaster – Hillsborough. It led to a complete rethink about football and gave us the all-seater stadiums. Because there was a cost involved that cost had to be recouped somewhere. Hillsborough led to a drop-off in hooliganism and a rise in middle-class attendance. There was a change in the demographics and they changed quite dramatically. People with more money who were willing to spend it, and not just on attending but on buying other goods, started to come back. If they were married, they were bringing their wives and their kids so it was becoming more family oriented, which was a massive change. There was no more of the standing in the rain or worrying about getting water down the back of your neck off the guttering on a stand – although you were lucky if it was water. The clubs just never saw themselves as businesses with a brand that had a value.

Fraher is not a football fan, preferring rugby union at the north London club Saracens. He does not like the atmosphere at football matches and believes that rugby is better because you are closer to the action. But he is a supporter of the business ethic in sport and is in the thick of the action as big money takes control of the beautiful game, in part via his company's involvement. He can spot a potential money-making opportunity and, like others, can now see that the vital safety work carried out after the horror of Hillsborough was the catalyst that helped create the conditions for the financial revolution.

The elements that would produce British football's big bang were being mixed long before Hillsborough. The top clubs had already been kicking around the idea of making more money out of television rights by forming a breakaway league which would give them greater control of their other commercial activities. They looked at the transfer fees that continental clubs paid and the wages they could afford.

However, in the pre-Hillsborough period English clubs had a slight problem when it came to competing with the European sides. They had been banned from UEFA competitions after the 1985 Heysel outrage. During the ban, continental sides came to lead the way off the field as well as on it. They developed new business methods, while the English could only stand and watch.

The Taylor report on the Hillsborough disaster and England's return to European club competitions unwittingly established new financial ground rules that gave the leading clubs the opportunity to cut off the other divisions that they felt had been hanging on the coat-tails of their success for so long.

There were already a few visionary businesspeople running major British clubs who were perfectly capable of matching the continentals in business. But most could not join the game until the necessary elements came together.

Irving Scholar, then chairman of Tottenham and now at Nottingham Forest part time, had established the City relationship with the 1983 stock-market flotation of Spurs and the introduction of Club Call premium rate information lines. David Dein, the head of an import-export company called London & Overseas Sugar, paid £290,250 for a 16.6 per cent stake in Arsenal in 1984, ultimately becoming vice-chairman. He also had strong views on the standards of stadia and marketing. In Scotland, metals magnate David Murray had moved in at Rangers for £6 million and he, at least, was finding that he could still tap into the European wealth stream.

It is undeniable that the European ban put the English game as a business back years. Between 1985 and 1991, Italy's Serie A re-established itself as not just Europe's financially dominant but also highest-quality league, paying the big transfer fees and salaries which brought in the star players. It attracted a different class of owner, such as former Italian Prime Minister Silvio Berlusconi at AC Milan, who used the club specifically to build his television interests and cemented the relationship between big bucks and big trophies. He was, to some extent, a visionary in European terms who recognized the importance of football in drawing TV audiences as the Continent saw a flurry of new commercial stations. The Italian experience and the deals being done in other European countries were ultimately to be the models for the BSkyB deal in the UK.

Meanwhile, a new breed of entrepreneur appeared at other continental clubs, drawn by the whiff of big money. The now-disgraced Bernard Tapie at Olympique Marseilles, who bribed his team's way to a European Cup, is only the most prominent of these characters.

At the same time, many of the English league's top stars had fled or were fleeing the country for European competition, success and riches, albeit with varying success. Among the sometime exiles of the 1980s and early 1990s were Ray Wilkins, Mark Hateley, Mark Hughes, Glenn Hoddle, Trevor Steven, Graeme Souness and Paul Gascoigne.

Over six years of English purdah, the gap between the national leagues grew to a point where it started to look frighteningly wide. They had started to build the Eurotunnel but, in football terms, the Channel seemed to be getting wider and wider.

However, the coming together of the lifting of the European ban, the Taylor report into the Hillsborough disaster, the foundation of the Premiership and the BSkyB deal was about to change all that. Out of a series of disasters came a once-in-a-lifetime opportunity.

A scum sport for scum people

In the late 1980s, it did not seem as though football was going to get a financial boost and the game did not really appear to deserve one. The late Lord Justice Taylor, who investigated the Hillsborough disaster and called for the stripping away of the terraces, was quite clear in his Final Report about what had gone wrong in football and how bad the situation was. One of the most damning sections summed up why the game was important, but then went on to say what had gone wrong. Taylor wrote:

> *Football is our national game. We gave it to the world. But its image in our country has been much tarnished. In my Interim Report I concentrated on overcrowding because it was the cause of the Hillsborough disaster. But wider and deeper inquiry shows that overcrowding is only one feature amongst a number causing danger or marring football as a spectator sport. The picture revealed is of a general malaise or blight over the game due to a number of factors. Principally these are: old grounds, poor facilities, hooliganism, excessive drinking and poor leadership.*

His pessimism and talk of 'malaise' and 'blight' in January 1990 strike a vivid contrast with the recent optimism about the game. Football has come a long way since the Taylor Report and is demonstrably a different game from the sport of the Thatcher decade.

Even die-hard supporters are driven to acknowledge that some things have changed for ever and that there is no going back. Sports Minister Tony Banks, a loud and proud Chelsea fan, recognized that very fact in an October 1997 speech. He said:

> *The new generation of modern all-seater facilities developed in recent years rank among the safest and most comfortable in the world. A return to terracing at our top stadia might not only risk crowd safety, but seriously jeopardize our chances of successfully bidding for top international tournaments such as the World Cup. As passionate as I am about football, and as much as I regard footballing heritage as being a unique part of our game, we must not let our nostalgic memories of life on the terraces blur the reality of what terraces were actually like.*

The former Conservative government supported Taylor's main recommendations on all-seater stadia and on pulling down perimeter fences because it saw serious issues involving public safety and public order. The opportunity to be seen taking straightforward action in these areas was the political equivalent of supporting motherhood and apple pie. For the same reasons, no New Labour government is about to roll back in bulk any of the Conservative-implemented legislation.

The diktats of the Taylor report which forced clubs to update grounds at vast expense were initially resisted or accepted only grudgingly by club owners and football's administrators. Clubs whined excessively about the cost of all the work that would have to be done, despite the stark, unanswerable fact that almost 100 people had died while watching football because the ground was unsafe.

Nostalgia fans have a more valid point to make. They are worried about the loss of the terracing community, citing the camaraderie of the crowd and the unique atmosphere in the ground. Groups like the Football Supporters' Association are also campaigning for some form of terracing to be reintroduced into the game, for the again entirely laudable reason that it would be cheaper for the fans who are currently priced out of Premiership and First Division football. They point quite correctly to the European experience, where it is still possible to be a fan without being that wealthy.

In major European countries such as Germany and Spain, there are still terraces and reasonably cheap tickets. In some German Bundesliga grounds it is possible to stand and watch a top-class match for around £5. Spectators in England are welcome to try and find a Premiership ground which will let them in for £5. In Spain, similar standards apply. Real Madrid's so-called Ultras Sur fans pay a mere £7 to get into one of Europe's finest stadia, the Santiago Bernabeu.

However, the English supporters are fighting a losing battle because people in authority and many fans still remember the problems there used to be in the game. During the 1980s, football changed from the national sport to a national pariah, partly because of Mrs Thatcher's personal antipathy, but mostly thanks to its own efforts. Hooliganism had taken root in the 1970s and in the 1980s groups such as the ICF, F-Troop and the Headhunters kept the headline writers busy. Going to football was at times unpleasant and increasingly unsafe. As the years went by, problems with so-called fans became enmeshed with concerns over ill-maintained stadia.

The two topics came sickeningly together during the May 1985 riot at Brussels' Heysel stadium as Liverpool and Juventus contested the European Cup final. Violence and intimidation by individuals in the Liverpool section of the crowd led to the collapse of a segregating wall and the deaths of 39 supporters, mostly of Juventus. Only a few days earlier, disaster had also struck at Bradford City's Valley Parade ground, when a fire that started in rubbish beneath the Main Stand caused 56 deaths – and, on that occasion, the infamous hooligans had nothing to do with it. The two horrific events hammered home the impression that football was a dangerous game to watch, not just because of the risk of being beaten up but because the stadia in which it was played were seriously dilapidated.

The familiar calls of 'something must be done' followed quickly. English clubs received the UEFA ban and the government toyed with ideas of a national members scheme which would have forced football fans to carry identity cards. Other, more radical plans were introduced by individual clubs. Luton Town, under its then chairman former Tory MP David Evans, banned away fans entirely. Chelsea considered the idea of an electric fence around its ground. Very strange things were happening to the national game.

Yet there were still nearly four more years until on 15 April 1989 the event took place that finally drew firm government action and the realization that enough was enough. An FA Cup semi-final between Liverpool and Nottingham Forest at Sheffield Wednesday's Hillsborough stadium had to be abandoned after 96 mainly Liverpool fans were suffocated by a combination of disastrous crowd control and inadequate safety measures. Claim and counter-claim over responsibility for the disaster continue to this day and successive governments have done themselves few favours by prevaricating over the matter. But while the establishment may have expected its original investigator, Lord Taylor, to channel national anger once more towards the supposed hooligans, he set his sights on some other targets. His bitterest criticisms were reserved for the game's chieftains, for example the administrators:

One would have hoped that the upper echelons in this hierarchy would have taken a lead in securing reasonable safety and comfort for the spectators and in enforcing good behaviour by precept and example. Unfortunately, these hopes have not generally been realised and indeed at times poor examples have been set.

Taylor noted:

In selecting Hillsborough as the venue for the Cup semi-final, the FA did not consider in any depth whether it was suitable for a high risk match with an attendance of 54,000 requiring to be segregated, all of whom were, in effect, away supporters lacking week in week out knowledge of the ground. No special inspection was made; no consultation with Sheffield Wednesday or the local authority took place.

He attacked football's owners:

In some instances, it is legitimate to wonder whether the directors are genuinely interested in the welfare of their grass-roots supporters. Boardroom struggles for power, wheeler-dealing in the buying and selling of shares and indeed of whole clubs sometimes suggest that those involved are more interested in the personal financial benefits or social status of being a director than of directing the club in the interests of its supporter customers. In most commercial enter-

prises, including the entertainment industry, knowledge of the cus-
tomer's needs, his tastes and his dislikes is essential information in
deciding policy and planning. But, until recently, few clubs con-
sulted to any significant extent with the supporters or their
organisations.

His attack on the owners and administrators of football was
echoed in the financial community, one of the first ports of call for
the club chiefs once they stopped moaning and realized they would
have to do something to raise the money needed to pay for Taylor.

In the late 1980s, Chris Akers, who was until recently chief
executive of Leeds Sporting, was a very young City and media
whiz kid and was in an ideal position to see what was going on.
He was just 25 when the football clubs started to come to the City
with their hopes of tapping investors, and claims now that he
could see the way the wind was blowing in football. Akers was
then a research director for Citicorp in London, concentrating on
media stocks and, in particular, rival satellite broadcasters BSB and
Sky's attempts to establish attractive programming. In 1988, BSB
went after football in competition with the traditional broadcasters. Akers says:

During the '88 talks, it was obvious that the clubs had no real plan
other than to get as much money as possible, and the only reason
BSB lost was because the clubs figured out that they would lose more
in sponsorship than the extra they would get from doing a broad-
cast deal with a satellite company. There was no real vision of the
possibilities.

The same thing happened a little later after Taylor. Man U and
Millwall went to the markets with some fairly good-looking ideas,
but there were half a dozen other Premier League or, then, First Divi-
sion clubs who also flirted with the City. They got told to go away
because the business plans basically said, 'The government's just
told us we have to spend all this money on making our grounds safe,
could you please invest?' Only United and Millwall were seriously
talking about expanding stadium use, developing new forms of rev-
enue and all those other, you know, profit things that an analyst is
likely to have a vague interest in. Even those two issues had

problems, because the overall impression of football was that it was running scared.

Akers' harsh but true views were also held by many inside the game. Football people were just as unimpressed with how the sport was being run. Crystal Palace chairman Ron Noades reportedly observed of his colleagues at the time:

Tomorrow is not a word that has any real meaning for these people and the idea of the day after tomorrow is completely abstract.

A leaderless, squabbling sport with no vision of the future does not sound like the sort of sport which nowadays commands the attention. But the effect of Hillsborough was not just financial but also cultural. It is a blistering indictment that it took such a tragedy to wake the game and the nation up, but seemingly it did. Lord Justice Taylor had been expected to say it was just a sad accident and leave it at that. Instead, his report and the national reaction to the disaster changed the way the game was viewed.

Liverpool fan John Williams, of the Sir Norman Chester Centre for Football Research at Leicester University, takes the view that Taylor and Hillsborough were the catalysts for the rebuilding of the game. No longer was the sport simply a national disgrace; it was being seen as something which had been important and valued and which perhaps could be again:

Taylor actually took the sport seriously and put it on the agenda, he challenged Thatcher's view of the sport. The Hillsborough disaster began to reshape public perceptions of the game. There was the out-pouring of emotion and the collective mourning of the people who died. You had Manchester United supporters turning up at Liverpool with wreaths and scarves. Supporters held hands across the country. Fans were finally seen as victims rather than perpetrators. The constant theme of the eighties was that fans were hooligans. At Hillsborough fans were self-evidently not the problem but the victims of mismanagement and the way that hooliganism was dealt with over that whole period.

Most important was the depiction of the people who died. These were not hooligans, these were people who were just like us, they had families, they had jobs. There were women as well as men. These were just ordinary people doing something that they loved and who were really committed to their clubs.

Taylor therefore presented a new recipe. Here for the first time was someone from outside the game, someone who was influential and important saying: 'Right, here we are. It is a mess. This is where we need to be in five years' time.' This had never been seen in the sport before. In the past it was just one spectator crisis after another and stumble on to the next. There was never any vision and no idea of the future. Here was someone telling clubs: 'We are in a bad place, we have to be in a better place.'

However, Lord Justice Taylor had a financial as well as a cultural effect. He served football with an enormous bill. The way that the game met the bill shows the process of change that has brought the sport to where it is now. The costs were not just, as is widely assumed, to replace all the historic terraces with seats and pull down perimeter fencing, but also to review the structural integrity of grounds as a whole through an Advisory Football Design Council. Taylor proposed that there should be some government funding and a lengthy timetable, deliberately biased towards poorer clubs in the lower leagues. Initial estimates nevertheless set the total cost of meeting Taylor's demands at a rather horrifying £1 billion.

Public aid was finally offered, but only at a modest level in comparison with the scale of the problem. The tax levied on football pools was cut by 2.5 per cent in March 1990, providing £100 million for reconstruction over five years. In October 1990, the Football Trust, the body charged by government with determining grant allocations, announced that it would provide £40 million over the same period from the revenues it received by a levy on 'Spot the Ball' competitions. This still only amounted to £140 million and that already small amount was later reduced by the impact of the National Lottery. The Lottery hit pools and Spot the Ball sales, forcing the government first to extend the pools tax cut, and then, in June 1997, to bail out the Trust's Taylor coffers with a further £35 million. Not that the government actually stumped up all the extra cash: the by then well-established and well-off elite of the FA Premier League was forced to come up with £20 million.

At best, Football Trust funding for the Taylor work might be estimated at £250 million, a quarter of the projected cost. Trust chief executive Peter Lee is quite clear about what was going on:

> *There was, I think, a deliberate political decision to put a major financial burden on football, in effect a fine on club owners for failing to run the game properly and keeping their business affairs in order. There may even have been a hope that it would push some of the more difficult clubs to the brink and, if possible, over it. That really was how government felt: 'Let's force them to clean up or close down.'*

Yet with 20-20 hindsight, football has been able to foot the bill without any great strain. In brief, the game was very lucky. The slump in the UK construction market was one surprise boost to the clubs by cutting the costs of both labour and materials. Even more importantly, satellite TV and Rupert Murdoch's desire for programming was to arrive on the scene and completely revolutionize the value of European sporting rights. But before that happy day, football still faced a daunting challenge from the Taylor demands and the figures spell out the scale of the challenge.

Rebuilding the game

According to Simon Inglis's essential reference work, *Football Grounds of Britain*, the bill for post-Taylor work had reached £473 million in England alone by early 1996. One can safely say that spending is now well past the half-billion point, as this estimate does not include the costs of new grounds opened since then.

A quick tour of Premier League grounds finds such gems as Sunderland's Stadium of Light costing £25 million, Bolton Wanderers' Reebok Stadium at £20 million, and Derby County's Pride Park which cost £24 million. Nor does the estimate take account of any of the investment in Scotland, including that by Glasgow's 'Old Firm'. Rangers and Celtic have each spent approximately £30 million on Ibrox and the new Parkhead stadia respectively since 1989. Indeed, Celtic has the UK's biggest football ground and is the country's best-supported team in terms of season-ticket sales.

Pushing ground expenditure still further towards the one-billion mark are a number of ambitious relocation projects, such as those already proposed by Luton Town and Blackpool. Arsenal is searching desperately for somewhere to play if it is not allowed to extend its Highbury ground, and West Ham is considering ambitious £30 million plans to expand Upton Park. Tottenham Hotspur has spent years developing and redeveloping White Hart Lane and still has one entire side of the ground to finish. All of these projects were entered into willingly and with little whining from clubs which had initially warned of the horrific effect of the Taylor Report.

There is something of a financial contradiction here. In 1989, football complained about the £1 billion price tag for legally required building work. That number should, thanks to dire economic conditions in the UK, have ultimately come in at far less. Nevertheless football went through a huge amount of money in pretty short order. And a few years later, the game seems poised to outdo that £1 billion figure of its own choosing and without being at all worried.

Where did the cash come from, where is it continuing to materialize from and how were clubs able to pull off the Great Escape from the horror of Taylor? How could a game on its uppers pay for all this activity, not to mention fund huge transfer fees and pull in the top international talent that now plays in the English and Scottish leagues?

When in doubt, tap the fans

Initially, clubs went directly to their fans and asked them to pay for the rebuilding and expansion of grounds. Arsenal and West Ham were but two of the teams that launched bond schemes, whereby supporters were asked to pay several hundred pounds to guarantee their rights to a seat in refurbished grounds with, inevitably, reduced capacity. Typically, such bonds did not include the price of the seat itself, merely the option to buy one. Bonds were marketed as a once-in-a-lifetime chance to ensure a place at your club and provoked anger and protests from supporters who feared that they were being excluded. Arsenal charged £1000 for its bonds and managed to sell enough. The value of the bonds, which were traded by stockbrokers Brewin Dolphin, initially slumped after the sale, falling as low as £750. Following 1997–8's double, however, Gunners fans are literally sitting on profits of up to £9000 if they choose to cash in.

But at many other clubs bond schemes had to be abandoned in the face of protests. At the same time, gate prices started an inexorable and inflation-busting rise to a point where a top-of-the-range Chelsea season ticket that cost £275 in 1989–90 is now priced at £1250, almost a 500 per cent increase. Chelsea chairman Ken Bates has been explicit about the reason for the price rises. Simply put, fans have to pay because the club needs the money to pay players and fund its plans.

Then the clubs turned to merchandising. In 1989, only Tottenham Hotspur had even a vaguely developed system of selling club products and this would later prove a burden rather than an advantage, almost bankrupting the company after an ill-fated expansion into sportswear manufacturing. Spurs was regarded as terribly daring and innovative with its merchandising ideas such as properly designed shops and large product ranges. These were introduced in the main by the then chairman Irving Scholar and another footballing revolutionary, Edward Freedman. Freedman later became the man who turned Manchester United's merchandising business into a monster and now works for consultancy Zone, which is attempting to work the magic again at Nottingham Forest, Spain's Real Madrid and Italy's AS Roma.

Most other clubs, including the future megastore men at Manchester United, made do by selling their wares in a chaotic fashion from tiny stalls outside huge and expensive 40,000 capacity stadia. Liverpool, in all its glory years during the 1970s and 1980s when it conquered Europe, never had a merchandising operation. The club had massive support across the Continent but did not think it worthwhile to sell the fans anything. Slowly but surely, though, things started to change throughout the game.

Manchester United director Mike Edelson says that some of it started even earlier at his club's local rivals Manchester City:

Malcolm Allison played with the idea when he was managing Man City in the early 1970s, but I think the first time you saw a modern English kit that had been designed more as leisurewear rather than for playing football in was in 1991, and it was one of ours, and it was bloody awful. It was this pale blue thing with what looked like tadpoles swimming all over it, and we dreamt it up with German manufacturer adidas. There was some resistance on the playing side, but it worked.

This was only the beginning. The build-up of the merchandising and commercial side of the business to include such exotica as Ryan Giggs duvet covers, branded wine and lager and even Chelsea's own Ruud Boy motorbikes (hurry while stocks last) was still some way off.

We are the men in suits

Clubs also tried to go to the City of London. By 1989, Tottenham Hotspur had already been a public company for six years, but no other club had yet followed its lead. Again, when Spurs took the stock-market plunge it was regarded as insane inside football and was not very highly regarded in the City either. Post Taylor, however, Spurs was soon joined on the Stock Exchange by Millwall in November 1989 and Manchester United in June 1991, both of which saw the opportunity not merely to upgrade but totally to overhaul their stadia, and began to meet such ambitions by raising City investment. Neither club was well received on its stock-market debut. Manchester United's share issue was an ignominious flop, in contrast to its current glamour rating as part of the FTSE Mid250.

Some heavy talent began to enter the boardrooms as individuals like property magnate Sir John Hall at Newcastle United and industrial *wunderkind* David Murray at Rangers arrived on the scene (Mr Murray, of course, initially considered buying the rather less mighty Ayr United). Yet even they were not prepared for what was going to happen. Craig Armour of Murray's financial advisers Noble Grossart acknowledges as much:

> *David Murray could see the potential in the business but was not aware, in fact nobody was, of how big a business football was going to become. Obviously there was a lot that could be done but nobody could foresee the TV money that would soon be on offer.*

Football, after all, was in the doldrums at this time. Its image could not have been much worse. So the real money-raising still had to go through traditional routes, convincing bank managers that clubs would be a good risk, often by tidying up accounting procedures that, being charitable, had suffered from years of neglect or, frequently, had thinly disguised more than the odd bit of naughtiness.

And football turned corporate. Despite its wider troubles, the introduction of shirt sponsorship in 1982 had generally been successful, contributing to the game's coffers also through the associated promotion of the executive box. These glass-fronted cocoons were first seen at Manchester United during the 1960s but were now becoming a feature at almost every ground, as local companies saw some value in touching their local club's hem. As yet this was not big business but, as clubs strove to underwrite the costs of Taylor, it was already shaping up as 'a nice little earner'. For a game with an image problem, the corporate route was always going to take some time to develop.

The men from Auntie ... and BSkyB

The decisive factor would prove to be television. As the clubs digested their first estimates for ground refurbishment, TV's intervention would not come for another four years. Although some directors could see that the avenue was already opening up, they did not have any idea of how wide it would be.

In 1988, the English Football League – still four divisions at this time – signed a four-year £44 million deal with the main domestic terrestrial network, ITV, despite strong competition in the bidding from the fledgling and ultimately doomed BSB, famous now for its Squarial technology and not much else apart from helping to catapult Andy Gray to national icon status. BSB bid higher – £12 million a year over 10 years – but lost out because of questions over satellite TV's likely popularity with the public. Owners, meanwhile, were still getting over their aversion to live TV football, which had seen broadcasters severely restricted in the number of games that could be shown because of fears over the effect this would have on attendances. Clubs and fans were also worried about the effect of a sellout to satellite television, which would only be available to a minority audience. These debates rumble on even now.

Nevertheless, as one Premier League chairman says, football was now aware that there was and could in future be much stiffer competition for its product:

> *Before 1988, we knew that we were being turned over by the broadcasters and had been turned over for years. Most of the time, the BBC and ITV had got together like a bunch of crooks and held down the prices, so that we, the English clubs, were getting far less than the Italians, Germans or Spaniards, even when teams like Liverpool, Aston Villa and Nottingham Forest were going to Europe and winning everything in sight. I mean Rai, the Italian state broadcaster, was paying over £40 million a year.*

In 1983, the combined BBC/ITV bid was £5.2 million for 10 English games. In 1985, a six-month contract from the pair was worth £1.3 million for six games. The following year saw a two-year, 14-game deal from the two terrestrial broadcasters, worth £6.2 million. BSB challenged the long-standing duopoly.

Football knew that it had a tremendous broadcasting value, but its attempts to extract a fair price – and there can be no doubt the game was undervalued – had been kept in check by a gentleman's agreement between ITV and the BBC not to let the bidding get out of hand. Even were this agreement to fall apart, ITV believed that it would not need to raise its price too high to outbid its publicly funded, eternally cash-strapped and, until satellite took off, solitary rival. The Premier League chairman comments:

> *The difference in 1988 was that suddenly there was competition. Back then, BSB and Sky were not selling that many subscriptions, so it didn't happen. But you could already see some people thinking that in four years' time, we have to do this all over again, and then the satellite people should have sorted things out one way or another. Then it could be very different. So different that maybe we could get £30 million a season and that was the target.*

However, 1988 also saw the first instance where major clubs stopped talking about a breakaway and tried to do something about it. ITV's head negotiator Greg Dyke initially struck a deal with what were then England's 'big five' – Liverpool, Arsenal, Manchester United, Everton and Tottenham Hotspur – with an option to expand it to include five more teams of their choosing, but which would see everyone else, including the then 12 other First Division sides, get sweet, fat zero. In part, it was his response to the breaking of the duopoly, but it also reflected a broadcaster's natural desire to secure only those clubs that will deliver viewers nationally. This was a worrying preview of what the Ted Turners of this world could do in the future. More immediately, it showed that the big clubs were now determined to get their own way at some point regardless of the consequences.

The proposal was blocked and ITV instead struck a £44 million deal with all the English clubs, but from then on there was a remorseless logic to the fact that someday, somehow, something similar would happen.

In football the winner might take all three points, but in British TV deals victory was more relative, as League chieftains tried to use much of the money to support clubs outside the elite. Circumstances, however, were making this position increasingly shaky.

In the years immediately after the last ITV deal, the clubs continued to exhibit their least endearing but most enduring attribute – a total lack of any long-term planning. By the end of the agreement in 1992, all football needed, as the song goes, was a miracle. The game had run up debts of £160 million compared with an already rather alarming £95 million in 1989. Much of the extra money had been raised to meet the costs of upgrading stadia, but there had also been a rush of expensive transfers following British clubs' return to European competition in the 1990–91 season. At the same time, another City source claims that four large clubs were also in near-crisis talks with their bankers over how repayments on overdrafts and loans would ultimately be met.

Mounting debts and existing pressures for an elite breakaway led the First Division to announce in Summer 1992 that it would be resigning from the League en masse and setting up the FA Premier League. According to the PR, this move would take football into the future on the pitch to the same degree that the ongoing Taylor programme was doing off it. The 17 clubs that had been outside the 1988 plan now realized that it was more in their interests to be in with the big boys than to stand in solidarity with the clubs in the three tiers below.

There were some justifiable observations that a dependency culture in the lower leagues had closed many minds there to the realities facing the game. One now First Division director says:

> *The decision to set up the Premier League was as much about merit as it was financial ambition. The Football League people refused to acknowledge that football began with a strong First Division which feeds into a strong national side, and that it is essential to develop that top flight financially, not to hold it back by worrying about how much Solihull Corinthians get paid to entertain and keep on entertaining a couple of hundred die-hards.*

Even though his club has been relegated from the top flight – hence his unwillingness to be quoted by name on the league's conduct – he remains convinced that the Premier League has:

> *brought a necessary financial hardness to the game. As a more commercially driven organization it has started to bring in appropriate sums of TV money and it has also educated the sport about sponsorship deals and other new forms of income. What the Premier League has done has also vastly improved the business skills in the divisions below it.*
>
> *Overall, football is now on a more secure financial footing and, from my point of view, that means it has a better future. The sensible people here in the Football League are now talking about catching*

up with the Premier League and adapting its good ideas, not about dragging it down to our supposed level.

And yet football's role in the 1992 round of TV negotiations was almost entirely supine. The game was desperate, and struck lucky because of the needs of an Australian–American called Rupert Murdoch.

Mark Ansell, financial director of Aston Villa and, at the time, a senior adviser to the Birmingham club, remembers things very differently:

When the First Division broke away to form the Premier League in 1992, it was seen as the only way to solve a political and financial mess. Some of the big clubs wanted to get much more money from television. In fact, everybody had wanted that for a long time, but the big clubs thought they knew the best way to get it and that was by going it alone. After all, four years earlier, ITV had tried to do a deal with just a Big Five and it almost came off.

By 1992 everybody knew that those clubs would not hold back again, because they had spent the most on their stadiums and the most on new players. For our part, we had also spent a small fortune on Villa Park and built a winning team. So, we ended up with a bigger split – 22 clubs rather than five – and [Premier League chief executive] Rick [Parry's] job was to get something from, we assumed, ITV or the BBC that would make everybody comfortable.

Ansell's is the insider's view and he is understandably worried less about the effects on fans and the culture of the sport and more about the finances. As an outsider, John Williams comes to similar conclusions, albeit in the different language of someone not quite as in love with New Football:

The old fraternal cross-subsidization idea of football that the large should support the small had been under attack for some time. New arrangements such as allowing the home team to keep all their gate receipts had changed the ethos already. That had made it less attractive for the small team such as Wimbledon to compete in the

First Division, as they had to rely on their own puny home gates rather than getting some of Man U or Liverpool's big gates.

Williams reckons that the switch away from the sharing of gate receipts was symptomatic of what was already happening. Entrepreneurs saw the arguments that were being put in the Taylor Report and saw that the game lacked decisive leadership able to formulate a plan. They were aware of what was going on in the TV deals, as were the administrators at Lancaster Gate, FA headquarters. Williams says:

> *The larger clubs got together with the Football Association, which itself was becoming more aggressively commercial about the possibilities of taking control of the game. The FA felt it should take a role because of its part in the control of the national team and the importance of that to players and clubs. It used Hillsborough as an opportunity to go for the main chance and establish a breakaway league. The premise of the league was that football in its new, repackaged form could be sold in a new way. Old football, which was 92 clubs, could give way to new football with just 22 or 20 shiny clubs to be remodelled.*

He believes it was:

> *entirely fortuitous that television came along and especially fortuitous that it was satellite TV.*

In the early 1990s, the two satellite TV competitors were in major financial trouble. BSB and Sky merged to form BSkyB as a last desperate throw of the dice before both went out of business. Williams comments:

> *Back then, BSB and Sky were in desperate straits, they were very economically troubled. They needed a single major product, which could rescue them from the hole they were in. New Premier League football emerged as the first form of the game that has been substantially shaped by television. Without this single major sponsorship and the television that is provided by this single major sponsorship, the Premier League doesn't make sense.*

Since then, Sky and the Premier League have been mutually reinforcing of each other. I think Premier League football for Sky as a product produced by Sky moved satellite television out of a cultural ghetto of being something that rather vulgar working-class people had and others shouldn't. Premier League football actually takes Sky upmarket with it. But Sky helped promote the idea of Premier League football as an exclusive good that is sought after and which you need to buy. You had this marvellous opportune moment when Sky and the Premier League sign up for their own mutual salvation. Looking back it does seem seminal.

It was certainly a marvellously fortuitous moment when the combination of Hillsborough rebuilding, the Premier League and BSkyB revitalized interest in football and entrepreneurs with an eye for the main chance came together.

Therefore, when Rick Parry, in his role as negotiator, received a phone call from Sam Chisholm, then chief executive of the Murdoch-controlled BSkyB, it must have felt like destiny. It certainly was the most exquisite piece of matchmaking. Chisholm, like his boss Murdoch, believed that satellite needed, in the unlovely phrase, 'tentpole' programming, a number of examples of expensively purchased exclusive material. On one level, it would support the rest of the generally mediocre and extremely cheaply bought schedule but, as one former aide explains, Chisholm had another equally pressing motive:

In the wake of the merger, there were all sorts of stories flying about, many of them true, about the new company being technically bankrupt, about losses of hundreds of thousands of pounds a week and so on. Sam basically told Murdoch that BSkyB needed to do something really big, something that would say, 'You say we haven't got any money, well take a look at this. You say we still haven't got any decent programming, well take a look at this.'

They sat down and asked themselves what was available, and there was the Premier League staring them in the face. Murdoch already knew that football sold more copies of the Sun [the UK's biggest-selling tabloid newspaper] than the topless women on page three, so that was that. The decision was taken in less than 48 hours and it was that Sky was to secure exclusive rights, whatever the cost – not 'within reason' but 'whatever the cost'.

Ultimately, BSkyB had to compromise, cutting the BBC in for a highlights package to assuage clubs' concern about taking top-flight football totally away from non-satellite homes (still over 80 per cent of UK households at the time) and the consequent wrath of sponsors. But the £380 million, five-year deal that the clubs ultimately accepted was an astonishing leap forward – the value of rights effectively rose by 900 per cent overnight.

It was an incredible break for a game which not very long before had been extremely wary about live football on television. Quite apart from embracing live TV, it was now looking at switching games to Sundays and Mondays and changing kickoff times to accommodate channels which could not be watched by a vast majority of the population. Clubs had taken one small but decisive step away from the old notion of community. Despite the very limited BBC deal, Sky Sports now had the field completely to itself and has maintained that position since.

Who has really won in Sky vs football?

With the deal struck, BSkyB then moved in to market football under the title 'a whole new ball game'. Chris Akers, who by then was getting ready for his move into football executive mode, thinks that the game again missed an open goal. Had Akers been around at Leeds perhaps the story would be different. Then again, perhaps not. He says:

> *The whole marketing exercise was sold to the clubs as Sky supporting football, giving it a new, sexy image, dressing it up for the super century. But, come on, this was a symbiotic relationship. Sky needed to sell sub-scriptions. It was committed to over £60 million a year here and was already paying out over £100 million for rights on the movie channels.*
>
> *Sky's objective was to finesse the clubs into doing what its research said would deliver the biggest TV audiences and the biggest number of subscribers. So you had things like Sunday games kicking*

off when the pubs were closed so you absolutely had to have a dish at home. [Until 1994, all English pubs closed on Sundays between 3pm and 7pm.] You also had Monday night games.

If you look at the proposals Sky was pumping out in spring and summer of 1992, they all say 'doing such-and-such will restore football's image and promote the game'. The clubs were told this was all part of a revolution for football, but it was a revolution in broadcasting. The clubs were still stunned that they had ended up with more than twice what they had expected, so they turned to Sky and basically told them to run it. What they did not realize was that there was so much money on the table because Murdoch was willing to do anything to get the Premier League because its value is absolutely massive. They should have kept more control and more rights for themselves. It's only now that clubs are waking up to that, and there are only certain things you can do about it. Even then you need to look very closely at the holes in the contracts.

In the most recent, 1997 round of negotiations with football, BSkyB ensured that there was more than enough money on the table to keep the clubs in awe, offering £670 million for exclusive live domestic coverage from the 1997–8 season to 2000–1. However, the fact that the clubs only agreed to a four- rather than a five-year deal and rumblings from within the game suggest that some chairmen do think the relationship needs rethinking.

Man United's Edelson, who has been a serial soccer entrepreneur, helping to bring Sheffield United and Leicester to the stock market, says:

Sky has been very good for football, but I do think that now football is pointing out that it has also been very good for Sky.

In 1998, his first and true love, Man United, struck a three-way joint venture with the satellite company to launch MUTV, a digital satellite channel dedicated to Britain's largest club. The ownership structure is important. Unlike the league deal with Sky Sports, United will get a direct percentage of the profits in MUTV, which could grow significantly over time if you add in live games, pay-per-view and so on.

This is the first sign of football exerting its power in the relationship with BSkyB. MUTV is one of only a handful of projects where clubs are moving from rights sellers to rights exploiters, the others being TV channels planned by Newcastle United, Middlesbrough and Leeds United. In this respect, Akers highlights where clubs may be heading into dangerous territory:

I think that so far football has been riding its luck. Clubs were forced to redevelop their grounds; they didn't really want to. But as a result of all that work, you find that spectators are coming to matches and not just behaving themselves, but also spending more money because the food and the merchandising are better. You are also getting families coming back, where 10 years ago parents saw football as too dangerous. And you are getting a lot of hospitality income. It's all very good, but if you can find one chairman who will say that was what he always knew would happen after Taylor, then I'll show you a liar. Some might have had an inkling of the possibilities, but they were just dreams rather than targets.

TV rights are not much different. There are still a lot of clubs who think they just have to sit back and the money will roll in. Even the analysts were thinking that when all the clubs were floating in 1996. The idea was that a football club was a great way to tap into that BSkyB money. Now the City is not so sure, and clubs need to wake up to that. What will happen if Man United can sell all its own rights? What does that mean for everyone else? United could probably get £2 million or £3 million a game for every game from ITV or Sky or by going pay–per–view, but how much will you give me for, say, Wimbledon against Bolton?

Football's wealth dream, as expressed in its belief that TV money will continue to flow, helps illustrate the business principle that the source of a company's ultimate failure can lie in the roots of its success unless action is taken. This may be exactly the threat facing British football today. The game has, after all, profited from an opportune moment when all the elements came together. The reaction so far has been good for some of the game, but the formula is unstable. Football has basically fluked it from the half-way line while believing that it meant the shot all the time and is reckoning on doing it again just as easily.

A government that basically wanted to chastise a disliked sport ended up causing that sport to reinvigorate its finances and its business activities. A broadcaster who had to make one last throw of the dice to save a multibillion pound satellite venture then swelled the game's treasure chest beyond imagination, but it was Rupert Murdoch and Sam Chisholm's gamble and BSkyB has written the rules ever since.

That gamble is now under scrutiny both by the European Commission and the UK Monopolies and Mergers Commission. BSkyB and Murdoch are putting their safety net in place by striking separate deals with big clubs such as Manchester United. Football, which never knew what the business game was about in the past, still does not know quite what is going on. The Premiership at the moment has plenty of money – but what will happen to the rest of football?

Quite apart from the TV problem, there are all the other issues that have been allowed to mushroom while the football boom has run along. Fans have been burdened with ever-increasing ticket rates, over-priced merchandising and often heavy-handed stewarding. Even popular and successful clubs such as Arsenal, Leeds United, Derby County and Newcastle United have all recently found themselves at loggerheads with their supporters, their customers.

One investment banker with close links to the football sector and also a Newcastle United fan takes the Geordie giants to task, although his comments could apply to many other clubs:

The people running Newcastle have blundered from one cock-up to another since [chairman and main shareholder] Sir John Hall first left the board. They try to build a new stadium on a natural beauty spot, Leezes Park near to the St James' Park Ground, and assume that because the city loves the club, no one will object. Instead you've got season-ticket holders of thirty years' standing passing anti-United petitions around inside the ground. Then, they go and tell a non-league club, Stevenage Borough, that they don't want to play there even though that's the draw in the FA Cup. Again, you end up

> *with Geordies telling the club to pack it in and stop playing big*
> *bully. You ask yourself, 'Do these people understand the business?'*

His comments came before the notorious performance of Newcastle directors Douglas Hall and Freddy Shepherd in Marbella managed to enrage the team's fans even further. On a drunken spree, the two men were caught on camera laughing at supporters for buying over-priced replica shirts, mocking star player Alan Shearer as Mary Poppins and claiming that they had offloaded another striker, Andy Cole, to archrivals Manchester United when they knew he was injured. Sir John Hall's reaction after the pair were forced to stand down as directors and he temporarily returned as chairman emphasized the continuing problems as the self-proclaimed leader of the Geordie nation showed himself capable of blaming everyone but his culpable son and friend. And then, after a remarkably brief rehabilitation, the two miscreants were brought back on to the board – they still owned more than 50 per cent of the club – with fans left to like it or lump it.

There is a strange and disturbing echo of Lord Taylor's eight-year-old criticisms in these comments. Is it still 'legitimate to wonder whether the directors are genuinely interested in the welfare of their grass-roots supporters'?

And then there is the simple fact that for all the financial success of the game and the new stadia and superstar players, it has been achieved at a cost. The fabulous prosperity at the top has not been universally shared. The three divisions outside the Premier League have received far less TV cash to meet their dreams, even if the sums they do now get far exceed those of the dark days of 1988. Meanwhile, the riches at the top have not filtered down. They have simply made the situation more desperate and increased the likelihood that very soon clubs will start to fall like dominoes, taking with them their idea of what the game is really all about.

CHAPTER THREE

THE INCOME GAP

We are getting to a very dangerous point with how the money is split. You could soon see a club get promoted from the Football League to the Premiership and go bankrupt as a result. There are plenty of First Division chairman who look upstairs and ask themselves if they can afford the risk.

> John Wile, chief executive, West Bromwich Albion,
> August 1997

THE MOST IMMEDIATE THREAT FACING FOOTBALL CLUBS TODAY IS how the big-money cake gets sliced, with particular regard to television income. The current deal for English Premier League coverage on BSkyB is worth £670 million over four years from 1997–8 to 2000–1 and covers 20 teams. BSkyB's deal with England's remaining 72 clubs of the Football League is worth just £125 million over five years from 1996–7 to 2000–1. There is no balder representation of how the Premiership's wealth translates into domination of the game.

The so-called income gap between the Premier League and the Football League is already at the centre of the debate over the football economy. It defines what is and is not a good investment opportunity or a good debt risk. At its most stark, it defines who has a future and who does not. However, there are a few more important wrinkles.

There is the question of the 'yo-yo' teams that bounce between the two worlds, clubs such as Crystal Palace, Bolton Wanderers and Sunderland. One season they are Premiership contenders and then they are dumped back into the First Division, only to return to the heights one or two seasons later. There are those who, once banished from the Premiership's Carling-sponsored Elysian Fields, enter periods of marked decline, clubs like Manchester City, Swindon Town and Oldham Athletic. But then, even more perverse, there are those teams that manage to stay in the Premier League without reaching the very top and still find that the costs of doing so eat up almost all the apparent riches they earn.

Ask some analysts about the income gap now and the shrewder are likely to shoot back: 'Which one are you talking about?' The one thing they all agree on, however, is that none of these differentials is particularly good news for the majority of teams.

The moneymen would be quite content if the richer clubs could hold on to some of the vast sums they earn, but football simply does not seem able to control its costs, no matter how fast its income rises. By contrast, there are deeper issues facing fans. Are some clubs being shut out of the top competition? Are their debt-incurring attempts to reach the heights or even just stay afloat putting many historic teams in jeopardy? Are some teams being rendered irrelevant and prepared slowly but surely for the knacker's yard by starving them of resources?

To suggest that there is a conspiracy among Premiership chairmen to shrink English football to 20 professional teams would be a wild overstatement. But there are a significant number who would welcome a sizeable reduction in today's 92 full-time clubs. The market, they say, is not big enough to support everyone. If this can be achieved through 'natural wastage' rather than some form of cull, all the better. That first route would lessen the likelihood of a national outcry – campaigns like Brighton & Hove Albion's Fans United aside – and tough government intervention.

The reality, however, is that even the most powerful clubs did not expect the basic Premiership–League income gap to grow to its current size. Like so many of football's current dilemmas, nobody ever anticipated that things would turn out quite as they have, and as many of those who could do something about it appear to be reaping rewards beyond their wildest dreams, there does not seem to be much impetus behind finding a solution. The income gap is nevertheless eating away at the game like a cancer. It is not incurable, thank God, but it has to be understood and treated.

Welcome to the Skydome – spaces limited

When in 1992 former BSkyB chief executive Sam Chisholm announced to Premier League chairmen that his company would offer a package worth £380 million (with the BBC attached for highlights to assuage sponsor concerns), football's leaders could not believe their luck. The sum was almost four times what the 22 chairmen had expected. Most cottoned on that Murdoch was prepared to gamble and gamble big to get football, because he and Chisholm saw the game as vital to boosting mediocre dish sales in the wake of Sky's takeover of BSB. They had never expected that he would go this far. But getting the cream of English soccer was Rupert's 'shit or bust' bet. Importantly, though, as in all matters Murdoch, there were strings attached.

To most supporters these became apparent in the form of subscriptions for all live league games, the shifting around of the traditional Saturday timetable to accommodate Sunday afternoon and Monday night fixtures, and some US ideas, mercifully soon dispensed with, such as dancers and fireworks after a nil–nil draw. But Murdoch's men, led by BSkyB head of sport Vic Wakeling, had some other demands of the clubs, as one director explains:

> *Very soon after the deal was struck, people from Sky were making it pretty clear that they expected their money to be well used. By that, I mean that they wanted all the clubs to start bringing in more big-name talent. England now had the world's richest league, so it should also have the best players. For them, it was all part of the marketing.*

Of course, the clubs probably did not need all that much encouragement. The original and the later 1997 BSkyB deals included significant financial bonuses for appearances in live games and a club's final league position. Spending money on improving squads made financial sense. There was also the threat of relegation to the now vastly poorer Football League, which in 1992 netted a mere £5.25 million for the season from ITV, rising to £8 million in 1993.

However, the pressure to do well meant that football's cost structure was about to change fundamentally. Almost automatically, Football League clubs greatly raised the transfer prices they were seeking, an understandable response to seeing the Premiership set sail with an average annual income 12 times as much as they would enjoy. Bigger clubs responded by looking overseas for players, but while this proved a useful alternative in the short term, agents on the Continent soon realized that they should now be charging the English similar amounts to the equally rich Italian clubs. Domestic players and their representatives were quick to become aware that if the game had achieved an eightfold increase in its income at the summit, wage packets should grow in sympathy. After all, whose skills were ultimately being paid for?

Rampant inflation throughout football had begun and it would not stop at the bridge between the Premier League and Division One, as John Wile, the former captain of and now chief executive at First Division West Bromwich Albion, explains:

One of the ironies of football life is that the Premier League did promise some sort of trickle-down income for the lower divisions, largely through transfer fees. Instead, it seems that much of that money has gone abroad for foreign players, and what we have had is trickle-down wage inflation, right through not just to the Third Division, but even the non-league Vauxhall Conference.

Ambition in the Football League played a part as its larger teams that had been excluded by the schism decided to invest heavily to join the elite. They would raise money to attract Premiership quality players to achieve promotion and, so the thinking went, untold riches. Add to that more general concern among talent about wage differentials and the pressures become obvious. The income gap was becoming the main force behind the temptation for clubs to raise ever-growing mountains of debt.

However, while Premiership outsiders understandably believed that there was a pot of gold just over the horizon, those on the inside rapidly discovered that there were two very different competitions within one division. As befitted its elitist philosophy, a viewpoint sanctioned and approved of by the FA, the structure of the Premier League was such that its internal sharing of the spoils greatly favoured clubs at the top, particularly when their additional access to big money-spinning European competitions was taken into account. Not one gap opened up but two or three.

What's the difference between Premier and First?

In the 1997–8 season, the first year of BSkyB's improved £670 million deal provided £152 million to split among the Premier League's 20 members. That was divided as a basic £3.3 million each plus £320,000 for every game a club played that was televized. In addition, there was a payment of £118,000 per position in the league.

On that basis, a team finishing tenth and featuring in six televized games would pocket £3.3 million plus £1.92 million for TV appearances and another £1.18 million for coming tenth. That is £6.4 million for doing not very well and exceeds even the £6.3 million that Manchester United received in the last year of the £380 million contract as champions.

More cash is today reaching the Football League, and the 1996 £125 million deal with Sky prompted that organization's president Gordon McKeag to claim:

> For many clubs, television rights money probably represents the difference between survival and extinction.

But there is still an enormous difference between what a good First Division club can earn compared to a Premiership relegation candidate.

TV money plus sponsorship and other activities, most notably the Football League-run Coca-Cola Cup, gives the Football League an average disposable income of £33 million a season to divide among its 72 members. This is split on a basis of 59.5 per cent (£19.6 million) for the First Division, 23.5 per cent (£7.8 million) for the Second and 17 per cent (£5.6 million) for the Third.

A rough calculation covering TV appearances and merit awards suggests that any team winning promotion to the Premier League will earn between £1.2 million and £1.3 million for its efforts from the game, while a mid-table First Division side pockets about £830,000. Both these figures are far behind the £6.4 million for a mid-ranking top-division side, but they are also less than the £1.65 million that a relegated Premiership club receives from its former partners as a parachute payment during the two seasons after its departure.

Every year of the Premier League's existence theoretically widens the gap still further, as the teams in the top flight supposedly build up bigger and bigger war chests to buy players, pay wages, market their brands and expand their businesses. Further financial comparisons support this view. An average Premiership club made an annual profit of £4.3 million in 1997, compared with losses for the average club in each of the other divisions of £0.5 million in the First, £0.4 million in the Second and £0.3 million in the Third. Total Premiership turnover was £464 million in the same year, compared with £346 million previously. First Division turnover was £131 million, Second Division £55 million and Third £26 million. Although turnover in the First Division was up from £104 million, almost matching Premier League growth, Second Division turnover growth was more modest and Third Division turnover dropped slightly.

Not surprisingly, some First Division clubs are less than enamoured of their richer neighbours' behaviour, as WBA's John Wile notes:

> *The Premier League is undoubtedly a very well-run organization and has had startling success in bringing more money into football than anyone would have expected. But when it was founded, it also had two other big things on its side.*
>
> *First, the circumstances were right. When they struck the first Sky deal, there was genuine competition for rights for the first time. I have no doubt that Murdoch would have paid the same amount of money for the whole Football League as he did for the Premier League. The numbers were inevitably going to go up and there would have been more than enough for everybody, whatever happened. Look*

back at the original talks and you can see that whatever Sky offered, ITV outbid, and then Sky outbid that and the process went on until somebody blinked.

The second point is that they had the elite product. Yes, the Premier League has shown the way in marketing. It has really shaken up the way clubs present to sponsors, advertisers and so on. And that revolution was long overdue. But, it also sliced off the cream of English football and was a pretty easy sell. Typically, taking on a football rights contract involves taking the rough with the smooth, so to speak, but this time all that was on offer was the Cresta Run, a fast slide all the way to some very big profits.

The longer-term implication of that second action is that the Football League appears to have been devalued as a product. So, yes, we are bargaining harder on TV rights and sponsorship these days, but you can see it in some people's eyes: 'This is really second rate.' Well, I would challenge that. I do not believe that the gap in quality between the bottom half of the Premier League and the First Division is that great. But if it is beginning to widen, it's nothing to do with teams outside the Premiership being inherently weaker than those in it: it's an artificial situation the leading clubs have created.

That said, the determination of many clubs to enter the Premier League further exacerbates the situation. Williams de Broe analyst Nigel Hawkins certainly sees this as a major contributory factor to the out-of-kilter economics of the Football League:

There are some teams in the Football League, including a few of the listed ones, and although they'll never put it in the business plan, their strategies come down to: 'We will get into that Premier League by any means necessary', and if that means paying over the odds for players and wages, then so be it. It's still one hell of a gamble. There are 12 teams working this way in every typical First Division season, and only three can go up. So most are going to be disappointed. But what makes it worse is that the same teams come back and do the same thing the following season. Carry on paying Premier League salaries, carry on trying to get up into the top flight, carry on building up debt. At some point, something will break.

The extent of risk was emphasized in the 1997–8 season when two of three clubs that were promoted to the Premiership, champions Nottingham Forest and second-placed Middlesbrough, were clubs that had come down from Carling Heights the year before, while the third fallen angel, Sunderland, only narrowly missed out on an immediate return in a play-off final penalty shootout against Charlton Athletic. The two successful teams had been the beneficiaries of Premiership money not just the year before but also from their parachute payments, extending their financial advantage over their rivals.

Forest, in particular, made no bones about the fact that it was going to buy itself back at the first attempt, controversially raising 1997–8 season-ticket prices even though the team had been relegated. Nevertheless, the privations of the First Division after relegation meant that the club lost £6.4 million in just the six months to December 1997. The deficit was entirely due to ambition, as the club spent on transfers and kept its wages at the same level as they had been in the Premiership. If these were the risks for a 'wealthy' First Division side, how did the finances stack up for the rest? It is instructive that, following Forest's conversion to a plc in 1997, chairman Nigel Wray was clear about what would happen if the club failed to win promotion at the first attempt:

If we are not promoted to the Premier League at the end of the 1998 season then appropriate measures will be taken to ensure that our cost base is compatible with our revenue base in future periods.

In other words, the axe would have fallen.

Chief executive Phil Soar emphasizes the role of manager Dave Bassett in all this. Bassett attends all plc board meetings, taking all the footballing decisions on transfer spending and which players he wants. He would play a role in any restructuring following a failure to win promotion. But again, Soar is blunt about the gulf between First and Premiership and its consequences:

The gap in television revenue has become quite enormous. Running a football club means tough decisions have to be taken over a period.

On the other side of the issue is Sunderland, which failed in its battle to get back up. In its results for the six months to 30 November 1997, the club noted that average attendances at games were 32,000 and for some matches at its new Stadium of Light crowds had reached 40,000 – a long way ahead of the majority of Premiership clubs.

The club has talked of bringing its capacity up to 63,000 within five years and has such passionate support that this is not beyond the bounds of possibility. Partly as a consequence of ticket sales, turnover was up nearly £3 million to £8 million, but profits were halved to £518,000. The main reason for the fall was £5.8 million spent on players in the bid to secure promotion and a doubling of players' wages from £1.3 million to £2.7 million. The wage bill was lower while the side was in the Premiership and chairman Bob Murray was up front about the reasons for the rise. He said the club was:

> *coping with a traumatic return to First Division football. All of us at the club are fully committed to returning to, and remaining in, the Premier League not only for the financial reasons but for the pride of all those working and supporting this great club.*

The City of London was quick to add up the cost of failure and success for the two quoted clubs. On 29 April 1998, Sunderland's defeat by Ipswich Town meant that Forest was guaranteed promotion. Sunderland's shares dropped in value by almost 13 per cent to 435p overnight, while Forest's rose more modestly by 1p to 76p. Then, on Tuesday 26 May, the day after the play-off defeat, the Sunderland shares which had recovered to 512p were slashed again to 415p, a loss of 19 per cent. By early June, the shares had fallen again to 400p.

The irony of all this is that Sunderland is seen by City analysts as a well-run club with the potential to be as big as teams like Liverpool and neighbours Newcastle United. Yet as long as it remains in the First Division, its attraction to investors is greatly diminished because the assumption is that it will have to keep on spending more than it earns to build a promotion-winning side while living off Football League money.

The modest rise in the Nottingham Forest share price also tells a story about the income gap, particularly since that rise had mostly fallen away one month later and the club was trading at around 56p. Getting up is good, but staying up is what really matters. For Football League clubs that arrive in the top flight without war chests to match their rivals this is no easy task, as was shown in 1997–8 when the two ex-Premiership clubs going up passed the three which had been promoted the season before and were going straight back down – Barnsley, Crystal Palace and Bolton Wanderers.

Wile, again, is clear on the problem:

When you look at the numbers, and bear in mind that promotion means competing with some teams that have been earning Premiership money for four or five seasons, you end up in a situation where a large number of First Division club directors are genuinely wary of what might happen if their teams go up before they are fully prepared, and in that sense, you are talking mostly about money. Winning the First Division has to be the team's objective, but that means promotion and you do find yourself thinking: 'Will we be able to live with these Premier guys?' or 'Will we just go straight back down?'

West Brom has floated on the Alternative Investment Market, although it has not as yet offered any new shares but merely translated those that were already held into a public trading environment:

AIM is a possible mechanism for us to raise extra cash quickly if we do achieve promotion or, indeed, want to expand other parts of the business through developing hotels or leisure clubs next to our ground [The Hawthorns]. In footballing terms we differ from some of the other quoted First Division clubs in that we would rather ask the City for money once we were going up to the Premiership, rather than in order to get there. This is a very difficult division to get out of and you can only ask for that really big City injection once.

The Barnsley story is instructive about what can happen even to a successful First Division team. In the 1997–8 season, the Yorkshire underdogs were probably many English fans' second team. Being runners-up in the First Division the year before had earned the club its first ever spell in the top flight, and even its own supporters saw the Premier League as probably a glorious 12-month adventure on a shoestring budget. Initially in order to prevent embarrassment but later as the chance of survival became more of a reality, some big numbers began to stack up.

Before the start of the 1997–8 season, the club's record transfer fee spent had been £310,000 in 1993 for Celtic's Andy Peyton. Between March 1997 and June 1998, Barnsley broke through that figure six times, its most expensive acquisitions being strikers Georgi Hristov from Partizan Belgrade for £1.5 million and Ashley Ward from Derby County for £1.3 million. Total outgoing transfer fee expenditure from June 1997 to March 1998 was £6 million plus an undisclosed sum to a non-league club. Transfer fees received over the same period were a mere £225,000. Barnsley's promotion reward from the First Division, and its share of Premier League money, will just about cover the outlay. Just about.

The club's manager, Danny Wilson, was phlegmatic in saying that he aimed to build a squad to survive that first season, nothing more. To do that, even in the moneybags Premiership, this new arrival spent just about everything that was available. And it didn't work.

Where profit fits into this equation is another matter. There will be the safety-net cash, but Barnsley now goes down with a wage bill that the club cannot cut and players that it may find difficult to sell.

The Barnsleys of the game have to pay the transfer fees to compete with the wealthier clubs or go down. All of that has to be achieved most of the time on a much lower turnover than the big sides. It even has to be achieved on much lower turnover than the established Premiership low- and mid-ranking clubs, because former First Division teams are relatively new to the other promotional aspects of being a leading side. Not every team has a national profile which attracts kids and adults around the country. Barnsley is regarded as a well-run club; its chairman John Dennis is widely commended for matching business acumen with an awareness of fans' needs and desires. However, the club's brand appeal only stretched to selling around 16,000 replica club shirts in 1996–7, according to insiders. That was double the previous season's sales and early Premier League sales figures showed strong growth again, but suffice to say that it did not worry the big clubs too much. As a result, the club's kit deal is rumoured to be worth just £10,000 a season.

It is no real reflection on the Barnsley management that the deal is so low; it simply shows that some clubs do not have the bargaining power of others. Man United is reputed to make £40 million from its six-year deal with Umbro. Other less illustrious clubs can look for at least £1 million a year. Even many First Division sides are reckoned to do much better. Yet Barnsley is a club which, during its season with the big boys, went to Anfield and won, and knocked Man United out of the FA Cup. There were a fair number of disasters early on, but the club's determined although unsuccessful attempt to escape relegation would also appear to justify comments that the footballing quality gap between the two leagues is not that great.

Barnsley may well make a quick return – by the end of its Premiership journey, the squad looked well equipped to play good football at any level. But for others the culture shock of a sudden return to Football League makes the numbers much harder to deal with. One example stands out in particular – Manchester City.

Man City's average gate is over 20,000, another band of support like Sunderland's that exceeds those for many Premier League sides. Moreover, City boasts this huge and hugely devoted following in direct local competition with Man United. Both in the past and at present, the directors have spent to match their supporters' ambitions, and the board includes more millionaires than at any other club. City should be a big, championship- and cup-contending side, but instead, it spent the 1997–8 season failing to fight off relegation to Division Two.

City's miserable season was due, according to former chairman Francis Lee, mainly to the problems of having a wage bill and a 40-member squad more suited to the Premiership. As a result, the club lost nearly £1 million in 1997 and had net borrowings of £6.3 million. City's experience helps demonstrate that it can become difficult to survive even if you have only a couple of bad years – and, let's be honest, the majority of teams do. The club went down from the Premiership not five years ago, but in 1996.

In part, clubs are hamstrung by agreements with the Professional Footballers' Association over contracts. These say that teams cannot reduce the terms and conditions of a player's contract while it is running and cannot sell him unless the buying club is at least willing to match the salary he already receives. When you have a situation where the Premier League is paying massive salaries even to ordinary squad members, while the other divisions cannot, the system starts to store up massive problems for any club that gets relegated.

City had some of its fabled bad luck. Its record buy, £3 million striker Lee Bradbury, picked up a long-term injury, for example. But boardroom battles and recriminations over the club's plight made a bigger contribution. One Second Division manager explained:

There were City directors and senior staff going around slagging off the squad and that became common knowledge throughout the game. The result was that nobody wanted to buy any of the players that the club was trying to offload. Then when they weren't making money from the players, nobody was willing to put anything into the club because they were trying to drive Frannie out. So, things just got worse and worse. The financial side of the club was under increasing pressure and that went straight into what happened on the pitch.

The City experience, in fact, stretches further than Division One. A director with one of the Premiership's top sides even admitted to the authors that:

I look at what has happened in just three years at Maine Road and it really is, you know, 'There but for the grace of God go I.'

What happened to City sounds like crass management, but given the risks involved in football at that level, it will happen at many more clubs before long.

The Premiership was damned for greed and for being exclusive when it first kicked off and the accusations had some force. When a Sunderland does not get the promotion it supposedly deserves or a Man City falls into decline, the accusations are repeated. However, as WBA's Wile admits, hurling insults upstairs is pointless because the Premiership is a done deal:

> *Nobody is going to close the Premier League down. But we do need to take a long, hard look at the real relationship between the Premier League and the clubs outside it. What are the consequences of having one very rich division and three others that scrabble around for cash? Or what happens to those teams that want to hunt the big game, but have to invest frightening sums of money to get up there and stay up there, basically by mortgaging their futures? The problem now is that much of the Premier League is doing very nicely, so it doesn't really need to negotiate.*

So if the Premier League will not talk – not on equal terms, at least – what can the First Division clubs do about it? Almost inevitably, some clubs have been talking about their own breakaway – a sort of semi-skimmed league to match the full-cream version above. In late February 1998, a project that had been talked of variously as the Phoenix and Premiership II took a step closer to reality at a meeting of Division One chairmen in London. Their demands? A greater share of TV revenues when the BSkyB package is renegotiated in 2000 and control over their own marketing and commercial activities. Four months later, League and Ipswich Town chairman David Sheepshanks headed off the threat for another year by getting 62 of the organization's 72 members to agree to most of these demands.

However, the plotting of a First Division breakaway did have something more to it. If the English and, more recently, Scottish Premier Leagues were based on their members' desire to get a 'true' value for their product, Premiership II is a project with more than a modicum of fear about it. The gap is now getting so wide that the First Division – or, at least, many of its members – is effectively contemplating the sacrifice of the two divisions below for its own survival. And even at that lower level, there are those who are upsetting the apple cart.

There are no prizes for second and third

Second and Third Division clubs have suffered the bulk of the real financial crises in the last five years. Brighton & Hove Albion, Hull City, Millwall, Bournemouth and Doncaster Rovers are the most high-profile teams that have stared extinction in the face. Doncaster, in fact, has now left the Football League after finishing at the very bottom and faces an uncertain future.

In many cases, what one might charitably term bad management that had nothing to do with the Premier League has played the major part in these difficulties. The destruction of Brighton's Goldstone Ground under a board led by Focus DIY magnate Bill Archer and Liberal Democrat politician David Bellotti was nothing more nor less than a crude act by a couple of chancers. Archer initially paid £56.25 for a controlling stake, and with his board colleagues changed the club's articles of association so that the directors could benefit from the sale of the stadium, a £7.4 million deal that was duly struck in Summer 1995.

The regime at Hull City, meanwhile, ran up £2 million of debt and failed to keep up to date with the tax authorities over a £240,000 bill, while the owners of Doncaster behaved in equally bizarre ways that, at one point, saw chairman Bill Richardson taking over team affairs despite having absolutely no knowledge of coaching – Mr Richardson, it might also be added, has put nowhere as much into his club as Ted Turner has into his. Richardson is also one of those in the unusual position of being both the club's largest shareholder and its largest creditor – never a good sign.

There is nevertheless an underlying sensation that some directors are coming to the opinion that lower-division football simply is not a viable business. Once a board goes down this route, it heads into very dark territory that almost encourages asset-stripping. Bournemouth's chairman Trevor Watkins took away one stark lesson from the near collapse of his club. The City lawyer, who has been a fan for 25 years and who saved the club by helping organize a community ownership scheme in 1997 to replace the previous administration, puts it this way:

If you go bust, you are out. The Football League have made it very clear over the last few years that clubs in financial difficulties are not going to get too much leeway. There won't be any Middlesbrough or Bristol City situation again where old debts disappeared and something called Boro brackets 19– whatever starts the following week. Gone are the days when you can wind a club down, start a new one the next day and keep your league status. Football clubs have to stand on their own two feet. Of all the 72 Football League clubs, most are making a loss and it is going to need radical solutions to deal with that.

The average loss at a club like ours is £275,000 and unless you sell players it cannot be done. It is commercial realism. We sold Mattie Holland to Ipswich for £800,000 and we lost a good player. But what has it done? It allowed us to bring in four new players a year earlier than we would have done. It allowed us to free our transfer embargo. It allowed us to clear some litigation. It allowed us to recruit a day-to-day chief executive, to recruit a receptionist, to give small pay increases to staff who deserved them and it has meant that we go home at night knowing the club is secure.

At Preston North End, also in the Second Division, chairman Bryan Gray is limited in his ambition, which is to reach the First, with the Premiership just a dream. He has built a strong, well-run business that is quoted on the stock market and respected by City analysts and institutions. The club comes up with ideas such as a FIFA-backed football museum supported by National Lottery money. It is innovative and does not pay too much for players. It does, however, have one of the higher wage bills. Despite the careful way the club is run, the City looks at its value of around £9 million and is not interested. The club is a viable long-term business that should be around in years to come, but according to analysts it will not really be a challenger in the money leagues.

The temporarily blocked threat of Premiership II and continued trickle-down inflation have had a wider effect at this level. In some instances, rich businesspeople have spotted that it might be better to acquire a club in the lower two divisions and buy that through to some form of higher-league glory than to meet the high asking prices of the established clubs.

The most famous example of this is at Second Division Fulham, where Harrods owner Mohammed al Fayed gave his pompously termed chief operating officer Kevin Keegan over £8 million to spend on boosting his squad during 1997–8. As the former Newcastle manager bought in players from higher divisions, like the Pauls Peschisolido and Bracewell and ex-England star Peter Beardsley, it had a predictable effect on other clubs – talent started to seek much higher wages and agents began to mention differentials. Some rival Second Division directors were actually disappointed when the club failed to secure a promotion, because they now expect the pressures on costs to continue being fuelled through 1999. Al Fayed has pledged a total of at least £30 million to Keegan for his five-year Premiership plan, so there is still quite a bit of spending to be done.

There is, even at this level, a definite jostling to grab a seat when the music stops, but there are some directors and potential investors who are working to prove that this need not be the case. Nicholas Bitel is a sports lawyer, chief executive of the London Marathon and the former owner of Wigan Athletic, now very much one of the ambitious clubs under its new owner, JJB Sports magnate and former Blackburn Rovers fullback David Whelan.

While Whelan is one of the lower leagues' big spenders, Bitel argues equally firmly for the prospect of smaller clubs that build on community links to both secure and justify their futures:

> *What surprises me is the fact that clubs do not see that they could balance the needs of running a club as a business with their social roles, and, for some, it is going to be a hard-learned lesson indeed.*

He takes the position that clubs must be run on proper business terms, delivering profits or, at least, meeting long- and short-term financial commitments without resorting to the begging bowl. He also argues that such conditions should apply to teams at both the top of the Premiership in England and Scotland and the bottom of the Third Division in the two countries:

> *If you are looking for financial aid from outside the game, forget it. Even if they wanted to help, government could not. It simply cannot afford to, so long-term subsidy is a non-starter at any level. So*

where does that leave you? Wherever they stand, but particularly in the lower divisions, clubs need to turn back to the communities they serve. They need to work in partnership with that community and recognize their roles, because it is good business.

He cites two examples of clubs that have taken this route to secure their futures, Northampton Town and Wycombe Wanderers:

Northampton used to have an appalling ground and staggering debts, now they have the brand new Sixfields stadium and are, let's say, comfortable. Yet by the time the administrators came in [in 1992], turning the club around was already largely down to its directors having gone to the local council and saying: 'Look, we matter to people round here, and they matter to us. They keep the turnstiles spinning. Can we work this out together?'

The result was that a new £5.25 million stadium was built for the club. On Saturdays it houses the team, but throughout the week it is also available as a conference centre, a gymnasium and has various other facilities open to everybody. Bitel adds:

There's also been an interesting side effect here. Yes, some people are coming back to football because of new, safe grounds, but Northampton have achieved above-average increases in gate attendances. Because Sixfields is a seven-day facility and is attracting people who were not football fans before, when they go to use the gym or whatever, they're also thinking, 'Well, maybe I'll come to a game here next week.'

Wycombe have worked in much the same way. The Adams Park ground is open all week long and has facilities – not just club shops, museums and over-priced bars, but proper facilities that are open to the community. Beyond that, the club also goes out and works the community hard. It promotes the team by being an active local participant in charities, in activities for school children and so on. Again, a small club with a pretty small catchment area, but it's not going to go bust. It's a viable, popular business.

The unanswered question in what Bitel says, however, is whether it is still possible to perceive the football business in these terms when income pressures surround even clubs like Wycombe and Northampton on all sides.

So why shed tears for the Premier League?

Given the circumstances facing clubs in the Football League, it seems strange to conclude this journey across English football's income gaps by talking about problems in the moneybags world of the Premiership. And yet, serious problems are beginning to develop because even the top division is split.

Merchant banker Tony Fraher of Singer & Friedlander is one of the prophets of football's financial heaven. He talks bullishly about every club having a brand and a worth and, while the performance of his Football Fund investment scheme had not been too impressive by mid-1998, there is a certain force to his arguments. Within the Premier League, he concentrates on the bigger clubs:

> *At the end of the day it is a business and it is about the strength of brands. You have a top eight or nine clubs. It's not about strength of play and it is not about results. Wimbledon have done well recently but they don't have the support. It's about the clubs that can deliver the TV audiences. They probably are Man United, Liverpool, Arsenal, Spurs possibly, Aston Villa, Celtic and Rangers.*

Beyond those, the City is not particularly interested and some teams which might be regarded in the outside world as Big Business United, such as Newcastle, are not rated very highly, particularly when directors are caught on cameras in Spanish *whiskerias* blathering drunkenly. Such 'companies' are seen as a possibility for the future, but that is about as far as it goes.

The stock-market values put on clubs demonstrate the point. Manchester United is worth around £400 million and has been as high as £500 million. No other club comes anywhere near. Rangers, which is privately quoted rather than being on one of the two main exchanges, comes next at about £240–250 million, but the remainder are all at least half the Man United value. Newcastle United is worth about £130 million, Aston Villa £74 million and

Spurs some £68 million. The lesson that only certain clubs count is hammered home.

Money has always played a major role in football. In the 1970s, Burnley was referred to as the 'Bank of England' club when it was a force in the land because of the power of the chequebook of its then owner Bob Lord. The formation of professional football was all down to some clubs paying for better players so they could beat their rivals. Go back to the literature of the 1920s or 1930s and you will find plenty of authors complaining about the damaging effects of ongoing commercialization. Money as such is not the sole issue. It is the sheer volume that is now flooding into the game and will continue to pour in and, most importantly, where that money is going. Predominantly, it flows into the different Premier Leagues, and at the summit that flow becomes a torrent, re-emphasizing the preeminence of the teams at the top.

Nottingham Forest chief executive Phil Soar sees the landscape as follows:

The step up to the Premiership is difficult but it is a problem that we are happy to have to deal with. There is an income gap definitely. At the start of each season there are just three or four Premiership clubs who can think seriously about winning the league. The rest are concentrating on staying up and trying to win a Cup.

The top of the Premiership is undoubtedly the profit pinnacle. Man United is the world's most profitable football club. Annual pretax profit in the year to 31 July 1997 was £27.6 million against a turnover of £87.9 million. But there are other wealthy and powerful teams. They are not the Big Five of old, Spurs and Everton having slipped in recent years, but clubs like Arsenal, Liverpool, Blackburn Rovers, Chelsea, Aston Villa, Leeds United and Newcastle United are also powerful in their own right. In general, though, the eternal verities hold, with each of these other super teams able to claim a strong history.

Of this group, three sides have the biggest supports. Continental Research estimates that 18 million people in England are football fans. Some 14 million of these are fans of Premiership clubs. Of these, 3.3 million are Man United fans, while Liverpool is supported by 2.2 million and Newcastle by 1.3 million. By that measure three clubs account for more than a third of the fans in English football.

The leading clubs are undoubted winners and genuinely powerful money machines with huge supporter bases. They are the clubs that are perennially 'there or thereabouts'. But can the same be said, financially if not sportingly, to apply to the rest of the Premiership? They also share the BSkyB honey pot, after all. The amounts that even an 'ordinary' club can earn are, at first glance, frightening.

The TV value of mid-table mediocrity is something between £6 million and £7 million, but it doesn't stop there. The biggest sponsorship deal in the Nationwide League in 1997–8 involved champions Nottingham Forest and was worth £2 million over three years with Pinnacle Insurance. That was a good piece of business for the new management that had bought the club, but hardly one to compare with deals that can be secured in the Premiership. Consultants estimate that teams comparable to Forest in size and support and in the division above in the same season could have earned between £4 million and £6 million.

The problem, of course, comes down not to income but to expenditure. The Premiership is a very, very rich man's game. Transfer spending in 1997 was £209 million, while transfer cash received from sales was only £130 million. That works out at £79 million net outgoings – virtually £4 million a club. And all this was in a year when the deals were not quite as big as had been seen in the past, being led by the £7 million spent by Aston Villa and Arsenal on Stan Collymore and Marc Overmars respectively, not £15 million for an Alan Shearer.

At the same time, the extra leverage in terms of merchandising, corporate hospitality and other new business areas that the super sides can apply is opening up a new mega-gap. United already has a higher turnover in merchandising alone – £28.7 million in 1996–7 and rising – than most Premier League clubs have altogether. But at this level improving income – if not always performance – in European competition is also critical.

United chairman Martin Edwards says that his club sees Europe merely as the 'icing on the cake'. If this is true, then we are talking about a kind of icing so rich that it would make your teeth rot to stumps on the merest contact. Europe is worth a lot of money as long as you are not Rangers and virtually certain to go out early on. Qualifying for the Champions' League, perversely also open to second-placed teams in the biggest TV markets, is worth a minimum £2 million plus £1 million from the television pool, followed by £500,000 for a win and £250,000 for a draw.

So, say a team plays in the Champions' League, draws three games, loses two, wins one and goes out – a pretty ordinary performance, you'd probably agree. Well, it will still make £4.25 million before counting in gate money for its three home ties. Even if it lost six out of six, it would pocket £3 million plus gate receipts. Do a little better and the numbers really mount up. Making the final is worth a minimum £7.5 million without counting the win bonuses along the way, and a team could make £10.5 million before gate money if it won all six of its league games yet was knocked out in the second-stage quarter final – just enough to buy a tough-nut Dutch defender.

On top of all that, gate money and other receipts at grounds such as Old Trafford can comfortably exceed £1 million per match given the premium ticket prices that European ties attract, as well as likely merchandising and catering sales on the night. United even tried to push Europe further recently by launching a kit in 1997 specifically for its Champions' League games.

Then there are the Cup Winners' Cup and the UEFA Cup, which give the individual club a chance to sell TV rights for matches in addition to gate receipts. In the UK that has become more lucrative recently as the football-starved BBC and ITV are keen to pick up matches and the newly launched Channel Five is also in the race (although BSkyB does not normally compete for European games because it does not believe they will provide sufficient added value over and above its existing packages).

The Five effect was clearly illustrated in the 1997–8 season when the channel snatched rights for three English clubs – Aston Villa, Chelsea and Arsenal - with each receiving at least £375,000 even if they were knocked out in the first round; more was on offer for progressing significantly further. British teams can also expect to see as much again, at least, if they are drawn against good opposition in TV markets where rights are in similar demand such as Spain, Italy, Germany and France.

Channel Five is thought to have budgeted to spend about £2 million on live club soccer during the 1997–8 season because it knew that football was the kind of programming it needed to build its audience. 'Live football coverage is a very serious way of saying you are a major market player,' chief executive David Elstein has said, in an echo of the strategy originally followed by his former BSkyB employer Rupert Murdoch. There can also be no doubt that Elstein is only interested in certain clubs.

This is just one side of the rewards on offer to teams that do well and have the big brands. Some consider that it is only right and proper for success to be recognized. Yet outside the top five of the Premiership and the cup winners that automatically qualify each season, the happy picture of profitable football clubs does becomes cloudy. Apart from the cost of staying up, relegation is a serious and genuine threat that removes clubs from the money pump of the Premiership and can put them in severe trouble.

So how far do they go just to survive? The average Premier League team made a £2.6 million profit in 1997. But these are average figures and mathematicians will point out to anyone who will listen that there are always more below an average than above it. For English and Scottish football the lesson holds good, but it applies most especially in the Premiership. BSkyB cash is, in some respects, an addiction for all clubs there and not just the Barnsleys. They are all spending fortunes to stay afloat, while only a few can be said to be reaping the richest rewards.

Alan Sugar at Tottenham Hotspur has long been an advocate of tough financial discipline. Yet between June 1997 and March 1998 his club splashed out £12.33 million on transfers of players such as Les Ferdinand from Newcastle for £6 million, Moussa Saib from Valencia for £2.3 million and David Ginola from Newcastle United for £2 million. During that same period, Spurs managed to raise only £3.8 million from selling players and if it had not sold Teddy Sheringham to Man United it would have made just £800,000. That adds up to a transfer loss of £8.53 million in 10 months. This is a fair bit more than the £5.8 million spent by Barnsley. But Spurs is an established Premier League team and has been a member since its inception. Therefore, it has been able to build up more of a war chest. It is also still one of the more highly rated plc clubs where Sugar turned the company around from near bankruptcy to a comparatively healthy financial situation.

For Spurs some of the problem lies, as with Manchester City, in its wage bill. In late 1997, the club's finance director John Sedgwick told analysts that he expected the club's salary costs to rise by 20 per cent during the 1997–8 season, even though they had already risen by over 14 per cent the year before. At the time, Sedgwick based his estimate on the recent renegotiation of contracts with existing squad players such as defender Sol Campbell and goalkeeper Ian Walker. However, Spurs' situation and its desperation to fight off an early season slump led the club to invest heavily in two 'star' players, a returning Jürgen Klinsmann and the established Italian international Nicola Berti. Klinsmann reportedly received £33,000 a week, while Berti pocketed £25,000. Ferdinand and Ginola did not come cheap either. By mid-1998, 20 per cent looked like a conservative estimate.

Spurs can be said to have tackled this problem by cutting its staff. In the 10 months under review, the data shows five players, all with substantial Premier League experience, released on free transfers. A sensible approach, you might think. Yet in November 1997, investment bankers UBS issued a report that accused the club of 'destroying' £13.5 million of shareholder value between 1995 and 1997. The decision to sell some players cheaply, even for nothing, was, the bank said, counterbalanced by a transfer policy that saw it buying older players at inflated prices. The £6 million paid for 31-year-old Ferdinand was cited as one example, as were the earlier purchases of 30-year-old winger Ruel Fox for £4.4 million and 32-year-old defender John Scales for £2.6 million. Between June 1995 and November 1997, Spurs had spent £30.5 million on players, yet failed to qualify for European competition or win any of the main domestic trophies.

For the Spurs management, UBS's findings were particularly galling. The company found itself between Scylla and Charybdis. For some time before 1995, it had been under attack from its fans for trying to build a side based on youth and not venturing too frequently or expensively into the transfer market. It was a policy that put Tottenham in reasonable mid-table comfort, not a bad place to be after accusations of corruption involving former manager Terry Venables and, before that incident, near financial collapse. But this, Sugar and former manager Gerry Francis were told, was not the Tottenham way – meaning the way of a big-spending club which had previously bought in talent like Paul Gascoigne, Chris Waddle, Glenn Hoddle, Ossie Ardiles and Ricky Villa, won cups and leagues, and been the first English side this century to do the League and FA Cup Double. The City of London, by contrast, had praised Sugar for keeping a tight rein on expenditure and turning around the failing business. Then suddenly, the City's attitude also changed.

Analysts began to say that Sugar's strategy had 'devalued the brand'. Cost control was one thing, but the football business also needed glamour. In a blinding Damascus-like flash, the men in suits realized that successful teams were winning teams. So Spurs began to spend. Now, here was UBS claiming that was also the wrong policy.

Premier League clubs are expected to spend big money to win things but also to support the image of the 'world's best competition' on which its marketing and, equally important, paymaster BSkyB's marketing depend. For the league's business to function, every game must be a clash of titans. What most fans see as a nondescript fixture like Derby Country vs Wimbledon must be something that the TV schedulers can hype up. Wimbledon is perhaps the one club that has escaped the 'spend, spend, spend' rule, but it has been forced to think again and consider a move to Dublin in search of the cash to preserve and develop its status. Even the plucky, shoestring Dons cannot continue for much longer as they are in this environment. As Wimbledon's Lebanese owner Sam Hammam has said:

> Dublin is a very sexy option. We can't carry on forever as we are because of the way the Premiership now works.

It is true that UBS was not questioning Spurs' decision to spend so much as the wisdom of how funds had been used, but the critical issue is the nature of a competition that prompted the club's knee-jerk reaction.

In English football there are only three major prizes – the league title, FA and Coca-Cola Cups - plus five more European places that teams compete for each season. That means that even in the Premiership there are typically 13 disappointed sides every year, although that can arguably be reduced to 10 if the objective of a promoted club is just staying up. So, while clubs might be making an average profit of £2.6 million a year, the fact is that most are losing money. Even though the new BSkyB deal has doubled their income, many expect that situation to continue because of outstanding debts and continued player and wage inflation. In 1996–7, 14 of the 20 Premiership clubs reported a pretax loss, according to consultants Deloitte & Touche, yet only three were in this position before transfers were taken into account.

The real risks that this presents are clearly illustrated in the City of London's changing attitude towards football. Many of the clubs in the Premier League's annual relegation dogfight and those in the First Division with Premiership ambitions turned to the City for investment to underpin basic income, either by flotations or by bringing in institutions as private shareholders. During the 1996 football investment boom, this appeared to pay off as the game was viewed as a potentially huge leisure stock. However, this door is now closed and several clubs in similar circumstances have abandoned or postponed their plans. As analyst Hawkins puts it:

> *Premier clubs in the bottom half of the table or First Division clubs looking to go up are huge gambles. They are not very attractive stocks because a Premier club that gets relegated is likely to go down with huge financial commitments, yet its income could be slashed by up to 75 per cent overnight. The teams in the bottom half of the Premier League are terrified of losing the Sky money, so they pay big money to players just to keep them afloat.*

Football is a drug but so, it would appear, is Premiership money. You can never get enough to feed your desires and objectives. Man United, ironically, is now the club that talks most about the need for cost control, but that did not stop it once more tabling a number of eight-figure offers during and after the 1998 World Cup.

United can complain because, to some extent, it can afford to complain. Its revenue streams are massive.

More and more managers have started to talk about building squads just to stay afloat, but this suggests that even Premier League football is becoming a one-sided competition that will ultimately be of little interest to anybody. Sport requires a changing cast and a sense of competition for places at the top. If the income gap continues, then most of the 92 English and 40 Scottish clubs will no longer be part of that competition and that will devalue the entire sport.

If football becomes dull, it will also find that its followers desert it quickly and in large numbers. After all, the 18 million fans of English football include 95 per cent who never go to a match. Only 750,000 actually turn up for at least one match a season. Those people are probably reasonably committed, but what about the rest?

The essential income gap has always been there, with the sides which pull in bigger crowds and wealthier backers able to lord it over the smaller teams. Some teams were never able to mount a serious challenge in the past, but every once in a while they might have a winning season. If current trends continue unchecked, however, the future will be a time when most teams will never be able to challenge for anything at football's summit, while those outside in no more than a survivors' encampment face a bleaker future.

It is a worrying climate and, for smaller teams, the prospects for speculative outside investment are slimmer still. Hawkins explains:

> There has been a major change in how the City views companies ever since the utility privatizations began in the 1980s. Before that a £9–11 million pound outfit could come in. It would still be difficult, but there was financing available. After the privatizations, however, ideas of what should be the base-level valuation for a listed firm have shot up. You're not even looking at £30 million now, but maybe as high as £70 million for a 'small' company. That makes it very difficult for anyone other than the big clubs. Second and Third Division flotations really are for the fans and the local business community.

Promoted teams are finding it harder and harder to survive in the Premiership and the whole dream machine ethos of the game is being brought into question. Dreams need to be sustained but the reality now is the growing and almost unbridgeable income gap. In the 1960s and 1970s, a fifth of teams which were promoted to the top division went straight back down again. (Manchester United, incidentally, was promoted in the 1970s after relegation and, of course, managed to stay up. Had football's revolution happened years earlier, would it have been so lucky?) Between 1992 and 1996, a third of teams promoted from the First Division were relegated the following season.

However you look at it, only certain clubs are regarded as proper investments, and by and large they are the members of the elite. Others can develop models of community ownership or partnerships with local authorities, but it is a moot point as to how much this technique will simply preserve a club's future, never mind allow it to expand and reach for the Premiership or even First Division skies. The City's participation in football is, if anything, crystallizing the income gap and the existing hierarchy.

And so, at football's time of greatest riches and popularity, more clubs are at risk than ever before. Recent seasons have seen several near-death experiences in England and in Scotland for Glasgow's forgotten third team Partick Thistle and for Falkirk. Clydebank, meanwhile, is challenging Wimbledon's attempt to become Dublin United because it also cannot find enough support north of the border.

The result is that in a sport which depends on mobility, diversity, promotion and relegation, the barriers are going up. Strategies are becoming increasingly defensive. The big teams are worryingly looking at their smaller counterparts and hoping to gobble up their markets with breakaway proposals rather than protecting the overall structure. The minnows, meanwhile, look to avoid the wolf.

Football could end up eating itself by choking off the competition which is needed for its financial and sporting health. This is not the game that the fans will want to watch or the men, boys and women want to play.

CHAPTER FOUR

ELEVEN NOT-SO-DAFT LADS

I never thought it would get to the point where just about everything depended on eleven daft lads.

Francis Lee, former chairman Manchester City,
October 1995

YOUNG BOYS WANT TO BECOME PROFESSIONAL FOOTBALLERS FOR many reasons. Kevin Keegan gave some idea of the motivation in his 1997 autobiography when he imagined a former player turning up at the local Job Centre and being asked what sort of work he is after:

Well, he replies, I want something along the lines of my last job. I'd like to start at around 9.30am and finish no later than 1.15pm. I want lots of leisure, a cracking wage, good bonuses, a car. And I want to travel first class, stay in the best hotels, meet interesting people and I want everything taken care of for me – my boots cleaned and my travel arrangements made for me so that I don't have to worry about things like remembering my passport.

The life of most footballers must be a bit harder and, in truth, the majority of British players start off as trainees at YTS rates with a modest top-up from the club, hoping against hope to outwit a very high failure rate – over 90 per cent, according to Gordon

Taylor, chief executive of the players' union, the Professional Footballers' Association.

Yet for all these 16- and 17-year-olds' undoubted love of the sport, some of the reasons for accepting the risks and the low starting pay do come with pound signs in front of them. Those who make the big time are incredibly well paid. With guesstimates of the superstars' salaries appearing daily throughout the press, they are among the most obvious beneficiaries of the game's current riches.

But they are also now portrayed as the greatest threat. Spurs chairman Alan Sugar has been vociferous in his denunciations of the economics of football. He has claimed that the finances are out of control, with football managers unable to resist the urge to spend their newly acquired riches on talent:

> *It's not the fault of the agents. The clubs themselves can't hold on to the money. They are like children in a sweet shop. There are awesome amounts of cash being handled by irresponsible people. They have what I call the 'prune juice' approach – what goes in one end must come out the other. It would not matter if they got £50 million or £100 million or even £200 million from television. They would still spend it.*

All good colourful stuff, but which chairman was willing to sign Jürgen Klinsmann on £33,000 a week when his club's season went pear-shaped in late 1997, even though he had been contemptuous of the player following an earlier spell in North London?

An arguably more independent view comes from analyst Paul Wedge of stockbrokers Collins Stewart:

> *When you have a situation where average squad members in the Premier League are being paid £500,000 a year and the better ones won't play for less than £750,000, it is a recipe for disaster. I believe that bankruptcy will be a major feature of the football scene in the next few years.*

So what is the dilemma that forces a supposed tightwad like Sugar to open his wallet quite so widely? If bankruptcies are a genuine possibility, why is football so determined to buy itself a Club Class ticket to catastrophe?

Who does the work around here, anyway?

Immediately before France 98, the UK sports agency Hayters published its roll of financial sporting honour, placing three footballers among its best paid Brits. Alan Shearer came second after boxer Prince Naseem Hamed with £7 million a year, while Ryan Giggs and Paul Ince were joint ninth on £1.65 million. Separate research by BBC Radio 5 Live had earlier found other £1 million-plus earners, including Les Ferdinand (£1.6 million), Teddy Sheringham (£1.4 million), David Beckham (£1.35 million), Stan Collymore (£1.3 million), John Barnes and Robbie Fowler (both £1.2 million), Ian Wright (£1.15 million), Paul Gascoigne and Paul Merson (both £1.1 million), Andy Cole and Graeme Le Saux (both £1 million).

These are just some of the British millionaires playing in England and Scotland. Apart from Klinsmann, many other foreign players were also thought to be in the £1 million-plus bracket in 1998 and, unlike their English counterparts, the figures bandied around for these superstars do not include earnings from product endorsements and other activities outside football. Arsenal's Dennis Bergkamp was reputed to be on £35,000 a week, Chelsea's player-manager Gianluca Vialli was supposed to be pulling in £30,000 and his colleague Gianfranco Zola made about £25,000 a week. Even Manchester United, which has always had a tough salary structure, was believed to be paying Ole Gunnar Solskjaer around £25,000 a week. The new high, as of May 1998, was the £50,000 a week used to tempt Brian Laudrup to Chelsea.

It is no surprise that terms such as 'mercenary' and 'hired gun' are bandied about, although British fans have typically been reticent about turning their anger over money directly on individual players or whole teams, other than in the most exceptional circumstances. The continuing popularity of Gazza is testimony enough to that. Despite incidents of wife-beating and Gascoigne's apparent scant regard for his own fitness, the majority of supporters prefer to think of him affectionately as the game's clown prince rather than offer moral judgement. Even his many critics were shocked when he was dropped from the England World Cup squad amid tabloid tales of drunken carousing with showbiz mates in the run-up to the tournament. And on top of that, Gascoigne was able to extract a six-figure sum from the *Sun* newspaper for his admission that he had sunk a couple of beers at the national side's Spanish training camp. Although national coach Glenn Hoddle would later extract a similarly large sum for a book offering a more 'violent' account, it was Gazza who emerged with more sympathy.

Plenty of sophisticated reasons have been offered for fans being so lenient, even though many recognize that wage demands are damaging the game. One academic has gone so far as to suggest that sportspeople represent the last collective memory of the 'dignity of labour' in being a manual worker. They push themselves to their physical limits to achieve their task, and a wider society largely transferred to a desk-bound, service economy accepts that and therefore sanctions their rewards. It sounds attractive, but the case does not really hold.

On one level, perceptions of players are wrapped up with the idea of belonging to a club and being addicted to its performance. As we all know, anyone who services an addiction can extract a high price, hence the repetitive bleating from chairmen about meeting the wage bill when season tickets undergo yet another inflation-busting hike. To a great extent, players have owners over a barrel. No matter how good the administration or the marketing, a team as a business stands or falls according to what happens on the pitch. Profits in football start with victory.

Four Premier League trophies in six years have made Man United England's biggest club. Nine of out ten league titles since 1988 have done the same for Rangers in Scotland. Even below that, the players are the stars in the weekly drama to which each club lends its name. Treating football purely as an entertainment industry is wrong – it is a mistake that many boardrooms are now making – but there are some powerful parallels, as the PFA's Taylor points out:

> There are obviously some major structural differences between football and music, film or television, but as far as the logic behind the cost of the best talent is concerned they are very similar. Top actors or rock stars are paid a fortune because they lead the film or sing the song, they sell it to the public; top players perform a similar role. They boost the gates, bring in the TV ratings and help a club to rise up the league to an extent that it makes more money.

Taylor might further have mentioned that film, music and TV have undergone their own bouts of massive inflation in talent costs during the 1980s and 1990s. The reasons behind these also allow some interesting comparisons with football. Hollywood marketing has turned from an insular, US-centred approach to a global one, exploiting the growth of the media to improve revenues from established territories and tap into new ones like China. This has brought greater financial rewards which actors' and musicians' agents have used to push benchmark salaries higher and higher. Improved selling skills, greater TV exposure and the frequent talk about making English and Scottish clubs more powerful in Europe, not forgetting their growing popularity in the Far East, raise the same issues in football. A European Super League, the real golden goal for some of the biggest clubs, would be yet another step towards globalization.

The idea of footballers as media icons is not particularly new. In the 1960s, George Best was the first superstar player and often described as the 'fifth Beatle'. Before him, Arsenal player and England cricketer Dennis Compton was plastered all over railway stations in the 1950s as the Brylcreem Boy, a mantle since inherited by David Beckham. However, as earning potential has changed, so has the quality – although some might challenge that word - of player representation. It is no coincidence that the country's most famous football agent, Eric Hall, started life in the music business as a talent scout and agent-cum-record plugger. When Ruud Gullit was sacked at Chelsea, the media were summoned to his press conference by First Artist, an international talent agency better known for representing actors, rock singers and those dreaded TV personalities. This trend can only bring closer the cost parallels between football and Vaudeville.

From the players' side, Taylor, himself Britain's highest-paid union boss on £305,000 a year plus £113,000 in benefits, places the responsibility fully on those signing the cheques:

I have never said and I never will say that any particular player is not worth his crust. My particular concern is that some clubs may be paying wages that are beyond their resources, but the question there is not the value of the individual but the quality of the book-

keeping. Any question of player wages ultimately comes down to what the market will support and nobody can deny that the money in football has shot up incredibly over the last decade. Since there is an undeniable link between profitability and sporting success, it stands to reason that the players, as the key talent, as the absolute essential for delivering those profits, will seek and get much bigger salaries.

This is cold comfort indeed, and it also tends to overlook two other parts of the equation. A player can secure earnings outside football, income so vast at the very top that it can make a key talent financially independent of his club, raising further questions about loyalty and commitment. And the market for players is now so great and made up of teams with so many different business agendas that stability still looks to be more of a dream than an objective.

Roy Race plc

As long as football maintains its fashionable profile, players' massive earnings on the pitch can be supplemented off it through an ever-widening range of outlets. Traditional earners such as media work have become more lucrative than in the past. More coverage of football means more space to fill in more publications, giving players the chance to pick and choose. Some particularly savvy players, like Liverpool's Steve McManaman and Chelsea's Frank Leboeuf, write their own columns rather than employing a ghost-writer. Most can sell an autobiography and Kevin Keegan's latest – in fact his third in a life of only 50-odd years – was one of 1997's most successful hardbacks.

But the really big money is in product endorsement. Advertising's love affair with the game leads to the production of about £100 million worth of football-related ads a year in the UK, and big stars are very big earners. Less than half of Alan Shearer's £7 million income in 1998 came in his wage packet. He is a popular face for a range of products, as are plenty of other players. Think hamburgers, computer games, building products and soft drinks. Shearer has backed brands in each sector. Traditional kit deals and boot contracts also pile on the cash but, like Shearer and Beckham, Jason McAteer (Head & Shoulders shampoo), Ian Wright (One-2-One mobile phones), Ruud Gullit, Gareth Southgate, Stuart Pearce and Chris Waddle (all Pizza Hut) have been advertising stars for more mainstream products. Even managers Kenny Dalglish and Alex Ferguson have been used to sell financial services – ironic given the game's own condition.

The concept of the player as a brand by himself has also arrived: Gullit has his own line of leisurewear and Leeds defender Lucas Radebe has a similar business in his native South Africa. Virtually any reasonably high-profile player can pick up some kind of deal from manufacturers desperate for endorsement. QPR player-coach Vinnie Jones may have been found guilty of assaulting a neighbour, but that has still not blighted his career as an actor and TV host. Meanwhile, Man United bad boy Roy Keane has secured jokey endorsement contracts with Snickers and Diadora sportswear, the first featuring a priest settling down for a very long chat in the confessional and the second carrying the forgettable slogan: 'We've sold our sole to the devil'.

In this arena, the agent's role is viewed with some ambiguity by clubs. One chief executive said that because some members of his playing staff had good representation and earned good money from outside activities, they had remained loyal to the club when other offers had come in:

> *There is a tension when the club would like a player for something and he is committed elsewhere through his agent, and similarly when we may have commercial reasons for not wanting him to endorse a particular product. But, by and large, it is an acceptable practice.*

However, Ruud Gullit's sacking as Chelsea manager suggests that not every director takes this view. The main reason given by the club's managing director, Colin Hutchinson, was that the board was not prepared to meet Gullit's £2 million net salary demand, which would have been more than double what any of his Premier League counterparts received. Later, however, it became clear that the Ruud Boy's wide range of outside activities had raised questions over just how much time he was spending at Stamford

Bridge and the training ground. This example raises the serious question of player independence.

John Barnwell, chief executive of the League Managers' Association, has commented on the difficulties that his members face when dealing with squads where a large number of players are already earning more in basic pay than their supposed bosses. Players draw the gates, score the goals and save the penalties and, as a result, easily out-earn their managers. Alex Ferguson is reckoned to be on £600,000 a year at Manchester United, which is considerably less than many in his team. In terms of the success of Man U as a football club and a business, he has been the crucial figure but never the highest earner. The same story is repeated at other clubs. Even George Graham, who built Arsenal's 1991 championship side on the specific basis that no player earned more than him, now has to accept second, third or, most probably, fourth place in the wages hierarchy at Leeds United.

Barnwell's concerns have been lent force in the press by a number of high-profile star outbursts against managers over team selection and tactics. Most famously, Fabrizio Ravanelli attacked the coaching practices followed by Bryan Robson and his assistant Viv Anderson while at Middlesbrough in 1996, and Klinsmann made similar complaints about the Christian Gross regime at Spurs in 1998. In both cases, the charitable said that the highly paid superstars were speaking out because that they could afford to and were expressing what lesser squad members could not. Sceptics pointed to the growing incidence of damaging power struggles between the big-money players and those in the traditional footballing hierarchy. It is plausible that under different circumstances and at different times either of these theories could be correct, but both are indicative of the growing power that some players can exert.

The issues raised are central to football as a sport. The game is built on ideas of loyalty, dedication and commitment, yet a player can now be servant to a great number of masters. In 1996, the clubs and the PFA agreed on the insertion of a standard clause in contracts requiring all team members to dedicate time each month to community programmes, but managers admit that this is seldom enforced and that participation remains voluntary. Officially, some do not want to overburden these highly trained athletes, but unofficially executives admit that pressure is applied to allow stars to pursue other business interests. Contractual obligations, meanwhile, are leading to a dizzying range of absurdities, the weirdest in recent times being Argentinian striker Gabriele Batistuta's refusal to appear in a photo shoot featuring some Italian cattle because he has a contract with his home country's beef producers.

Worryingly, there are signs that outside interests could take an even greater role in the future. US sportswear giant Nike is understood to have 'oiled the wheels' of Ronaldo's £17 million transfer from Barcelona to Inter Milan, according to a senior source at the Spanish club. Nike already had the star on its books but all his Barcelona apparel was tied up in that club's separate deal with Benetton subsidiary Kappa. By contrast, Nike had a merchandising deal with Inter, so the link with the Italian club was more attractive. Nike's supposed intervention came when Ronaldo first had to buy out his contract with the Spanish side before the formal deal went through. One Barcelona executive confirms that the Brazilian found the cash, adding tartly that 'he did not get it from his bank manager or from Italy. So where did it come from?'

Nike has also struck a $250 million deal with the Brazilian national team, which has given it control over which opposition the Samba boys face in friendlies across the globe. Its fans are already voicing disquiet that many of these choices are being made for commercial rather than sporting reasons. This reached a peak after 1998's World Cup final when Ronaldo played even though he had suffered a fit the night before. There were dark mutterings that Nike executives forced coach Mario Zagallo to deny his instincts and let Ronaldo play, a charge denied by the company.

A time may come when sportswear companies and others lease players directly to favoured teams; another aspect of the corporate takeover where those who sold the greatest number of replica kits and had the largest global support would find it even easier than now to get the best talent on the pitch. In Spain, Atletico Madrid president Jesus Gil has contracted star players to his own companies rather than to the club. This is one way of ensuring his re-election, required in Spanish clubs that are still run as members' associations. The precedent has been set. The ability of players to link to companies, almost to become limited companies in their own right, has been further enhanced by the moves towards free agency after the Jean–Marc Bosman case.

Football clubs created many of the difficulties for themselves. In the past, they were never that good at maintaining equitable employer–employee relationships, and almost feudal practices led to the greatest example of player assertiveness to date. Belgian player Bosman sought a ruling from the European Court on the refusal of his club, RC Liège, to allow him to leave or to play even though his contract had expired. The Court ruled that registrations – previously used to keep such players on the books until a good enough transfer deal could be found – were invalid once the contract was over and that the player was then a free agent within the European Union. It decided that the transfer system's use of registrations impeded the freedom of movement of workers set down in the Treaty of Rome. Bosman was undeniably badly treated by the club in denying him a move at the end of his contract to French club US Dunkerque in 1990, and he was not a lone case. In Scotland another player, Chris Honor, claims that he suffered similar treatment at Airdrie and has threatened the club with a six-figure claim. A soon-to-lapse aspect of the transition to full free agency – that clubs within the same country can hold on to registrations – has previously prevented Honor from taking advantage of the change.

For those who have suffered abuse, Bosman is a positive move, a reward for some pretty poor behaviour from directors. It has prompted clubs, players and their agents to respond in two ways. They can either agree longer contracts – typically around seven years – which include guaranteed pay rises and bonuses, or they can seek or offer big-earning short contracts. With players under free agency, clubs argue that they can afford the higher wages because they no longer have to pay a transfer fee.

Brian Laudrup is a case in point. His alleged £50,000-a-week deal at Chelsea makes some sort of sense because he was a free agent and no transfer fee had to be paid to his previous club Rangers. If he stays two years and pockets £5 million in wages, that will be the total cost to Chelsea instead of £5 million in wages plus a similar sum on a transfer payment. Laudrup was one of the stars of France 98 and would have cost a great deal more – probably upwards of £8 million – via the traditional route with a still hefty salary package on top.

Bosman can benefit players in other ways. When the ruling first came into effect, there was a noticeable and sudden drain of fairly ordinary English players to foreign clubs. They went because they were out of contract in the UK and could leave without a transfer. The clubs to which they went were willing to take them because they did not have to pay a transfer fee, so they were happy to give signing-on fees and short contracts to the players who, in turn, were perfectly happy to stay for part of a season before suddenly developing homesickness and a desire for a transfer home. The English club buying them had to pay a transfer fee, of which the player received a 10 per cent cut. A quick few months of travelling and playing on and off for a continental club could make an average player a nice sum of money.

Foreign footballers have also taken advantage of the ruling and of the generosity of British clubs. The number of overseas players in the UK has soared, with most top clubs now boasting several. This has added to the diversity of the game and brought some charismatic talent to the country. Premier League players appeared in the squads of 14 of the 32 countries at the World Cup. However, Bosman has also brought a lot of run-of-the-mill journeymen who some believe are keeping home-grown talent out of teams.

The bottom line is that taking on a foreigner is cheaper than buying British. At the start of the 1997–8 season, 123 foreign players were registered with Premiership sides – an average of six a club. The biggest collections were, unsurprisingly, at Chelsea with 13 and Arsenal with 12. The club with the fewest foreigners was Wimbledon, who made do with Nigerian Efan Ekoku (although some of its British-born players did sign up for Jamaica). The players came from all points of the globe, with the traditional European countries making up the bulk, although a few more exotic countries were also represented, such as Trinidad and Tobago, Uruguay, Costa Rica, Australia and Ghana.

The PFA is consulted by the Home Office each time a player from outside the EU is about to be bought by a British club, and it has been instrumental in tightening up the regulations on admission. Players should now appear in two-thirds of their club's first-team games for their work permit to be renewed after the first season, and should also have a track record in their national side before they arrive. Gordon Taylor defends this stance:

> *People accuse us of xenophobia over this, but clubs are using the system at all levels in a way that will hamper the development of English talent. Many incoming players do not bring extra skills; they arrive because they are cheaper than the domestic equivalent. The biggest worry from my point of view is that many of the imports actually stop better English players from getting into squads.*

Again, the business decisions involved can raise questions about loyalty and commitment, even when the alternatives are of less polished quality and inhabit British football's lower divisions.

The problem may soon end. From summer 1999, domestic English players over 24 will be allowed to move within the country on a free transfer, ending the last vestiges of any restraint of contract. This free-for-all will be entirely official.

In that environment, players will cease to be team members and become suppliers or even subcontractors. Another entertainment analogy comes to mind. In 1997, David Bowie floated in New York. The Thin White Duke had not discovered some kind of yogic karma, but launched himself as an artist with ongoing proceeds from his back catalogue via a Wall Street share offering. Bowie undoubtedly has a much longer shelf life than the typical footballer, but the potential may soon be there for a Ronaldo to do the same.

Stemming the tide

As players have gained more independence, money has flowed into the game, and various other factors have encouraged clubs to seek out talent from overseas, the shape of the football transfer market has radically altered.

England's quoted clubs may be big spenders, but they are also the ones who complain the most about wages and fees. The plcs especially have a duty to be seen to be doing something to control costs, even though their balance sheets frequently tell a different story.

The most recent figures from accountants Deloitte & Touche showed that the total salary cost for all English football in 1996–7, rather than just the Premier League, was £361.5 million, compared with £288.9 million for the previous season. That was paid for from total turnover of £675.7 million, compared with £517.2 million previously. Turnover therefore rose 31 per cent while wages climbed 25 per cent. Not many other industries are as kind to their staff.

In the Premier League wages made up 47 per cent of turnover at £218.2 million out of £463.9 million, while in the First Division they accounted for 67 per cent at £87.4 million out of £131 million. Keeping up with the Premier League Joneses is expensive. In the Second Division clubs spend 69 per cent or £38.1 million of their £55.2 million turnover on wages. In the Third Division 70 per cent of the £25.2 million turnover goes to employees in the shape of £17.7 million in wages and salaries.

Of course, not all the money goes to the players. After all, clubs have plenty of other employees. Taking two annual reports at random, Tottenham Hotspur lists 84 players and football administration staff, 47 administration staff and 28 retail and distribution staff for a total headcount of 159 employees. Chief executive Claude Littner was paid £233,632 for 14 months. Chairman Alan Sugar earned £58,333 and finance director John Sedgwick £81,967. And according to Nottingham Forest's most recent report, it employed 66 playing staff and 113 non-playing staff for a total of 179. Chief executive Philip Soar was paid £130,000, which rose to £150,000 following promotion. However, it is obvious that there are not that many employees on minimum wages eating into the budget. The big spending is on talent.

Focusing just on talent on the pitch, West Ham United, with a first team squad of 20, has a wage bill of around £7.5 million. Wages on offer range from the £100 or £200 a week for youth team players up to £600,000 a year. Of the 30 players on the club's books, around 60 per cent have agents to negotiate for them.

Wage inflation is the biggest business challenge for the British football industry, which until 1964 had a maximum wage. Fulham's Johnny Haynes was the first £100-a-week player and was regarded as incredibly well paid at the time, but would barely recognize the money on offer now. Haynes's £100 a week at today's prices would be about £930 a week or £48,350 a year. That would be a good enough wage for most people, but would leave Haynes a pauper when he mixed with the current stars. Even an average Premiership player is reckoned to be on around £7000 a week. That is a handy £364,000 a year – three and a half times Prime Minister Tony Blair's salary and nearly 20 times the average national wage. In Scotland the average Premier League players are on about £4000 a week.

And these are just 'ordinary' players. Fabrizio Ravanelli's £42,000 a week at Middlesbrough was the amazing statistic of the 1996–7 season. A club which had within recent memory been bankrupt and quite literally operating out of the back of a director's car was suddenly willing to pay a salary of nearly £2.2 million. Boro was also relegated in the same season. That salary seemed incredible, but it has since been eclipsed by the £50,000 Brian Laudrup deal. Laudrup came from Rangers, where he was already on more than £1 million – one of three at the Ibrox club in that bracket alongside Paul Gascoigne (now at Boro) and his former striking partner, the Italian Marco Negri.

The market cannot support these figures on any broad scale for too long and everyone running clubs knows that. Yet a subsequent Deloitte & Touche report showed Premier League inflation for 1996–7 rising from 23 to 35 per cent. So why can't this process be stopped? Before answering that question, it is only proper to acknowledge that many UK clubs are trying to derail the gravy train.

One of the critical changes in transfer negotiations has been a move in control of the process. The days of the Matt Busby-style manager as lord of all he surveyed have disappeared and there are very few old-fashioned gaffers left. Even though Alex Ferguson inherited Busby-like powers, he has willingly ceded many of them and still believes that the position as it stands is 'too big for one man'. The fashion now is for a head coach and a general manager or chief executive. The coach is in charge of football and that alone.

He can pick the players he wants to recruit, but the other half of the duo does the deals. This keeps a manager's hands clean: from the temptation of transfer bungs, and having to refuse a pay rise to a player he then wants to do a job for him on Saturday afternoon. West Brom's chief executive John Wile explains:

> It has always been difficult for a manager to be both the main route for contractual negotiations and the team motivator. Telling a player to get stuck in when you have just turned down his request for a pay rise the week before is obviously going to have mixed results. I had the same experience managing Peterborough [between 1983 and 1986]. Almost all the main clubs have now split off that kind of work for the chief executive. It's easier for him to say 'no'.

West Ham United's managing director Peter Storrie also handles wage negotiations rather than manager Harry Redknapp, and he emphasizes the need for direct boardroom involvement:

> Most clubs are employing chief executives or managing directors and we are the people who deal with players' wages and transfers. Managers now are coaches and they pick the players they want to buy and sell and they agree valuations, but it is up to the chief executive or managing director to do the deal. And it needs to be. We used to have negotiations with players where an increase on £1000 a week would be about £100. Now the figures involved are more likely to be increases to £2000 or £3000 a week. There's a lot of talk but you never know the facts. Wage inflation is a big problem but clubs have to get used to it. Clubs will have to say here is my budget for wages and here is my budget for transfers and just stay within them.

At every level, packaging has become important. Many of the figures quoted for a player's weekly earnings are misleading. One of the challenges facing the chief executive is to wrap up a player's goodies with enough incentives not only to improve his performance but also to ensure that the club can meet the final bill. An actual amount per week is usually only part of something much more complex. Storrie explains how West Ham typically sets about this task:

A standard contract will normally include a basic signing-on fee, an amount for playing say 20 to 25 times a year, money for finishing in a certain place in the league, money for qualifying for Europe and so on and so on. If players want to earn a lot of money they can, but we will be happy paying it out because the club will be successful.

This still means that a club may have to give up in merit payments much of what it stands to earn after a good season but, again, it can be asked who exactly brought the team to that point. Other forms of performance-related incentive are emerging alongside hard cash. As one example, the British game's rush to the stock market has opened up another way of attracting and retaining stars, although at the moment it is being used mostly for managers rather than players.

Sunderland manager Peter Reid was induced to stay at the First Division club when Blackburn Rovers was offering him a salary of up to £500,000 by more than the intermittent prospect of Premiership football. Chairman Bob Murray sold him a 5 per cent stake for £300,000, on the understanding that when the club joined the stock market he would make money. On flotation the shares were worth £2.8 million and increased in value to as much as £3.6 million at one stage. Share prices, like Premiership football clubs, can go down, but Reid should be reasonably cheerful about the result of an investment which he is now free to sell.

Shares and share options – under which recipients are granted the right to buy shares at a discount to the current market price in, typically, three years – are other similar devices. Former Newcastle United manager Kenny Dalglish is known to have had around £1 million in share options. Stan Collymore's agent Paul Stretford is understood to have asked about the possibility of options in the package when Collymore moved to Aston Villa. It is probably just as well Collymore did not get any, as the Villa share price performance has not been impressive, listing at £11 and sliding to as low as £6.12. Loftus Road, which owns Queens Park Rangers and rugby union club Wasps, gave share options to current England rugby captain Lawrence Dallaglio, but not in this instance to any of its footballers. The explanation for the discrepancy was: 'Well, footballers earn enough anyway, don't they?' How long this argument will hold up is open to question.

Other players have bought shares in their teams and have been encouraged to do so. Alan Shearer, David Batty, Peter Beardsley, Robert Lee, Warren Barton, Robbie Elliott, John Beresford and Pavel Srnicek took a punt on Newcastle's flotation, although they are not all still with the club. Gareth Southgate is a Villa shareholder and has paid the penalty in the share price slump. Trevor Francis and Steve Bruce's share-buying at Birmingham City was used to help push the club's flotation.

In a traditional industry, this kind of performance-related pay packaging is commonplace and has proved relatively effective in keeping income and expenditure in reasonable balance. There is just one problem with football, the reason that share options are not yet popular in squad deals. Players and their agents tend to see such perks as *additional* to the shape and content of the basic package, not as complementary in the sense that they gamble something against their own achievements.

In part, this comes back to the point that the players know that they have chairmen and other executives where they want them. If football is the drug of the masses, players are the drug of those seeking profits in the boardroom. But the market is even more complex than that. Business managers such as Aston Villa financial director Mark Ansell talk about the inevitability of wage inflation:

We can only play in the marketplace we are playing in. All the people inside the industry are forecasting significant increases in playing and managing costs. Some clubs are going to find it very difficult to meet salary demands. A sensible industry will make sure it will only pay what it can afford.

And Storrie's view is:

Players' wages have gone up 30 to 40 per cent and you have to keep up.

The global marketplace

So what forces keep driving up the price? One factor is that foot-ballers and their representatives have a suspicion that in global terms they are – please don't laugh - underpaid. Football is the world's most popular sport, but its top players are still not the world's best paid sportspeople. Megastars like Shearer, Ronaldo and Alessandro Del Piero of Juventus covet the serious money made by US athletes and, with Del Piero having just signed a £5-million-a-year contract for just playing, they are beginning to get it. The Inter fans call Ronaldo 'the phenomenon' for his footballing skills, but here is a man who is also one of the top 10 best-known sports-men in the world, taking home an estimated £12 million a year. By comparison, basketball's Michael Jordan slam dunks $78.3 million, boxing's Evander Holyfield knocks out $54.3 million, For-mula One's Michael Schumacher crashes through to $35 million and golf's Tiger Woods – closest to Ronaldo in profile, age and youth appeal – sinks a sweet $25.4 million. In fact, no footballer featured in *Forbes* magazine's most recent list of the world's 40 best-paid sportsmen, published in December 1997. While some may believe that this is because football is less well paid as a team rather than an individual sport, the rankings do contain plenty of basketball, ice hockey, gridiron and baseball players. One British agent said:

> If you look at what the Americans earn, you immediately think, 'Why shouldn't Ronaldo be up there?' And it's not just Ronaldo; in the UK, it's Shearer and it's Beckham. I don't like predictions but, given the time it may take to catch up with the US, I think that Ronaldo will reach those levels and after him, I'd put my money on Raul [Gonzalez of Real Madrid] and [Liverpool's] Michael Owen. These guys are going to make some very serious money. And there is absolutely nothing that the club owners can do about it.

From this perspective, clubs are powerless because the market rate has already been set.

Free agency and Bosman could well encourage the upward trend. The US is the best guide to what will happen in British football. There, big money and free agency have long been the norm. Jordan, Dennis Rodman, Shaquille O'Neal *et al.* can become movie stars and sell books and merchandise in the UK, even though no one is totally sure what they actually do.

The free agent concept came into US baseball in 1976 when the average player was paid $51,500 – worth around £125,000 in today's money. By 1987 the average was up to $412,454, with the superstars regularly pulling in $2–3 million. By 1992 the $1 million man was the average, with the top stars pulling in $5–8 million. The highest-earning-player tag was being tossed around liberally. Trivia fans might be interested to know that Cecil Fielder of the Detroit Tigers took the prize in 1992 with a $7.2 million contract. Mr Fielder was probably a very good player, but his is not a name to conjure with the world over, in contrast to those of many European footballers.

Baseball led the way, but other sports were not far behind, with basketball players such as Larry Bird making $7.4 million in his retirement season and Dan Marino of American football's Miami Dolphins pocketing $25 million over five years. US commentators pin the blame for the salary inflation firmly on the free agent concept. Players were free to move when they wanted and the rules of the free market applied. Clubs responded by offering longer and longer contracts to make sure that players would not jump ship whenever it suited them. In the US, 10-year contracts are not unusual. In British football, 10 years with one club is enough to earn a player a testimonial match – and you don't see many of those nowadays.

Baseball has recognized the problem and struggled to control salaries. The most notable instance was when the annual free agent sale, which usually produced a flurry of mad bidding for players, ended with no one making an offer. Some 32 players declared themselves free agents and open to bids in 1985. Just four, who were being dumped by their teams, actually moved. The rest had to sign again with their clubs. The Players' Association took the club owners to the courts, which eventually ruled that the owners had acted illegally in their attempts to limit spending.

The baseball commissioner Peter Ueberroth later commented:

There was no actual collusion. I don't think there was collusion involved because I don't think the owners could collude if they were forced to do so by threats on their lives.

I think the owners operate like sheep. Sheep go in one direction or another. Right now, the owners are going in a spending direction. There'll come another time when they absolutely run out of money, and choking with losses, they'll try to go in the other direction. The problem, though, is that there will still be one or two of them who can afford to pay high prices for players.

Some aspects of US sport have forced collaboration through salary caps, but they generally do not prove as effective as intended and already British directors can see that this is not a way around the problem. Peter Storrie comments:

Wage caps and transfer limits will never work. What will happen is everyone will go for the highest wage and the highest transfer and find other ways around the limits. You could buy someone a house or extend a contract over a much longer period so the annual pay comes down.

However, Ueberroth's observation that there will always be someone who can foot the bill points to another aspect of the problem. Plcs with wage structures and budgets are, after all, often competing with clubs run by philanthropists and/or rich lunatics willing to stake everything on a player who can bring them glory.

English football may be the richest in the world and leaps and bounds ahead of the rest in commercial terms, but it is Italy's Inter Milan which broke the bank to buy Ronaldo. And the club which held the biggest transfer record as of mid-1998 was Spanish. Seville-based Real Betis paid £22 million for the 20-year-old Denilson. He is on a 10-year contract worth around £5 million a year. Betis is owned by Manuel Ruiz de Lopera, a rich man with a mission to make his relatively unglamorous club a power in the land. He took control in 1992 when the team was near-bankrupt and in the second division. Yet within six years he was able to sign Denilson against the competition of Barcelona, Real Madrid and Lazio – because he was willing to pay. A determined, rich boss will probably always win out.

Aston Villa's Ansell admits that both directorial egos and the increasingly international transfer market have imposed difficult-to-resist pressures on wage inflation:

> *You need to remember that we are not always competing for a player's signature with another plc that will think about its wage structures and the size of a transfer fund. In England, there are owners who let their emotions take control; they're like kids who have got to have some toy for Christmas, so they agree silly fees or wages and all of a sudden the industry benchmark goes up another 3 or 4 per cent. Either that or they get caught up trying to keep the fans happy, without looking at the real consequences. The fan thing is actually worse when you're competing with European sides because many of them are still owned by their members and they elect the president, the guy making these decisions.*
>
> *The hope, and it's not entirely forlorn, is that as more UK clubs become plcs or bring on board institutional shareholders, and as the same trend takes root on the Continent, you will start to see things balance out. Everybody will be using the same rulebook. But almost everybody, anyway, knows there will always be at least one misfit.*

The flaw in Ansell's argument is that the European sides are only slowly turning towards flotation, largely because of the way they are run and the objectives of those in charge. Available figures show that two years ago AC Milan had a total wage bill of £31 million, at a time when Man United was paying out £13 million. Comparing a selection of European clubs shows the top two wage places going to Milan and neighbour Inter, followed by another Italian club Juventus on £21.5 million, Newcastle on £19.7 million, Spain's Barcelona on £17.5 million, Germany's Borussia Dortmund on £14.8 million and Bayern Munich on £13.4 million. Man United on £13.3 million, Rangers on £10.9 million, and Celtic on £6.3 million are still some way behind. Man U's wage bill has risen by around £3 million since these figures were released and Newcastle's has fallen, but neither will get anywhere near the Italians for quite a while.

There is still a long way to go and if media groups and sporting companies move in to control clubs, regarding their main profit streams as businesses off the pitch, this kind of big spending can only be expected to rise further. Already, the tacit acknowledgement that any Premier League, English or Scottish, functions in marketing terms as a league of stars (although it is the Spanish who have taken that particular slogan) means that clubs will inevitably find themselves competing with what a Milan or a Juve can offer. On top of that, once a club moves to match these levels, it heads into the awkward area of differentials and the need to bring other players closer to the leading talents in financial as well as sporting terms.

Living with it

Chris Akers, when he was at Leeds, said the following in terms of pay structures:

> *It all comes down to team spirit. If some regular first-team players are earning substantially more than others are, it is likely to demotivate the team. One or two very highly paid players can actually do more harm than good.*

In the season before the consortium led by Akers and former QPR owner Richard Thompson took control at Elland Road, Leeds had taken on a number of 'superstars', including Tomas Brolin and Tony Yeboah:

> *There were guys in the squad who had won the championship and yet were earning half or two-thirds of what the newcomers were getting. Some just wanted to leave, others simply stopped playing at their best.*

That Leeds side only just pulled out of a disastrous slump that saw it take a mere nine points in the second half of the 1994–5 season, narrowly avoiding relegation. In 1996–7, Middlesbrough was not so lucky. Despite its glamorous stars – including the Brazilians Juninho and Emerson as well as Ravanelli – the team fell to Division One. Dressing room discord between those with seven-figure wage packets and the lesser paid players who had won promotion for the club two years before played a major role in the collapse.

Spurs chief executive Claude Littner seconds this view and sets the question of differentials in a wider context:

> *You can't try and buck the industry. When players go on inter-national duty, obviously they compare notes and we can't pay them less, nor would we want to pay them less, than the competition.*

The point can even be made that wage restraint is not a good idea for clubs. Alan Sugar is, or was, the high priest of the cult of salary controls and he has paid for it. His strictures on holding down pay and not spending heavily in the transfer market were well com-municated and easily understood. That led to the stock-market-quoted club receiving a high rating during 1996 and early 1997 as a sensibly run business with a hard-nosed attitude to cost control. For many in the City it was second only to Manchester United as the favoured stock. The share price soared as high as 170p, putting a value of £171 million on the club.

And yet the image started to come across that the club was not succeeding on the pitch because of its parsimonious attitude to transfer dealing and wages. The image was perhaps not correct, but it hit the share price. The perception that Spurs was not spend-ing enough on players and wages damaged the brand. At one stage its market value fell to less than £70 million.

Merchant banker Tony Fraher of Singer & Friedlander outlines the dilemma:

> *Business managers should be making sure the advertising is the highest quality and in football by that I mean the players. It is up to the management to make sure that the product is right on the pitch. The football played on the pitch is what advertises the brand. Bad advertising doesn't work, good advertising does. By not putting the money into his advertising – i.e. the team – Sugar ended up with bad advertising so he lost fans, he lost merchandising opportunities. The club has a lot of loyalty but that can be lost or devalued. Sugar has created a lot of loyal non-attendees. The perception of Spurs is pretty bad compared with the reality.*

This does not mean that the City wants clubs to throw cash around like drunken sailors. Fraher himself admits that wage inflation is a major problem. And the analysis undoubtedly seems a bit harsh on Spurs. The club has spent £28 million in four years on its White Hart Lane stadium and is professionally run with well-motivated staff. It is building a youth team and spending money on training facilities. It has gone to all the schools in Essex offering to run coaching sessions. It has built relationships with specific schools under which it helps develop boys into footballers, while making sure they are educated. It is adapting ideas from European sides such as Ajax and FC Stuttgart on youth development and claims to be ahead of the game in the UK.

But Littner himself admits:

We have not fulfilled the ultimate objective, which is to win trophies. The main test for Tottenham Hotspur is to succeed on the pitch. We think we are doing things in a professional way, but for all that and for all the money we have spent on players and all the things we are doing to attract players, it pales into insignificance if we do not perform on the pitch. If we can get the performance on the pitch right we will hit the jackpot. It is very easy to accuse people of lacking ambition because it is very difficult to demonstrate ambition.

Littner acknowledges that it is a difficult balance to achieve yet, as the global market, player ambitions and the general economy of football push the numbers upwards, he warns that there are already worrying signs:

We are not unwilling to spend, but it is possible in the future that two or three clubs could go bankrupt because of spending on wages. We have already had situations where we have been selling players to other clubs in England where they have been asking for more time to pay. All transfers are supposed to be settled within a year, but we have had people asking for more time, presumably because they do not yet have the money.

At a club such as Celtic, the attitude is taken that they must spend on players and management but, again, balance that against success. Finance director Eric Riley says:

> *Sometimes it comes across that the management of the operation do not have a perception of what happens on the football field, but that could not be further from the truth. All our revenue streams come from success on the football pitch and if you are doing well your income streams get a benefit. We are very conscious of the need to try and make further progress.*

After one more season of disappointment in 1996–7, Celtic decided to split management roles between a general manager and a head coach. That lost the club its then manager, Tommy Burns, and provoked anger among fans and much public mud-slinging. Under the new structure, the coach Wim Jansen concentrated on the football, while the general manager Jock Brown took on player contracts, youth development, public relations and other details. At its first attempt, the plan appears to have both succeeded and failed. Celtic won the Championship for the first time in a decade, but Jansen quit amid much acrimony between him and Brown over how his transfer proposals had been dealt with.

Celtic remains phlegmatic about what happened, however, and intends to continue with the format. Eric Riley points out:

> *The proof of the pudding is in the eating and whether you get any success. The fans won't care whether you get it with a head coach or whether you get it with a general manager.*
>
> *As far as players' wages are concerned, you have to look at the deals that are done, look at the money that is being invested in wages. If you want to buy the better players, you have to realize what the market price is. Most of the problems are overcome with success. If a team is winning there are not problems. When a team is not winning people turn around and say you have to spend money and that is not always the solution. What is quite difficult is that so much is subjective. In many industries you can say you will go out and buy a piece of equipment and you will know what it is going to do for you. In terms of football, you are backing someone's judgement and you can only hope you have done your due diligence and checked out his background and hope he fits in.*

Manchester United is often held up as the exemplar of how to do it. Until the start of the 1998–9 season, its net transfer spending in the previous five years was around £1.5 million, which is, as David Coleman might say, quite remarkable considering what has been achieved. It has spent on developing players such as Ryan Giggs, David Beckham, Paul Scholes, Nicky Butt and Phil and Gary Neville, who are highly paid but dedicated to the club in ways seen rarely in contemporary football. These players and other unsung prospects are also signed to long-term contracts. If they want to leave, United will be able to recoup something of its investment. The club has also shopped well in Europe. Ole Gunnar Solskjaer cost a tenth of Alan Shearer's £15 million but has been a big hit with the fans and a success on the pitch. Ronny Johnsen cost just £800,000, which in the transfer market is a Poundstretcher-type buy compared to the Harvey Nichols prices paid by others.

Finally, another key factor in United's make-up has been its close attention to differentials, not only between itself and other clubs but within its own squad. It has missed out on deals which could have been important because it was unwilling to break this structure – the most recent example being Brian Laudrup. It has often been criticized for this attitude, with many fans taking the view that if all United needs to win the European Cup is one or perhaps two players, then it should pay. Yet it has found eight-figure talent in Dwight Yorke and Jaap Stam who have a great desire to play in the Red Devils' colours and consequently are willing to receive wages within the existing system.

Part of the response from United and the possibility that other clubs are now looking at is, in effect, catching them young, developing talent that can be both a financial and a sporting asset. The normally astute pundit Alan Hansen famously dismissed Manchester United's youth policy and its 1995–6 double-winning side with the unintentionally accurate double negative: 'You don't win nothing with kids.' He was not entirely wrong, as it is certainly difficult to win very much with a team of youngsters. And he helps make the point in reverse, as football is not a game with a long-term view. A run of bad results can put a team in trouble and a manager's job in jeopardy. Youth policies are not a quick fix, as Gerry Francis, for one, discovered at Spurs. He placed the focus on developing in-house talent but, as regulation loomed, the buying started again.

However, almost all clubs now chant the mantra of youth policy, schools of excellence and scouting networks. The teams that have tried to buy their way to success have in the main failed, although Blackburn Rovers can at least point to the reward of one Premiership title from its spending blitz. The other big spender of the 1990s, Newcastle United, lavished £40 million without winning anything beyond admiration for its style some of the time. It also did it without having a reserve team or a youth policy. Even though Alan Shearer is a Geordie, Newcastle had to spend £15 million to get him to play for the club. As part of its £193 million stock-market flotation, it had to emphasize that it was setting up a youth policy on which it was staking £10 million.

But what of the players themselves? Do they think that the situation is getting dangerously out of control?

The 1997–8 season in Germany was marked by the unusual sight of fans at many Bundesliga clubs backing Bayern Munich manager Giovanni Trappatoni when he accused the game's stars of outright greed. Fans held up banners to support the Italian coach and some even went so far as to turn their backs en masse on their supposed heroes.

Would English fans do the same? Similar protests in Britain only tend to occur when a player commits one of three sins.

First, as was the case with Arsenal's former striker Ian Wright, the player leans out of the dressing room window after a game and shouts abuse at the leaving crowd after the home team was barracked. The fans below chanted a not-so-gentle reminder to Wright about who pays his wages.

Second, as has happened to the likes of David Beckham, Stuart Pearce and Gareth Southgate, the player screws up big time in a major – typically World Cup – game by missing a crucial penalty or being sent off. Torture here is typically a rapid assessment of the individual's wage packet and more terrace and tabloid abuse.

Third, and the greatest sin of all, is when a player comes right out and admits that he is in it for the money. Players like Arsenal's Nicolas Anelka and former Middlesbrough star Fabrizio Ravanelli, who mix comments about being unable to fit in and not getting a decent enough salary, are usually, although not always, out of the first team before the supporters get their right of reply. Needless to say, if they make a return another long barracking awaits.

This third issue comes down to football's equivalent of the Mafia rule of *omerta*. Questions such as 'Do you think you are fairly paid?' or, more appropriately, 'Don't you think you are paid too much?' will be blocked in most cases by the PR person or agent sitting in on the interview, a particularly effective technique if, as is often the case in the Premiership, an interpreter is required and the subject is one of the league's highly paid imports. Occasionally, nevertheless, a glimmer of how players perceive life at the top of the game does come through, usually from a younger star who has yet to be 'monstered' by the sporting press.

Danny Cadamarteri, the 19-year-old striker who broke through into Everton's first team in 1998, is one who has let the mask slip. In a recent interview, he acknowledged:

> *It's fantastic getting paid for what I love doing and I know foot-ballers get paid well. I do think wages are going a bit over the top though when you start looking at £40,000 a week and I sympathize with the fans over some of the gate prices.*

However, he is already equally sure of his place in the way of things football. He told the same reporter:

> *Football is a big business now and it is really drummed into us by the club that we might be earning a lot, but it is a short career and if you are injured it could be even shorter than you expect. As soon as you turn professional you have an accountant, a coach and an agent. That's quite something for a teenage lad. So there's a fair bit of advice being given to us. We probably know more about PEPs than champagne.*

By contrast, tales of conspicuous consumption are positively encouraged. We all apparently want to know which designers our favourite footballers prefer, what kind of car they drive and how they acquired their luxuries. It sends a frisson down the spine to hear that Liverpool and England wonderboy Michael Owen was able to pick up a Rover Coupé with his first wage packet, although generally that kind of thing passes without comment.

If there are dissenting voices within the playing community, they come predominantly from the lower divisions. Garry Nelson, commercial manager of the Professional Footballers' Association, has written two books about life in the Nationwide Football League. An admitted journeyman footballer, he paints a different picture of playing life, worrying about the consequences of a long-term injury not just for depriving him of the opportunity to play the game he loves, but for what it could genuinely mean for the mortgage and general future of his family. Yes, he used to make more than the national average wage, but not so much more as to put him on the Mount Olympus inhabited by Premiership superstars.

At this level, the uncertainties of a football career and the pressures it places on players to find ways of boosting their income to save for the inevitable rainy day when they are ruled too old, too crocked or simply surplus to requirements are wholly understandable. The fact that it almost certainly feeds into a much more venal culture higher up the food chain, where even mid-ranking squad members of a Premiership side will seek, literally, hundreds of pounds to give you the benefit of 30 minutes of reportable platitudes, does not and should not cast a similar shadow over those toiling below. Instead, it merely highlights some of the absurdities that remain in the current climate.

Nelson's own reaction to Alan Shearer's £15 million signing by Newcastle United in July 1996, completed while he was player-coach at Torquay United, is instructive:

> *On our way in Hodgie and I discuss the implications of [the Shearer deal] for the Torquays of the game. Neither of us begrudge the man his fortune: he's operating so far out of our sphere no comparisons are meaningful. (For the record, though, Shearer earns more in a week than I do in a year; [Gianluca] Vialli's weekly tax liability would pay Torquay's entire operation for the same seven days; [Fabrizio] Ravanelli's National Insurance contribution would pay the wages of our top three players. But who's counting?) However, as Shearer's fee is 15 times Torquay's 1995–6 turnover, this does give*

us pause for jaundiced reflection. Torquay are not the most direly strapped club in the Nationwide by any means. That the millstone of a massive, interest-gathering debt is not round our necks is due in large part to the chairman working full time as an unpaid chief executive and constantly subbing the club out of his own pocket. And ... when it comes to competing in the transfer market, we're hamstrung to the point of being crippled out of the game. Not merely as buyers but as sellers too. In 1993–4 the two bottom leagues' share of transfer monies realized £7 million. A single year later, precisely one-tenth this sum was generated. This is pre-Bosman.

What is more, later the same day, Nelson finds that a trialist's request for travelling expenses has to be turned down, observing gloomily:

Alan Shearer, £30,000 per week? No problem. Simon Dawe's £30 petrol expenses? No way.

Footballers buy into a dream. All begin by believing that they might make it to the top and reap unimaginable rewards, both in terms of trophies and (although it is bad form to admit it) financially. That dream is encouraged by the fact that most who start the journey are forced to make major sacrifices. Academic work is usually the first to go, making alternative career options limited if they fail to make even the most basic grade. They also gamble on their fitness holding up in what remains, despite FIFA chief Sepp Blatter's best and worst efforts, something of a contact sport. And even if they do make it, most know that their success will not last that long. Opportunities in coaching and management are limited to, at best, 10 per cent of those who play professionally.

On top of this, many still come from poorer backgrounds, an extreme example being current world superstar Roberto Carlos, who began his life in the very depths of Brazilian poverty. He was willing to talk about money and was refreshingly blunt. He told Spanish television:

When you have had nothing and get the chance to have everything, you do not think twice. You go for it. You always think that it might end tomorrow.

And yet, encouraged by agents and other advisers, those at the top of the game do not appear to appreciate the damage they are doing to their colleagues in leagues below. They also do not understand that, like the big clubs, if they push the smaller teams to extinction they too stand to suffer greatly from the financial backlash.

CHAPTER FIVE

FOOTBALL'S WEALTH DREAM

*We don't pay Umbro or Nike to put their names on our shirts. They
pay us. Clubs like Man United are far bigger and far more powerful
brands than they will ever be.*
Ed Freedman, Zone, merchandising consultant to Manchester
United, Real Madrid, AS Roma and Nottingham Forest,
Financial Times, March 1998

NEW LABOUR TOLD US THAT 'THINGS CAN ONLY GET BETTER'.
New Football seems to believe that it can only get richer. Unfortunately, the game has signed up for some of the greater business fal-
lacies – the conviction that those parts of the industry that
currently bring in pots of cash will always do so; and that any
other enriching scheme will only add to its fortunes. But hard-
headed City investors have tested out football's wealth dream and
found it wanting.

To be fair, it was the institutions that did much to encourage
football in this belief. Usually sober and cynical analysts fell madly
in love with the game during 1996 and a vast array of consultants
matched them in competition to come up with increasingly daring
and outrageous projections of the profits that could be earned.

Merchandising and the idea of the football club as a brand
promised a brand new game. Pay-per-view television, in which
armies of devoted armchair fans who could not make it to already

packed grounds paid £10 a time to watch a game at home, was another predicted winner. BSkyB and its pay-channels had made football fabulously wealthy – just think what pay-per-view could do! The prospect for new competitions, which would be even more attractive to broadcasters, also held out the hope of a permanently gilded future for the beautiful game. A European Super League could make so much more money than the UEFA Champions' League was already coining in, the argument went. All of these ideas played their part as football consummated its affair with the City.

By the end of the 1997–8 English and Scottish seasons, 21 clubs were listed on the main Stock Exchange in London or the lesser Alternative Investment Market. Another three were listed on the more loosely regulated OFEX market. In continental Europe, Denmark led the way with four clubs – Brondby, AGF Aarhus, Silkeborg and most recently FC Copenhagen – publicly quoted. Italy was catching up, with Lazio and Bologna taking advantage of changes to stock-market rules and floating in 1998. Ajax of Amsterdam also joined in with a stock-market launch in May 1998.

In Germany, Bayern Munich is planning to float, as is rival Borussia Dortmund. Club members at Dortmund, the 1996–7 European champions, voted to change their club into a share-owning company rather than a mutually owned organization. In Spain, the two giants Barcelona and Real Madrid are also looking at ways of tapping outside investors without necessarily floating on the Bolsa. Real has already launched a debt offering. Portugal's clubs are taking similar steps, while one of the first clubs to float in France is expected to be the infamous Olympique Marseilles, now headed by former adidas and Saatchi & Saatchi chief Robert Louis-Dreyfus. Moreover, French football's marriage with capitalism is being officiated by a Communist sports minister.

The Europeans appear to be some way behind, but several clubs respond by pointing out that, as pioneers, the British have shown them how to avoid some of the pitfalls and problems. On 1 April 1997, British football first truly encountered these risks when Newcastle United's stock-market debut, backed by a very ambitious share prospectus, broke the financial consensus. There had been soccer sceptics before then in the Square Mile, but the majority had been positive. Suddenly, two distinct and equally widespread views were being expressed. On one side were those who still believed in profits coming home; on the other were those who argued that football had tapped into fashions and that, in the longer term, the fashions promoting the game would inevitably change. Since then, the doubters have increasingly had the upper hand.

At the beginning of the 1997–8 UK football season, British clubs on the stock market were valued at £1.2 billion. By the season's end they were at £1 billion and falling, even though more clubs had joined the stock market in the shape of Leicester City and Nottingham Forest. Several clubs were looking particularly sick. Loftus Road, the parent company of First Division Queens Park Rangers and former English rugby union champion club Wasps, had been floated at 72p a share, with a special 68p offer to fans in early 1997. It started the 1997–8 season at a disappointing 52.5p after failing to get back into the Premiership, and ended at a disastrous 18p after almost falling into the Second Division. The value of the shares was a quarter of their launch price. Analysts scoffed at the company, run by music and media mogul Chris Wright whose Chrysalis subsidiary produces UK television coverage of both Italian and Spanish football. They pointed out that its prospectus had been reduced to listing slot-machine income. 'When a company is doing that, you can be sure you are not talking about a major international business success,' one analyst says.

The way in which Wright has supposedly got it wrong at QPR is only one example. The City's coolness shows that the bubble of optimism that buoyed up the game's finances during the boom of 1996 and 1997 is easily pricked.

The view of the bears in the City is that if football exhausts some of its current income streams, it does not appear that well equipped to replace them. If merchandising sales slip or TV income runs flat, how will the game move forward? This is not simply an issue of how well football can grow its revenues, but whether it can maintain them at current levels. As a business, the game could be compared to an ageing team reaching the end of a season that had promised much but is now too exhausted to make that final push for glory. Bereft of trophies, the game could find itself all played out.

But the beautiful people of New Football point to the success that has been achieved. And there is undeniably a success story to sell. Football can point to phenomenal growth in club revenues. Turnover for the English game as a whole has increased by more than 75 per cent in four years to around £675 million. Attendances are rising and commercial performance is improving rapidly. The boys have done good and reckon they can do even better. There is more TV money to be chased, more merchandising profits to be made, more cash from sponsors, a European Super League in prospect and ideas for a British Cup. The game still has plenty of ideas to expand and, if only some of them pay off, there will still be enough money to provide the resources needed for success in the sport. That, at least, is the bull market view.

Big-money TV

Television money has been the financial fuel for the growth of football, and not just in the UK.

The Italian clubs until recently out-earned the English in the TV stakes. AC Milan, for instance, received £11 million from television in 1996–7 and has already started to develop pay-per-view revenue. Relatively unglamorous sides such as Vicenza make around £8 million from TV, which would not leave them feeling hard done by in the Premiership.

In Germany, Borussia Dortmund was making £7 million from TV as long ago as the 1994–5 season. Annual contracts for TV rights to the European home games of German clubs cost around £40 million. Prices are about to rise following a ruling by the German Federal Court, which rejected the Soccer Federation's claim to exclusive rights to sell matches. The Federation now has to sanction a free-for-all in which the big clubs sell their own rights to European games and ditch an arrangement under which clubs which were not competing in Europe received some of the revenue. With media groups such as Axel Springer and Bertelsmann, the world's number two media company, competing with Bavarian tycoon Leo Kirch, clubs will not have to worry about where their next mega TV deal is coming from.

In Spain, two pay-per-view broadcasters scrap for TV rights. Sogecable, which runs the Spanish version of Canal Plus, teamed up with Catalonia's TV3 and Antena 3 to pool rights but was challenged in the courts by the rival Via Digital and Telefonica partnership. That led to broadcasts being blocked and an interim settlement whereby viewers saw the same pictures of the same game at the same price on different channels. More broadcasters equalled more money for clubs.

However, the next big step to boost the TV cash is supposed to be pay-per-view television. This is only in its infancy in the UK, but the few experiments so far have been fairly successful. When BSkyB tested PPV on Frank Bruno's brief fight with Mike Tyson on 16 March 1996, it managed to entice 600,000 people into paying to watch three rounds of boxing in the middle of the night. Live and exclusive football during the afternoon would surely be an even bigger draw. Vital World Cup qualifiers, crucial Championship games and relegation dogfights would presumably pull in bigger audiences than a convicted rapist beating up a much-loved but never entirely convincing Great British hope.

Research companies have come up with a bewildering variety of figures for how much PPV could be worth in Britain, with the wilder estimates going as high as £2.6 billion a season. That figure is based on every one of the seven million households that currently support Premier League clubs being willing to pay £10 a time to watch all 38 of their clubs' games. More sober analysis by Fletcher Research estimates that PPV will be worth an extra £450 million a season by 2003–4. The scaling down of the figure is based on around 2.5 million homes being willing to stump up £10, following market research which showed that only that number of homes would consider PPV.

However it is sliced, PPV is potentially lucrative and undeniably it is technically possible. BSkyB launched digital satellite TV during the summer of 1998 and terrestrial and cable digital TV was available in time for Christmas 1998. Digital TV makes PPV easier to market, as viewers will no longer have to phone to make their order. Just flick a switch and make your selection. Marketing experts believe that customers will then be more likely to buy.

Digital satellite offers the option of up to 200 channels of television and broadcasters will have to show something. Live PPV football is an obvious way to fill the void. Under the current Premier League TV contract, BSkyB has the exclusive rights to PPV (with Premier League clubs' approval) until the end of the 2001 season. At present it only shows 60 live games a season; PPV would give it the right to broadcast another 320 every season and fill up some of the gaps in its schedules.

Analysts at Charterhouse Tilney concluded in April 1997, in a major report on football, that PPV 'could be massive'. They wrote:

> *Clubs are in a very powerful bargaining position when it comes to renegotiating the BSkyB package towards the year 2001. According to Sky Sports, of the total 5.16 million homes receiving satellite TV, 3.84 million homes subscribe to Sky Sports – i.e. 74 per cent of all subscribers – and it is probably fair to assume that a significant proportion of these Sky Sports subscribers have joined the network for the football package. Therefore BSkyB will be keen to keep the rights to broadcasting Premier League football even under some PPV arrangement.*

Clubs themselves are already considering launching their own TV channels. Chelsea, Newcastle and Leeds are investigating the possibilities, and Manchester United has unveiled plans with BSkyB and Granada. MUTV will not as yet show live Cup or League matches and will initially be used for friendlies and testimonials. United was expected to be first on the air, but was beaten by Middlesbrough. Boro TV is a joint project involving the club, Visionsport International (VSI) and cable company Comcast Teesside. At the beginning of the 1997–8 season it was a match-day-only operation, but it has now been expanded to a three-day-a-week service.

VSI director John Gubba said:

> *It's too early to talk about pay-per-view. The emphasis will be on exclusive behind-the-scenes features and interviews. This is an exciting formula that has evolved after eight years of working closely with the club in our role of video producers and servicing rights-holding broadcasters.*

Manager Bryan Robson and his players are regular contributors and match highlights focus on youth and reserve team games. Presenters include the former Boro star Bernie Slaven.

All of these claims and counter-claims focus solely on the UK TV market for British football. However, it is also big around the world. In 1997, the Premier League's international contract with Communications Services International was worth just £8.5 million a year, which gave each club a mere £425,000 – about enough to cover the wages of an average player. It has since been re-negotiated to £28 million a season, a threefold increase, for the 1998–9 season, giving each club £1.4 million – enough to cover the wages of a superstar.

It is obvious that more TV money will come. Clubs are also setting out their stalls on other media. Chelsea, for instance, has a match-day radio station, as do a raft of other Premier League and First Division clubs. As the government frees up the airwaves still more will follow, and because radio is cheap to produce – Chelsea's licence and overheads are estimated at about £2000 a game – similar services look likely. Leeds United, for example, has pioneered the rather depressing prospect of live Internet broadcasts. Exiled Yorkshiremen, or those who cannot quite bring themselves to leave their computers, will be able to follow matches via the World Wide Web. The Leeds United Website, launched in January 1997, receives 95,000 hits a week and could be heading for five million a year. It already offers daily interviews and on-line shopping and plans to introduce video interviews, match highlights and on-line ticket sales. All of these ventures are today in their infancy, but they are another definite source of new revenue for clubs.

Leeds Sporting's former chief executive Chris Akers has seen the future and reckons it will work. He says:

The Internet represents a very cost-effective way of communicating with fans. It allows a club to respond quickly to rumours and bypass a sports media which many in the game regard with suspicion. It also gives the club a daily programme that is far more detailed and up to date than what is traditionally sold in the ground. However, the Internet as a broadcast medium in the medium term has tremendous potential. You can run audio, but you will soon be able to offer higher-quality video packages of highlights and, a little further down the line, live video coverage. In that scenario, there is obviously scope for cutting out the traditional broadcasters as the middlemen in distributing your signal.

Got any badges, posters, stickers or t-shirts?

Merchandising is another side of the business supposedly ripe for growth. Replica kit sales alone are estimated to be worth £200 million a year in the UK. A wide range of weird and wonderful products is already on offer. But advisers and executives of clubs believe that the clubs can and should do better.

Merchant banker Tony Fraher reckons that clubs as yet have no concept of the potential:

If any club that has a loyal support base can put its brand on a product and sell it cheaper than the high street, then fans will buy it. That applies to any club from Manchester United to Leyton Orient to Bournemouth. It's potentially very damaging to the High Street. You can take it to ridiculous lengths, and it is not going to happen, but you could have Manchester United water or gas or electricity.

Fraher warms to his theme by taking a swipe at an international icon:

Take Richard Branson, a man who never had an original idea in his life, what does he make? Well, he makes money and he does that by selling the Virgin brand. He exploits a brand. Why can a commercial entrepreneur exploit a brand and be called a hero when a football club cannot? The people who believe it is only a sport are the ones who have not thought about it. What it is about is brands and media rights.

That essentially is the business case for the financial expansion of football and the pump for the bubble of optimism. Brands are the clubs' ability to sell spinoff products and media rights are their ability to sell television pictures and other media. However, Fraher reckons that football is unique:

> *Can you show me any other business where there is such brand loyalty and where that loyalty is exclusive and it is total? It is to one brand and it is for life and it is hereditary. The exploitation of a brand has not even been started by the clubs. Flogging kit is just scratching the surface. That brand loyalty can be exploited and I don't mean exploited cynically, I mean developed. What do Marks & Spencer make? Nothing. They provide space for other people to sell things in and put the M&S brand on it. But you have a choice with M&S. If you don't like it you can go to Debenhams or wherever. If you support Arsenal, for instance, you don't have a choice. It is Arsenal or nothing. Show me another business where they are paid to advertise. The advertising of a brand for a football club is on the pitch and people pay to watch, to see the advertising.*

Clubs are waking up to this gospel and making strenuous efforts to build their commercial operations. These are, after all, solid earners, which should be relatively safe from the depredations of the 11 men on the pitch.

Tottenham Hotspur's finance director John Sedgwick, whose previous job was with underwear emporium Knickerbox, says:

> *The risk is quite low. We could have six or eight shops. We could possibly own a shop in Ireland and go as far as Northampton and out to Cambridge. We have a 120,000 mail-order database and quite a few are from overseas. Invariably at a home match we have supporters' clubs from Scandinavia, Ireland, Israel. We have had a load of people over from the Far East.*
>
> *We have proved that we can make consistent and improving profits without having any success on the pitch. People want to be associated with our name. We are halfway through a four-year sponsorship deal and our sponsorship income in 1996–7 was £5 million. When we negotiated those deals in 1995 they were fantastic deals. But two years later you look back and think we could do a whole lot better. It would not be inconceivable to double it and if we won something it would be even more.*

Despite its total lack of recent footballing success and at times unprepossessing public image, Spurs is still chased by companies keen to make a killing on the back of the ailing north Londoners. Sedgwick explains the sponsorship process and how the brand that is Tottenham Hotspur works:

> *It is good business for us. If we like the look of something we will charge, say, £50,000 and then a 20 per cent royalty on top. We get more than that from some companies. If they don't sell a single product we are guaranteed the money. We always have the right to audit their books and we exercise that right quite frequently. It has got to fit in with the Tottenham Hotspur image, so I can't see us letting someone put our name on condoms, for instance. We are more aggressive now and demand money up front so that we can be sure they will market it properly and make a real effort.*

Clubs such as Spurs can afford to pick and choose. They also have a better idea of their own worth. Sedgwick explains that certain deals are just not worth doing, pinpointing a proposal from the Premier League as one case in point:

> *The Premier League causes problems sometimes. They went out and did a deal with Marks & Spencer for Premier League polo shirts and we all thought, 'What's the point of that? You're either a Tottenham supporter or an Arsenal supporter, you're not a supporter of the Premier League.' Previously they wanted to do Premier League towels with all the teams' names on the towels and they offered to give us £500 to use our name on the towel. Ridiculous amounts of money, so we said no. First of all we didn't think anyone would buy the towels and secondly we are not interested in £500. We sell our own towels and get much more for them.*

Abdul Rashid, commercial manager of Aston Villa, echoes Sedgwick's complaints:

> *With the Premier League the biggest problem comes down to who gets what and why. For example, the Premier League runs a sticker album deal with Panini and all the revenues are equally distributed*

*from that. The argument, and it's a fair one, is that kids are col-
lecting all the teams, not just one, and they do not particularly
know what they are getting when they buy a packet of stickers.*

*However, the League has been involved with some other pack-
ages where it has said this money should be split equally, but we
have not agreed. An example there would be the club razors that are
marketed through Wilkinson Sword. There the consumer does choose
whether he wants a Villa, a Spurs or a Man United branded product, so the clubs feel that income should be divided according to
sales. Those who sell more should get more.*

On continental Europe, merchandising as an idea is nowhere near
as developed. Some businesspeople will see that as an opportunity,
while others might think it shows that Europeans are not as interested in spinoffs as the British. The answer is a bit of both. The
only foreign clubs earning anywhere near the same as the British
are Bayern Munich, with an annual £18 million due to a tie-up
with adidas, and Barcelona, which recently signed up with Nike. In
most other major countries merchandising earnings are very mod-
erate, with the exception of Ronaldo fever at Inter Milan.

Barcelona eschews shirt sponsorship as it will not allow colours
based on the Catalan battle flag to be besmirched by a commercial
name. However, the club is very busy in other areas. The Barça-
mania fair, held in the shadow of the city's Arch of Triumph during the regional holiday each September, features over 500 different
licensed products connected to the club. The Magic Barça themed
restaurant has 200 covers and requires reservations each weekend
before and after a game.

Yet what the club is capable of earning from any of its deals or
outlets is some way behind what the English have extracted from
the market; some 30 per cent behind a Man United or a Newcastle,
according to one internal source. Part of the question comes down
to different levels of disposable income – although Catalonia is
Spain's wealthiest region – with, for example, the family spend at
Magic Barça coming in at £25 for two adults and two children,
compared with £40 for the same group at Manchester United's Red
Café. People are used to spending more to eat out in England, but
the difference remains substantial.

A similar issue is replica shirts. In Spain these retail for £30 to £35, whereas in England the figure is upwards of £40. In this case, cultural differences are also important. Continental supporters will only buy kits to wear at games, if at all. You will not see very many adults wearing football kit on the Ramblas in Barcelona. Some children yes, but adults no. Instead, the club is looking to promote added-value products like health insurance, bank accounts and credit cards as more appealing to its stylish followers.

Barcelona has its fair share of strange licences, nevertheless. Fans can eat an entire meal of ham and eggs with a vegetable side salad and wash it down with wine. All the food and drink is available under club brands. They can even eat the meal outside using Barça-branded garden furniture. And there are Barça cigarettes to finish with. But, hey, this is all higher-quality tat.

This view of more discerning continentals is echoed in Italy. British financier Stephen Julius, whose Stellican company own a stake in 1997–8 European Cup Winners' Cup semi-finalists Vicenza, says:

> *Italians are more interested in football than all the other commercial parts of the business. I think it is a cultural difference. We have got a lot to learn from England. Italian football is still a very rich market, but the commercial side is negligible. There are scratchcard games, but the prevalence of counterfeiting and fake goods makes merchandising very difficult to start. You have to wonder whether some of the other English methods will work. In Italy there is no real tradition of corporate hospitality at football. It would be a major gamble whether we would get corporations buying boxes and people paying to eat in them. The biggest threat to football is that here the whole business is based on football. Football earnings are highly volatile and that is why we have to develop other business on top.*

Merchandising is difficult to set up because the Italians have a culture of counterfeits and fake goods – the almost-Gucci loafers, the nearly-Rolex watches, the sort-of-Armani suits. Why anyone would want to rip off, for instance, an Alessandro Del Piero duvet cover or a Paolo Maldini clock is another point, but that at least is Julius's experience:

*With fakes, if the police would cooperate with us then there is no
reason why merchandising could not work. But it is an industry
problem, not a problem just for us. Saying all of that, I think Italian football will develop at a huge rate over the next 10 years. A
huge amount of action will take place in Italy, because the best
teams are here and there are an awful lot of rich people really focused
on football and not just interested in it to make money. Even I am
becoming a passionate Vicenza supporter. When you are playing at
this level it is a beautiful sight and it is difficult not to get hooked
on the stuff.*

European scepticism aside, there is support for the idea that the
commercial side of football will continue to grow. Analysts reckon
that the sponsorship deals currently in force in the Premier League
can easily be improved. Many clubs are caught in long-term deals
negotiated before the football boom. Manchester United was tied to
a 16-year, £24 million deal with Sharp, which it renegotiated in
1997 to bring in £6 million for two years. It has struck a six-year
kit contract with Umbro worth £40 million.

Man United's pulling power is greater than that of most other
clubs, but that does not mean the others cannot do better. The
1997–8 double winner Arsenal might think that its three-year
sponsorship deal with JVC, worth £8 million, could be improved.
Aston Villa is tied to a six-year deal with AST worth £6 million,
Blackburn a four-year contract with CIS for £8 million, Middlesbrough with Cellnet for £3 million in three years and Spurs with
Hewlett-Packard for £4 million in four years. They might all take
Everton as a guide. It recently secured a new deal with the
MediaOne–Cable & Wireless mobile phone venture One-2-One,
worth £2 million a year compared with its previous £1 million a
year with electronics group Danka.

Merchandising sales at many leading English and Scottish clubs
have still to develop. Man United is always held up as the example
to follow, but in fact the club is so far in front it is embarrassing. In
the year to August 1997, Man United made £28.7 million from
merchandising. Tottenham, in a comparable period, made £3.7 million. That might seem dismal, but it is quite good in comparison
with other relatively big clubs. Sunderland, a massive club pulling

in 40,000 crowds in a footballing hotbed, manages to make just £1.3 million from merchandising. Leeds, which has recently been much more successful than Spurs, pulls in only £3.1 million. Sheffield United, a big club in the First Division, has a total turnover of £4.9 million, with very little coming from merchandising.

Nottingham Forest, which was promoted to the Premiership in 1998, is another merchandising failure. Chairman Nigel Wray, a Spurs supporter as a boy, says:

> *Nottingham Forest is a big name. It has won the European Cup. It has a great local franchise. It has always been the strong club in its neck of the woods. But turnover in total is £13 million.*
>
> *You have got to remember we haven't started yet. We had virtually no commercial activities; very poor catering activities, poor sponsorship and we can get much better attendances. But we have got to work at it; we have got to merit it. It is nothing yet to what could be achieved. Comparisons with Manchester United are almost not worth making. United is a global brand name. Nottingham Forest is a strong local brand name. I don't think it is realistic for us to become a global brand name. We can become very strong locally or even nationally. We have got to establish ourselves with our community, not because we are a benevolent institution but because it is good business. I can't see why we cannot double our turnover in the next four or five years if we work at it. It comes from more sponsorship, better catering and also playing good football.*

Even a major club such as Rangers had done very little until recently. Craig Armour of financial advisers Noble Grossart says:

> *They have really only got it moving in the past year or two. They have moved from selling on the High Street where the chain shops take all the profits to setting up their own shops, bringing in George Davies who ran Next, getting swifter on the videos like Manchester United have done. It is getting successful.*

Clubs are taking to the business of the sport with the zeal of converts, but they have a lot to learn. Villa's Rashid says:

I wouldn't say that we are even halfway there yet in terms of what can be achieved. Part of the problem has been that several different income streams have developed simultaneously. It has not just been the transfer from souvenir kiosks to merchandising megastores; you have also had the corporate hospitality angle, the general catering angle, the seven-day stadium and so on. In most clubs, all of these areas are still in the hands of one person, the commercial manager or director, whereas they are now growing to a point where each really needs one strong executive running them full time. Things will change as you see more targeted responsibility in each of those areas so that you don't have one executive who is, frankly, run off his feet.

Big money from big games

The final sequence of the wealth dream is the potential for new money-spinning competitions which can be sold to broadcasters for more money, will pull in extra crowds and will sell more merchandising and corporate hospitality. The hardy perennial here is the European Super League, which, it is widely assumed, will be another money pump for the clubs that are allowed to enter it.

The cream of English, Spanish, German, Italian, French and Dutch football playing each other week in and week out is reckoned by many to be a tremendous draw for TV and the fans. The countries which can guarantee the biggest television audiences would be guaranteed a place in the League, with the possibility of lesser countries such as Portugal, Belgium and Scotland plus Scandinavian sides and Eastern Europeans also being allowed on board. TV rights would be keenly fought over and television audiences would be enormous. That is the theory.

UEFA has acknowledged this by changing the rules for entry to its competitions. The Champions' League is now anything but. Newcastle and Manchester United were England's representatives in 1997-8 and only one of the teams was a champion. Germany went one better with three entrants – Borussia Dortmund, Bayern Munich and Bayern Leverkusen. Dortmund was at least the European champion.

Yet the European Super League is still a serious target, despite UEFA's reforms. Powerful forces in the continental game, led by AC Milan's Silvio Berlusconi, are anxious to wrest control of such a competition away from UEFA to swell their coffers still further. Certainly, for Rangers in Scotland it is regarded as the target. Craig Armour puts the club's view:

> *Rangers are paying the price for being trapped in the Scottish League. What they would like is some form of European dimension. That is why they are building up the player base and making sure they have a strong team, so that as the European discussions continue they are considered. If you are competing in the transfer market and getting the TV audiences, the chances are you will be considered.*
>
> *The '98 season failure in Europe hit the club hard. It was partly bad luck and partly bad management. They didn't think they were going to win it but thought they could do well. If you are looking at it from a business perspective of a club being run from profit, then it is the TV contracts that are going to drive it. TV contracts in Scotland won't be enormous, so they really need Europe. Unless you get decent competition, then how are you going to attract players? Who wants to just play in the Scottish League, win it every year or come second and then get knocked quickly out of Europe?*

Nevertheless, Armour recognizes that Scottish teams may have to struggle to be allowed to board the Euroleague train, despite the undoubtedly passionate followings for the Rangers–Celtic axis:

> *From a purely commercial perspective, for a European League you would want a couple of English, a couple of Germans, the Italians, the Spanish, the French and that would be about it. If Rangers are going to succeed and enter, then the next two years are going to be very important. If they don't compete on the pitch then it is going to be difficult. Nobody wants to have a team at the bottom of the Champions' League all the time. That is not an attractive product for the advertisers. The challenge, therefore, is to get a successful playing unit on the park. It is all down to eleven men really.*

His argument is perfectly clear and apparently sensible, but emphasizes why the game is on the brink of trouble. The potential is there for growth, but the potential is being assumed to be actual. And the potential is also there for growth to slow down. Football does not seem to have grasped that fact, believing instead that it has invented perpetual motion. The boom can easily go bust. The basic weakness of many of the expansion plans is that in one way or another they ignore the supporters.

It could be you ... but not necessarily

The European Super League idea shows how clubs might be getting carried away with their dreams. Would it necessarily be the huge success that everyone assumes?

Summer 1998 saw the most concrete proposals yet for such a competition come under public scrutiny when word leaked about the Continent-wide networking underway by a combination of consultancy Media Partners – a company with close links to Italian magnate Silvio Berlusconi – and US bank JP Morgan. They had set themselves the target to have the league up and running by August 2000.

Official confirmation of the discussions came in late July, first from Spain's Real Madrid (which was looking for institutional finance) and then via a stock-exchange announcement from Manchester United, which had categorically denied any involvement only days before but which ultimately found that its City investors could force it to declare its hand.

On the face of it, there were vast sums on the table – the hype around the plans started at £20 million per team per season, but within days rose to £100 million each.

Meanwhile, the roll call of those invited to discuss the idea – AC Milan, Inter, Bayern Munich, Barcelona, Ajax, Arsenal and Liverpool among others – was undeniably dazzling (although some crueller folk noted that neither AC nor Liverpool had won anything of note for several seasons).

Almost immediately there were those, with Man United manager Alex Ferguson as the biggest surprise among them, who joined the traditional FA, UEFA and even FIFA administrators in worrying about the potential and consequent devaluation of national leagues. Fergie said that such a league might – for which close observers read 'should' – be a decade away (that is, well after his retirement to Chester races).

There was talk that the 16 biggest Super League clubs were to be guaranteed six years with no threat of relegation or expulsion, while another 16 would be allowed what was tantamount to associate membership. There were threats of a breakaway from football's traditional structures that had eerie echoes of the foundation of the UK Premiership. It all sounded depressing, if not downright evil.

Offering one traditionalist's view, Keith Wiseman, chairman of the FA and a director of unlikely Super League member Southampton, bluntly observed:

> *This suggested league is quite literally unsanctioned football and if it came into existence I think clubs and players might well find themselves excluded from a whole world of sanctioned football.*
>
> *I don't think the fan in this country would have the slightest interest in what would be exhibition games. It would be Harlem Globetrotters stuff. With no promotion or relegation people will tire of it. It may be interesting for a year, but it would fade away. The whole concept of football in this country is promotion and relegation on merit. Any competition that suggests that is not applicable is going nowhere.*

Another popular perception was that here, once again, were the rich planning to get richer, with the attitude that if it happened to be at everyone else's expense then so be it. But pause for just one minute and ask whether this Super League would make sense even to the biggest sides.

Never mind the fact that promotion and relegation (after that lengthy moratorium) could possibly see a Manchester United and its charter flights replaced by Wimbledon and its supporters' club taxi – no big advantage for the media moguls behind that possibility. It might be what competition is all about, but there you go. That's business.

Instead, consider the fact that a European Super League could actually damage the biggest sides commercially. The big threat would be brand devaluation.

Say that Manchester United and Bayern Munich are both members but when they meet towards the end of the Super League season, neither is in contention. This is no 'Big European Night' for armchair fans to watch on TV, but a meaningless mid-table clash between two now ordinary-looking teams, despite their statures in their domestic leagues. How many fans would turn up? It is possible to take a pretty good guess based on events in 1997. When Barcelona met Newcastle United in the Nou Camp leg of their Champions' League group, both sides had already been eliminated from the competition. These may be two of the most passionately supported sides in the world, but only 20,000 fans turned up, leaving the cavernous, 120,000-capacity Nou Camp looking embarrassingly empty. Given that performance, just how many fans would have elected to watch the same game on PPV?

Williams de Broe analyst Nigel Hawkins believes that the league could be started, but is not hopeful about its future:

> *I can see a Super League happening, but the major difficulty may be maintaining its impetus. If, as already tends to happen in European competitions, you really have only six or seven sides regularly securing top honours, how will the remaining 14 feel about carrying on with a competition that makes them look like also-rans? Already, you can hear some clubs applying the old big fish–small pond, big pond–small fish equation to this and sounding less and less enthusiastic.*

A convinced sceptic about the European Super League is West Ham's managing director Peter Storrie. He says:

> *I don't see it. I'm not sure it is ever going to happen. What are you going to have in this country if you have a Super League? One or two clubs are going to go into it. The others are not going to be happy and I can't see it happening. Even when you talk to the clubs they just see it as a supplement to the league. Supporters still want to see the leagues going on, they don't want to see just the European games. So I think you will only see expansion of the games on offer rather than an out-and-out Super League. The Champions' League is a Super League already to some extent.*

Similarly, pay-per-view sounds a good business idea in principle, but it is based on assumptions that fans would switch on in droves. Ignoring the fact that the Premier League has already made plenty of money from TV by going on satellite, PPV is reckoned to be a way of making even more money. However, the assumptions forget that fans will not only be able to choose which match to watch but whether to go to the game or stay at home. Under the current BSkyB deal, live games are only shown in the UK on Sundays and Monday nights (and in exceptional circumstances on Saturday mornings). The simple reason for this is that clubs are worried about attendances at grounds. Broadcasters are also worried about attendances at grounds. After all, part of the attraction for showing games on TV is the crowd. What will happen if fans at home have more atmosphere in their sitting room than there is in the half-empty stadia?

It is not an empty worry. Some clubs where there are waiting lists for season tickets, such as Manchester United and Newcastle, won't suffer. But analysis by Fletcher Research showed that attendances at many grounds will fall by up to a tenth. This leads to debates about enforcing local blackouts so those fans living near a ground cannot watch the game on TV. That will suit the many Manchester United supporters who live far from Old Trafford, but will not be much good for Coventry and Leicester in their attempts to win PPV audiences. What will the demand for a clash between these two be outside the Midlands? Or, taking the usual cruel comparison, how many people will want to watch Wimbledon on PPV when home gates have been as low as 7000? Similarly in European terms, Manchester United fans, for instance, only really 'respect' Juventus and Inter Milan, in the same way that they feel passionate about their rivalries at home with Liverpool, Arsenal and Leeds. Fans of all clubs have favourite games and that would apply to PPV.

And again, there is the basic argument about PPV. The benefits are obvious for the big clubs with huge unsatisfied demands for tickets. They will be the PPV earners. However, like football as a whole, any PPV deal needs other clubs to provide the competition for the big draws. Manchester United cannot really expect to take all the money on offer, as it will need to play other clubs which will also need a financial incentive to play. Introducing PPV will reignite the old arguments about dividing up the TV spoils that led originally to the breakaway of the Premier League. That essentially boiled down to the question of why the big clubs should subsidize the small clubs. In 1992 they were at least arguing about 92 clubs. The PPV argument would be concentrated on 20 clubs, which would appear to be the new number under threat as football reduces itself to an even smaller universe.

The UK's only experience of PPV so far has been with boxing and it has been a success to some extent. But the big difference between football and boxing PPV is that boxing only calls on its supporters to choose a 'major' event every once in a while, whereas football plans to make its call once a week. Moreover, boxing events have to be carefully packaged to provide added value. It is not enough just to show Prince Naseem Hamed or Lennox Lewis, even though these are the two biggest British draws in the sport. A strong undercard including the likes of, say, Nigel Benn and Chris Eubank is seen as essential if the fight is to retail for the basic £10-plus level that covers the overheads of marketing, covering and administering such an event.

Gary Newbon, the head of ITV Sport's football coverage, is a sceptic about the supposed boon of PPV for football:

> We advised Carlton on its bid for the new Premier League contract and we also saw some of Sky's projections for PPV. The bottom line was that the really big clubs could justify the outlay – facilities every week, marketing, subscriber management. Man United, they'll make a fortune, so will Newcastle, Arsenal, Liverpool, Rangers, Celtic. But after that you were talking about take-up of 5000 or 10,000 at best.

The overheads of setting up PPV could reach £60,000 or £70,000 per game. That means that a Wimbledon or a Coventry would need to find between 6000 and 7000 individuals willing to pay £10 on a Saturday afternoon just to break even. Since neither club regularly fills its own ground, PPV may not have any real value for them unless they are playing a 'big' side, in which case it seems inevitable that such major teams will demand a larger part of the revenue split. PPV could be useful extra income, but it is no pot of gold. Worse still, and one of several factors that lay behind the Premier League's surprise rejection of BSkyB's first formal PPV proposals in Summer 1998, what if this outlet just ended up making the already rich clubs even richer and left the rest further behind?

Merchandising is not quite as difficult to judge, but nor is it quite the money tree that everyone assumes. It is based on fashion and fashions change. There will always be the die-hards who want to buy everything connected with their club. However, as football analyst Nick Knight of Nomura notes, they are not everyone:

> *Clubs are projecting vast income from merchandising over the next few years, but they forget that their current success is a consequence of fashion and in fashion everything changes at some point. In other words, a day will come when fans don't want to walk around with MUFC or Rangers on their chests – not to the extent that they do today anyway.*

The first signs of this decline came in 1998, when a number of clubs, including Spurs and even Manchester United, confirmed that kit sales had declined.

Lance Yates, the chief executive of clothing firm Hay & Robertson, is building his company by buying famous old clothing brands that have fallen on hard times. Dunlop and Kangol, famous for its customers such as the Gallagher brothers from rock band Oasis and movie star Samuel L. Jackson, are two parts of the business. The other is the sportswear brand Admiral, which was the kit supplier for England, Scotland and a host of clubs in the 1970s. Yates sees it as crucial to his firm, but not in the old style of supplying clubs. It has deals with Barnsley, Portsmouth and York, but that is it. He aims to compete with Umbro but is wary about the football merchandise boom going bust. He has experience of what has happened in other once-booming sectors of the market:

> *I think the fashion of wearing replica kits in the streets will go. I've been involved in my career with merchandise for the Rolling Stones and the Sex Pistols. I did Frankie Goes to Hollywood and the whole*

'Frankie says Relax' project. It all had a shelf life and so does the phenomenon of wearing replica kits in the street. It will just be considered one day that it has started to look naff. At the moment it's all tribal and looks great, but sales will drop off and any self-respecting supporter with an element of style won't want to wear it any more. Having been involved in fads and youth culture, I saw the trend go away from kids walking around in Metallica T-shirts and soccer coming through.

Soccer is the world game. It really was a working-class game up until recently. It is now firmly a middle-class game as well as a working-class game. It transcends all social classes, as do the major American sports. The game is now seen as sexy but everything is cyclical. In the 80s music was king for young people, but now it is soccer. Fashions at the moment are being very kind to us. Some 80 or 90 per cent of sportswear is worn on the street, it is not worn on the pitch or the court, but I suppose in five years' time everything will change and we will all want to wear more formal gear again. I don't know. For the foreseeable future there is a very large market for sportswear.

Yet, argues Yates, to keep the market alive merchandising must become more sophisticated, a challenge that the current displays in most club shops markedly fail to address:

Soccer-branded merchandise has got a long way to go but it has got to become a lot more streetwise and sophisticated, because it is going to start competing with Calvin Klein or Tommy Hilfiger or Levi's or Ralph Lauren. It needs to come more away from sportswear and become more, as the Americans call it, 'athleisure'. Too much European sportswear is designed to play sport in but is bought to wear in the street. Generic sportswear will remain, but consumers will also look for something far more sophisticated.

His view is that companies such as Umbro, which is focused exclusively on football – in contrast with Nike and Reebok, which cover all sports – will have to choose between supplying clubs and focusing on personalities. Currently, Hay & Robertson has deals with the unlikely quartet of former Chelsea manager Ruud Gullit, Terry

Venables, Sir Bobby Charlton and TV personality and footballers' fan Dani Behr. It is all a matter of taste, but for Yates they are the right sort of personalities to sell sportswear:

> *We have world-wide exclusive deals with Ruud Gullit and Terry Ven-*
> *ables and are in talks with Bobby Charlton about working with him*
> *in an ambassadorial role. We have insured both Ruud and Terry for*
> *a lot of money. Dani Behr has the right sort of attitude, so does*
> *Ruud. We attach personalities to our brands. Ruud Gullit, for*
> *instance, is articulate, stylish and generally liked and transcends*
> *the tribalism. Terry is a cheeky chappy and, despite all the business*
> *problems, is not someone who is hated like an Alex Ferguson or a*
> *Kenny Dalglish is by certain fans.*
>
>   *We have rights for children's branded underwear and pyjamas*
> *with all the major Premier League clubs such as Manchester United,*
> *Leeds, Liverpool, Villa, Everton, Arsenal plus Rangers and Celtic and*
> *Inter Milan and Juventus. But our strategy is not to attach our-*
> *selves to Premier League clubs. We feel that if you attach yourself to*
> *Manchester United then you alienate every other supporter in the*
> *country. A Liverpool fan won't wear Umbro because it is Man*
> *United, they will wear Reebok. A United fan won't wear Reebok*
> *because it is Liverpool, they will wear Umbro. I think Diadora gave*
> *Roy Keane £1 million to wear Diadora boots and leisurewear. But so*
> *what? I think it is barking up the wrong tree. Anybody outside Man-*
> *chester United supporters is not going to want to buy it just because*
> *Roy Keane does. That's where it is also dangerous getting attached*
> *to individuals who are particularly closely associated with a club.*

So, who else is in and who is out?

> *You wouldn't want Shearer even though he is the England captain*
> *and whatever. He just hasn't got enough personality. Arsène Wenger,*
> *the Arsenal manager, is maybe one person because he has that little*
> *bit of mystique about him which, even though he is a bit boring,*
> *makes him a possible.*

Rival Pentland, which makes the Pony brand, backs his views. It has abandoned the kit-sponsorship market because prices are rising too fast. That means that as well as Spurs and West Ham, Southampton, Norwich City, Oldham Athletic and Huddersfield Town all had to look for new kit sponsors for 1998–9. Umbro's largesse in its kit-sponsorship deals may also soon be a thing of the past. The FA took its time over the renewal of its £50 million, five-year England kit deal while it awaited financial guarantees from its US parent, which has announced a restructuring and repositioning of the brand. Umbro has spent big in Britain and elsewhere to build up a name that will compete with Nike, adidas and Reebok, but there is growing concern in the US that the popularity of replica kits is on the wane.

Just to add to the pain, the replica kit market is facing an investigation by the Office of Fair Trading, which is looking at claims that manufacturers have forced shops to keep prices high and refused to supply chains which discount. It has also been singled out as one of the strands for further investigation by David Mellor's government-backed Football Task Force. Recent kit launches are simply a red rag to a bull. Double winners Arsenal celebrated in 1998 by putting £5 on the price of a replica kit. Adult kits now cost £68.97, while kids' versions cost £42.99. The National Consumers' Council was not impressed. A spokeswoman said:

> *Children are being exploited by big clubs like Arsenal. They are pressurizing kids into buying these kits. There should be lower prices and they could at least change their kits less often.*

Of course, Arsenal was not the only offender, with Liverpool, Chelsea and Man United also launching kits earlier than usual.

Newcastle United's errant directors Douglas Hall and Freddy Shepherd recently highlighted the cost of replica kits when they boasted about ripping off fans. Their figures were slightly wrong, as adidas pointed out. The correct figures are that the average shirt costs between £6 and £8 to make. Wholesalers sell it to retailers for £20 and the retailer sells it for £40. The company making the shirts can depend on £12 to £14 profit on every shirt and the shop takes £20.

It makes sense on these figures for Umbro to pay £40 million for Man United's kit deal, as around one million United shirts are sold a year. It does not make sense for firms to pay very much for just about anybody else's kit deal, with the possible exception of Celtic, as they do not sell anywhere near enough. Yates makes the point:

> *We could have got West Ham and paid them £1 million for a sea-son. Liverpool was £5 million, but it is not for us. What's the point of having footballers running round on Match of the Day? It does not really give your brand much of a profile and might not make you much money.*

What is worrying here is that a supposedly key source of club rev-enues is playing down what it is willing to pay up front to a club, never mind the royalties that these clubs have been assuming would follow off the kit boom further down the line. As a reassess-ment takes place, therefore, the kind of competitive bidding that has boosted many a Premiership side's income from these licences may also be starting to slacken off.

Similarly, it does not make sense for clubs to allow the shirts to be sold in the high street as shops make £20 a time. Football clubs are presumably not in business to make money for chain stores. But if they break the relationship with shops, will they still be able to sell as much product through their own embryonic high street outlets and mail-order businesses? And nor does it make much sense for fans to pay the high prices.

Sponsorship is still a developing and fluid market but there are limits. Japanese electronics group Canon recently abandoned its sponsorship of the English national side because it thought that as a multinational firm it would achieve more as a sponsor of major tournaments rather than of single teams. Ford has adopted a sim-ilar strategy by concentrating on the promotion of BSkyB's foot-ball coverage.

Like kit sponsorship, club sponsorship is beginning to be seen as a bit of a mixed bag. Certain big clubs will always have certain degrees of success and get frequent coverage from the TV companies, but teams in a slump may not. In situations like that, many spon-sors are being asked to pay large amounts of money to be associated with unsuccessful brands. As a result, attracting sponsorship for lower-division teams is often limited to local firms and small sums, with many firms saying that they would rather deal with a competition like the Coca-Cola Cup where they are guaranteed exposure all the way through, regardless of a particular team's performance.

Getting sponsors is harder than it looks for the majority of clubs. Turning fans into walking billboards has been seen as a cost-efficient way of advertising a company, until, of course, rumours of falling sales have hit the market. Like Hay & Robertson, many mainstream industrial firms are also wary of the effect that 'backing' a particular club might have among their customers. The FA secured the supermarket Sainsbury's as an official and high-profile sponsor of the England World Cup side, but a spokesman for the company said that this was as far as his firm would go:

> *We are a national company and for us there would be inherent dangers in associating ourselves with one club in one region. I mean, if we put our name on Man United's or Arsenal's shirts we would probably end up drumming up business for Tesco.*

Football has assumed that its wealth dream will simply float through the window, but the reality is that it may need to work harder and harder just to keep some of its revenue streams flowing to the extent they are already. That raises the question of management structure.

Talent off the pitch

Clubs will have to become more professional in their business dealings and better at running their operations. They need to put a more effective infrastructure in place to protect and develop their businesses. That will be a change for many. Nigel Wray talks about his incredulity on taking over Nottingham Forest, which had just been relegated from the Premiership at the end of the 1996–7 season:

> *They had no executive directors at all, no finance director. It was amazing; there were barely any computers. It was run by non-executives, local guys who had the club at heart, but that's not good*

enough when you are handling huge sums of money and trying to compete with Manchester United, which you have to do. You cannot be good on the field if you are not good off the field and you cannot be good off the field if you are not good on the field. The two go hand in hand. If they were where they were with an organization like that, then hopefully you should be able to improve on it. In any business, be it engineering or football, if you don't get the management right then you get everything wrong.

His chief executive Phil Soar, a Nottingham Forest fan who is also a businessman and author, adds:

They managed to win European Cups and the league with that organization. But then again, they did have Brian Clough at the time. All their success proves is that if you have Mr Clough on board you will do well until he is no longer up to the job and then you will suffer.

Essentially, many football clubs are still family affairs or run by local businesspeople who lose their financial acumen once they get into the boardroom. Sunderland's millionaire chairman Bob Murray, who made his fortune as one of the founders of the kitchens and bathrooms group Spring Ram, fell foul of the City during the club's flotation when he said: 'I'm not worried about the business, I'm more concerned with the football.' They were noble sentiments, but they did not wash with some bankers, who consequently decided not to bother with Sunderland shares.

Wolverhampton Wanderers is challenging for the Premiership and rightly regards itself as a big club. Its owner Sir Jack Hayward, however, lives in tax exile in the Bahamas and has only one executive director, his son Jonathan, running the business for him. Sir Jack is currently looking for other investors to come into the club and his advisers have been to the City of London. People there were less than impressed with the business organization once they found out what it amounted to. 'It still looked like the family firm,' said one possible City investor.

Clubs are realizing that they are running big businesses and that they need people qualified for such jobs, but the change is a slow process. Many backroom jobs are still filled by devoted fans who remain supporters first and employees second. Tottenham Hotspur's chief executive Claude Littner explains that devotion to the club is important:

But we don't want people who go weak at knees when they see David Ginola or Les Ferdinand. They have to be able to do the job. It's never hard filling jobs here though. People always tell us that it is their biggest ambition just to work at White Hart Lane. That's great, to some extent.

Former players are often found on the staff of clubs, which can be a good idea if the player has the skills required. John Williams of Leicester University says:

The game is still very traditional in many respects and recruitment is often inward looking. You would be surprised by how little people look outside the game to recruit people with particular skills. Although that is changing, it is changing very slowly.

For example, the community officer at Sheffield United is Tony Currie, who was a great star at the club and is well liked. It may be that he delivers a lot in attracting people, but does he know how to work with ethnic minorities or women, and is he good at raising money to support the scheme?

Successful examples may be people like John Wile, former club captain and now chief executive of West Bromwich Albion, and less successful ones could include Francis Lee, former chairman of Manchester City. Both made money outside football after their playing careers were over before jumping back in, although in Lee's case it was a move he came to regret. Wile makes a strong case for bringing in people with experience of the game and business at the top executive level:

There is a certain resource of knowledge out there, although I wouldn't say it was very great. The player-turned-entrepreneur is a rare beast. However, it is a useful knowledge that brings a sense of balance to the boardroom. I think if you are going to communicate with playing staff and managers, you do need people at the top whose judgement they will respect because they know the game and they know a balance sheet.

Whoever is in charge, the clubs will still have to become more professional in the way they run their businesses. Small examples help illustrate the point. Many fans queuing to get into Wimbledon v Chelsea at Selhurst Park in 1997 missed the first 30 minutes of the game because the club did not have enough ticket offices open to fans who had already booked and were collecting their tickets on the night. This was not an unexpected situation, but it was one with which the club failed to deal because it had a bigger crowd than usual and these were customers who had taken the now supposedly more 'convenient' route of booking their seats via credit card.

Many clubs have failed to handle their expensively imported foreign players because they have not looked after them on arrival. One success has been Chelsea, which has done well because it has a personnel department. That department has proved crucial as the club has recruited its United Nations FC. Who else is supposed to help out players arriving in a strange country (England is odd, after all) without being able to speak the language? Gianfranco Zola is reckoned to have adapted so well because of the help he has received, and there is a similar view about Franc Leboeuf and Roberto Di Matteo. Other clubs, however, have had terrible experiences with foreign players, often blamed, admittedly by the imports, on the fact that nobody made them welcome.

All of this should be obvious business practice of the sort that is needed to make sure firms prosper and keep on prospering whatever the vagaries of football. Yet these kinds of ideas are only just sinking in throughout the game, where major clubs expect to compete without bothering to have anyone running the business.

Even at those teams which have floated on the stock market, the benevolent, or not so benevolent, dictator model remains. These clubs are more professionally run and boast the requisite executive directors, because that is what the City requires. However, ownership at many of the clubs is concentrated in the hands of one or a few major shareholders. At Newcastle United it is the Hall family, at Aston Villa it is Doug Ellis, at Tottenham Hotspur Alan Sugar and at Chelsea Ken Bates and the estate of Matthew Harding. Sunderland has chairman Bob Murray as a major shareholder, QPR's owner Loftus Road is dominated by former Grimsby fan Chris Wright, and Birmingham City has the porn baron David Sullivan plus the Gold brothers of Ann Summers lingerie fame.

Dominance by one individual or clique is a major reason that clubs are finding it difficult to attract investors in the City. Stockmarket rules stipulate that one investor can hold only 70 per cent of the shares in a company. However, institutions are never keen on backing clubs where a shareholder or a group of shareholder allies rules the roost with more than 50 per cent of the shares. Their reluctance is based on the fact that when push comes to shove, the person with majority control can tell everyone else to shove off. These kind of concerns are known to have blocked the flotations of Liverpool, Arsenal and Everton, all of which were confidently tipped as coming to the market during 1997.

The City experience has in fact turned sour for many clubs who have seen the valuations put on teams slump dramatically. Football has gone from being a £1.2 billion stock-market sector on the verge of outstripping textiles in value to a stock-market relegation candidate. The share price of many clubs has more than halved from the highs they hit during the heady days of 1996 and early 1997. And that process has stopped many from joining the stockmarket rush. West Ham United is known to have been dreaming of a £100 million stock-market value during 1997, according to people involved in negotiations, when it was considering flotation at the same time as Leicester City. The East Enders' directors abandoned the idea when they were bluntly told they would get nowhere near their asking price, and Leicester was the team which did float at a more modest £30 million level.

The City, of course, has other financial fish to fry. The continental rush to the stock market looks somewhat better organized than the comparable British race. It will also be carried out with the benefit of hindsight. The recent mixed performance of British clubs on the stock market has shown that plenty of unreal assumptions were made and a lot of mistakes happened in valuations. This is certainly one time where weakness is strength. European clubs are financially not as powerful as their English counterparts, which makes them cheaper to buy and more attractive to someone aiming to develop a business. Nigel Hawkins of Williams de Broe comments:

> *European clubs will undoubtedly have an opportunity to learn from British mistakes. The pity is that British clubs will have more difficulty in this respect, because the UK sector is not at a point where a flotation would now be advantageous, unless it was Arsenal or Liverpool. The bottom line, though, is that the big European sides and so forth have a much clearer idea of what bankers are looking for and the valuation levels they can seek. They also can pitch themselves as offering better value. You are now looking at an impending wave of big clubs – Bayern, Inter – hitting the international markets rather than just a few smaller British teams. I'm sure there are people in the City who are more aware of Ajax than Coventry City, for example. There are some doubts about how certain clubs run their businesses and about accounting procedures in their home countries, but if there are attractive brands on offer, there will be interest.*

The stampede to the stock market appears to have stopped for the moment, killed off as much by football's overweening sense of its own worth as the City's unrealistic expectations. It was stock-market analysts, after all, who believed the stories about every Premiership club being guaranteed at least £30 million a season from pay-per-view.

For all its alleged hard-headedness and eye for the main chance, the City does in fact have a rather dippy side when it comes to football. Executives at the clubs talk exasperatedly about the tensions of meetings with fund managers or analysts who turn out to be fans as well.

Newcastle United's former joint chief executive Mark Corbidge steered the club through flotation, collecting a £300,000 bonus on the way, only to depart with a £500,000 payoff after falling out with the rest of the board. He told of meetings with fund managers during the flotation which were businesslike, and others which were childlike:

Some investors focused purely on the business and asked about rev-enue streams and debt and so on. The rest were just strange. They would nod off while you talked about business, only to perk up and start lecturing you about buying a new keeper and not playing Shearer alongside Ferdinand and so on.

Tottenham Hotspur's chief executive Claude Littner and finance director John Sedgwick make regular visits to City institutions to explain strategy. Sedgwick says:

Your heart just sinks when you are in the taxi going to one of these meetings and you hear the guy is a Spurs fan. You know then you are in for a strange time.

None of this means that City investment in football is finished. There are 21 clubs floated already and they will remain on the market, gradually building stock-market records and followings. More will probably follow in time. Deals will be done by the stock-market clubs. There have already been rumours of takeovers, with Leicester City seen as vulnerable, mainly because it does not have a major investor. Manchester United has long been rumoured as a takeover candidate and indeed did have talks in 1996 with video company VCI (which is now incidentally around an eighth of United's stock-market value). United and Tottenham Hotspur have both recently changed merchant banks, with United going for HSBC and Spurs for Deutsche Morgan Grenfell. Companies usually change merchant banks if they are planning to launch takeovers or negotiate joint ventures. Spurs is rumoured to be looking at buying a stake in a Chinese club and Man United is reckoned to be considering deals in the Far East. This kind of move will continue to demonstrate football's profile in the City.

Meanwhile, clubs are bringing broader business skills into the boardroom. Former ITV Sport boss Greg Dyke is now a Man United director, while Spurs has signed up Sam Chisholm, the former BSkyB chief executive who masterminded the first Premier League deal.

And the game still needs new investors, who at the moment are likely to be either wealthy individuals or venture-capital firms.

Sheffield Wednesday and Derby County are currently tied up with venture capitalists – Charterhouse and Apax respectively – who will in two to three years' time want some kind of return, to be extracted by demanding flotation. The wealthy individuals, like the poor, are always with us and they will continue to play a role.

But the role they play is open to question as the game gears up for the next stage of its development. Clubs have built their hopes on dreams of wealth, which will not be realized to the extent that they hope. And they are competing in a game that is becoming more and more expensive, against teams that have developed stronger businesses. The off-the-pitch battle has become as important as the on-the-pitch game. And we all know which team is the one to beat off the pitch...

CHAPTER SIX

READ THIS IF YOU HATE MAN U

Which three English teams have swear words in their names? Can't guess? I'll tell you. It's Arsenal, Scunthorpe and Fucking Manchester United.

A Blackpool cabbie vents his spleen to the late *Guardian* columnist Vincent Hanna, November 1996

EVERY COUNTRY HAS ONE: THE TEAM YOU LOVE TO LOATHE, unless, of course, you are one of the sizeable minority that supports them. Take these comments from US sportswriter Bert Sugar's introduction to his cheerfully aggressive collection of invective, *I Hate the Dallas Cowboys*:

Enough! Enough already with that 'America's Team' crap! Every time I hear the Dallas Cowboys referred to as America's Team, I feel like tossing my cookies – preferably somewhere in the direction of Dallas. Like Peter Finch in the movie Network, *'I'm as mad as hell and I'm not going to take it anymore.' I'm not going to take having the Cowboys constantly rammed down my throat as America's Team. I'm not going to take having the rest of the NFL relegated to second-class citizenship because some ill-mannered, beer-burping Bubbas – with typical Texan hubris – think they're better than the rest of us.*

Substitute 'England' for 'America'. Replace 'NFL' with 'Premiership'. Adapt a couple of terms for British consumption – we don't toss our cookies here, after all. And then, critically, take the words 'Dallas' and 'Cowboys' and replace them with 'Manchester' and 'United' respectively. What you get is a rant that can be heard in pubs, schoolyards and academic commonrooms across the land. These are emotions that the genius, the sensible and the subnormal can share – abhorrence biliously directed towards one particular team above all others. As the great sports author Budd Schulberg observes in his contribution to *I Hate the Dallas Cowboys*:

> *It's bigger than politics. It's deeper than regional rivalry. And even broader than decent standards of morality.*

Should Man United move to the US?

For English football fans the stadium chant of 'Stand up if you hate Man U' sums it up, albeit less eloquently than Schulberg, the writer of classics such as *On the Waterfront* and *The Harder They Fall*. Of course, such hatred is really a backhanded compliment. It is born from envy of a team that achieves an outstanding level of consistent success or quality. Think of how in England the early 1970s Leeds United team became 'Revie's Robots' or the entrenched dislike that its successor Liverpool attracted before the tragedies of Heysel and, more potently, Hillsborough wiped that from the zeitgeist. Rangers in Scotland attracts similar disgust. To some extent, so it is now with both the Dallas and Manchester superteams. In the middle of the decade, the Cowboys won gridiron's SuperBowl in the 1992, 1993 and 1995 seasons. United, too, has dominated its main domestic competition, lifting the Premier League's hideous trophy in 1992–3, 1993–4, 1995–6 and 1996–7. In the years they missed out they were the team to beat.

But whatever envy the two teams have generated by their achievements on the pitch, opposing fans also attach opprobrium to them for their activities off it. They are seen as having reshaped the financial landscape of their different sports, not merely to their own advantage but to the specific disadvantage of every other competitor. They are, the complaint often goes, 'ruining the game' or 'spoiling the competition'. Alternatively, they are 'the best teams that money can buy'. They are too rich and too business oriented. They win everything not because they are better and play better football, but because they have more money than other teams. United, like the Dallas Cowboys in the US, is seen as being an exemplar of the New Football where money matters more than football.

The hatred levelled at these teams is different from the contempt piled on the all-conquering sides of the 1970s in England. The Leeds Uniteds and Liverpools were disliked because they kept on winning. Nobody hated them for their merchandising. The dislike aimed at the invincible sides now is tinged with a fear that they will be unbeatable for ever and that the game will die as a result.

In Dallas's case, the team's active role in changing gridiron is indisputable. The driving force behind the transformation of the Cowboys is owner Jerry Jones, a buccaneering and outspoken Arkansas oil and gas magnate who bought the team for $150 million in 1989.

Here is a man who knows how to throw money at a problem. In his team's 1995 winning season, Jones's salary bill was $62 million: $22 million in basic salaries, but $40 million in bonuses. The NFL had set a $38.8 million salary cap for the year on all its member teams, but Jones avoided this by having only part of the money accounted against NFL regulations, including a mere $15 million of the bonus cash. According to most US commentators, it was a very clumsy sleight of hand but it worked nonetheless.

The Cowboys have led the way in the development of businesses off the field as well. The team's 66,000-seater Texas Stadium has 370 'skyboxes' – the US equivalent of executive boxes – with firms willing to pay well into six figures to lease the largest. The ground alone produces annual revenues of more than $40 million, well ahead of rivals. And just as the Cowboys have sidestepped rules on player salaries, they have swerved neatly round restrictions on selling merchandise. Under NFL rules, teams have a joint marketing agreement where revenues from all spinoffs are equally shared, regardless of which team sells the most. Like the salary cap, this is meant to ensure that no club can financially dominate its rivals.

Dallas, however, pioneered 'identity rights' and then struck a separate and additional deal with sportswear firm Nike, worth upwards of $100 million.

The Cowboys do not win all the time. They have not been helped by various player scandals (comparisons with a former French international and Man United captain may not be amiss here, or even comparisons with an Old Trafford superstar sent off in a vital World Cup game). But they still have much more money than the average NFL side and no one is catching them. US gridiron fans believe that the Cowboys will be back and lording it at the summit of the game some day very, very soon.

Substitute the words Manchester and United again for Dallas and Cowboys. Much of what gridiron did a decade or more ago is happening in Europe and in football today. So, given that the British game is comparatively unregulated, the doom and gloom that many rival clubs and their supporters feel when they survey United and its activities appear well founded. Man United has several advantages over the Cowboys thanks to the lack of any regulatory system in football. The maximum wage was abolished long ago, totally centralized marketing would be opposed by many more Premiership teams than the Red Devils, and steps already taken to limit clubs' ability to attract or steal young players are widely and frequently circumvented. United has indeed had its wrists slapped on more than one occasion for exactly this, but it is hardly the only club to bend the rules.

The comparison with the Dallas Cowboys holds good for one major reason – the simple matter of money. The jibes about Megabucks United and Merchandise United are not without foundation and that foundation has been laid with lots of cash.

United plays footsie

Every January, the *Financial Times* prints the UK 500, a ranking of full Stock Exchange and Alternative Investment Market member British companies according to their market value at the end of the year just gone. In the 1998 version, Manchester United occupied 289th place, with a stock-market value of £435.8 million. This was far behind the leaders such as Midland Bank owner HSBC Holdings (£56 billion), oil giant BP (£53 billion) and drug group Glaxo Wellcome (£49 billion), but way ahead of any other quoted football club. In fact, only two other teams figured on the list and both were less than half the Manchester club's size: Chelsea Village (471st at £175.6 million) and Newcastle United (484th at £166.9 million). The bald statistic is impressive enough, but United's financial preeminence over the rest of football is only part of the story.

The list allows some comparison between the Red Devils and other more traditional companies. According to the *FT*'s snapshot of UK plc, United is bigger than such firms as auctioneers Christies, brewers Greene King and the Savoy Hotel. Charting United's growth over 1997, it shows that during those 12 months the club overtook Capital Radio, bankers Hambros, minicomputer manufacturers Psion and that most PC of retailers The Body Shop as it rose from 338th place. The lesson to be drawn is simple. Man U is not only the biggest club in British football, it is also one of the biggest and fastest-growing companies in the country.

Ask anyone in the City of London how United got to this position and the response is usually the same and comes in two parts. Here's the first, from Bill New of the DEMOS think tank:

Man United is a very strong, efficiently run business both on and off the pitch. It is the most sophisticated football club in the world in a financial sense, and it is far ahead of anybody else in the UK or in Europe. Its history matters, but it is the way in which it has built on that over the last decade that has made United so extremely powerful.

Nigel Hawkins of Williams de Broe expresses the second part of the equation:

The other important thing about United is that they look and behave very much like a traditional business from a corporate point of view. They have a strong brand and they have worked to maximize its value by bringing in good people to develop it. Throughout the company, you don't find just football men, but businessmen from traditional sectors in key executive positions. They have innovation in that they operate one of the best youth policies to bring through new talent. They act and think like a national business rather than a regional one – they want supporters everywhere. And they control costs.

As we saw earlier, Singer & Friedlander's Tony Fraher is the evangelist of football as a stock-market sector. He takes a historical tack when explaining why Man U is the super club:

Manchester United is a big name in the UK and it is the big UK name internationally and that came out of a disaster which was the Munich air crash. Now they had been doing impressive things before that – there were the Busby Babes, they were among the first UK teams to go into Europe – but the crucial thing was the air crash. So out of that disaster United's international reputation was born.

Football fans won't take the word of some City slickers when it comes to deciding on how big Man United is. However, facts and figures are harder to argue with.

To begin with, there is the hard cash. Despite the BSkyB riches, roughly two-thirds of Premier League clubs make a loss. Manchester United delivers profits, nothing piffling but serious and consistent profits. In 1995, at the pretax level, these reached £20 million, dropping to £15.4 million in 1996, but rising again – actually nigh on doubling – in 1997 to £27.6 million. The dip in itself is instructive. The club said it was because of a reduction in Old Trafford's capacity while it invested in topping out the vertiginous North Stand, thus bringing the stadium up to 55,000 seats, and United's unusual failures to win the league in the season before and then to carve out a reasonably long run in Europe's UEFA Cup. There is no reason to doubt either of these observations.

The most recent figures for the six months to 31 January 1998 might be seized on by the anti-Red Devils majority as evidence that the colossus is cracking. They showed United's profits plummeting nearly £5 million to £14.8 million. The shame, the horror, the totally misleading reading of figures. United's pretax profits only fell because it spent £5 million on defender Henning Berg during those six months and therefore lost money on transfer dealing in the period. In the comparable six months to 31 January 1997, it had made a £3.7 million profit on transfers. Once the transfer dealing is stripped out, United's profits actually rose £2 million to £17.5 million. Figures that will follow completion of this book may show similar dips, given a Summer 1998 spending spree on Dwight Yorke (£12 million), Jaap Stam (£10 million) and Jesper Blomqvist (£3 million). But United can afford it and, remember, it did not win the league in 1997–8 and was never likely to take that indignity lying down.

Then there is the brand, one of the foundations for that kind of financial performance. In 1997, the club's merchandising activities turned over a staggering £28 million. This was up from £18.7 million in 1996 and a greater turnover in itself than most other Premier League clubs achieved from all their activities. In the six months to 31 January 1998, merchandising sales were down £2 million to £15.5 million. Evidence surely that the nation was tiring of Ryan Giggs duvets and the other paraphernalia of Megastore United? Well, the jury is out on this one for the moment.

Deputy chief executive Peter Kenyon claimed that the problem was, in the new language of football, 'cyclical'. That means that United's new replica home kit is launched every two years and in the second year of its life sales are lower. Not that United is standing still and just taking the fall in sales. The new 1998–9 season's kit was launched in May rather than the traditional August so that merchandising sales for the 1997–8 financial year would look a bit better.

The man credited as the architect of the brand-building programme, former merchandising manager Edward Freedman, left his full-time post at Old Trafford in Summer 1997 but continues to work with the club. He believes that the United name also has more clout than those of Nike and its competitors Reebok and Umbro. Umbro is paying the team a guaranteed minimum of £58 million for the privilege of producing replica kits and some other items of spinoff clothing under a six-year agreement running until 2002.

Unlike other clubs and fashion experts, United is not worried about the death of the replica kit as a fashion item. Peter Kenyon, a former Umbro executive himself, is having none of it:

*There is a lot of speculation in the market but we have not seen any
slowdown. The big properties in the market will always command
more money. The UK is unique in terms of the replica kit market but
there are only about half a dozen clubs that really sell – us, Newcastle, Arsenal, Chelsea, Rangers and Celtic.*

But United's brand development does not stop there and Kenyon
is now driving it forward. There are definite moves for global
domination. The club already publishes the UK's bestselling
monthly sports magazine at over 100,000 copies. This is also
translated into Thai, selling 20,000 copies. Mandarin and Can-
tonese versions look certain to follow, along with, according to
some reports, the franchising of some 50 dedicated shops across
the Far East. Plans are far advanced for a chain of shops in the
Middle and Far East, with United teaming up with a retail group
in a joint venture. Part of the scheme will include United's themed
Red Café in shops.

The Red Café has been tested in the Old Trafford stadium and has
been a success as part of the club's tour business. Currently around
200,000 people a year visit United's museum and go round Old
Trafford, paying £7.50 a time and £4.50 just for the museum. A
new, improved museum was opened in April 1998 with Pele as the
guest of honour. United aims to double the number of visitors to
400,000 a year and chief executive Martin Edwards says:

*We believe it will be the best sports museum in the world. This
museum is many times the size of its predecessor.*

That is a small but significant measure of United's ambition and
confidence. The club is also investing £500,000 for a 25 per cent
stake in a hotel being built by a consortium of leisure companies at
Old Trafford, at a cost of between £4 million and £5 million. It is
intended to be used by overseas visitors coming to Old Trafford for
matches and to visit the stadium. The 110-bedroom, three-star
hotel opens in early 1999. Edwards says:

*We think it is an exciting development, but you shouldn't get carried
away that it is going to be a huge business.*

Unlike other clubs such as Chelsea and Aston Villa which are developing their own hotels, United was approached for the idea as it is approached regularly by people wanting to be associated with the Old Trafford success story.

Britannia Building Society is the latest firm to grab at United's coat-tails. It has opened an account for United fans across the country, paying 5 per cent interest on balances over £100. For the privilege the society has to pay United 1 per cent of the money paid into the account. That is reckoned to be worth around £100,000 to Mr Edwards and his friends, which means, of course, that Britannia expects £10 million to be deposited by United fans. United has also expanded its Mancunian network of megastores by opening up a concession within the most famous toy store in the world, Hamleys on London's Regent Street.

The development of the business carries on and on. In September 1997, the club struck a three-way deal with broadcasters BSkyB and Granada to launch its own digital TV channel broadcasting for six hours a day during prime time. This is not the much-vaunted pay-per-view project, but a magazine service showing reserve and youth team games, testimonials and exclusive interviews – hardly top-notch stuff. Nevertheless, sources close to the negotiations say that both the winning consortium and its main competitor, the BBC, were 'doing some very interesting contortions' in their attempts to secure Edwards's signature. United has received an equal third stake in the venture with its partners, but in terms of capital investment 'is doing little more than turn up'.

Of course, pay-per-view is a contentious issue, with many clubs wary of the possible effects on attendances and concerned about how the cash will be divided up. Such factors saw the most recent attempt to launch a service voted down by chairmen in May 1998. United is not so concerned. Edwards says:

I would like to see an experiment sooner rather than later. At some stage the market needs to be addressed. With pay-per-view you can actually assess performance. You know who is watching who and I think that whomever we are playing revenues should be shared. Everyone thought that when you allowed live TV attendances would fall but they have gone up. People like to see the product live.

United but anonymous

Mention of Edwards inevitably leads to the issue of people. The chief executive himself is a surprisingly and deliberately anonymous character, a cut apart from the stereotypical image of major sporting club owners. His father, the late Mancunian butcher Louis Edwards, was more an example of the flamboyant breed of owners and passed control of the club to his son on his death. If United had been a good business for the ebullient Louis – one that he acquired by fairly devious means, as superbly documented by Michael Crick and David Smith in *Betrayal of a Legend* – Martin initially seemed to want to sell up, wooing but never finally accepting bidders such as property developer Michael Knighton, now at Carlisle United, and the infamous press baron Robert Maxwell. When that did not work, however, he 'knuckled down to make the best of it that he could'.

Thus, whatever is said about Edwards's personal business skills, two things he did get right were to hire people who could fill in for any of his own shortcomings and to give them the investment to get on with the job. This was the case with Freedman, the merchandising director of Tottenham Hotspur who found himself out of favour following the 1991 Alan Sugar–Terry Venables takeover and rescue.

Edwards fully recognized what White Hart Lane's new tenants possibly did not: that the merchandising of the club, Freedman's responsibility, was working perfectly and that it was Spurs' move into manufacturing sports goods, nothing to do with Freedman, that had played a role in nearly bankrupting football's first plc. The subsequent growth in United's merchandising activities – which were turning over just £2 million a year when Freedman arrived – is testament enough to the executive's skill, but further evidence comes from his subsequent engagement as guru to, among others, Premiership rivals Nottingham Forest and European champions Real Madrid. He has even worked for those icons of our age the Spice Girls.

Other appointments appear equally apposite. Manchester United's plc board is headed by Professor Sir Roland Smith, famous in the City as the 'serial chairman' for his large number of FTSE

100 and other directorial positions, which at one point peaked at 17. Although he was ousted as chairman during the near collapse of British Aerospace, he is regarded as a safe pair of hands and is widely liked as the man who, when at House of Fraser, told tycoon Tiny Rowland to 'get your tanks off my lawn' during the Harrods takeover battle.

The gap left by Freedman's departure was partly filled by the appointment of Peter Kenyon as deputy chief executive in May 1997. He joined from the international division of kit supplier Umbro, where he had already built up knowledge of the UK market and those in the Far East that the club is eager to develop. A competitor described him as 'a good bloke and a sharp bastard'.

The board added another formidable figure in September 1997, by signing up Channel Five chairman Greg Dyke as a non-executive director. Between 1988 and 1992, it was Dyke who led ITV's Sport's rights negotiations, proposing the first breakaway deal with the 'Big Five', but later seeing the Premier League snatched away by BSkyB. With the ink on the BSkyB–Granada deal still drying, Edwards allowed himself what may amount to a slightly ironic understatement:

He is an ideal appointment for Manchester United at this stage of the development of our business.

Finance director David Gill completes the executive team.

These, obviously, are just the leading positions, but the philosophy of putting appropriate business skills before a knowledge of or even attachment to football permeates United's whole employment policy, according to one senior recruitment consultant who has dealt with the club. A rough initial idea of who Sir Matt Busby was is useful but not essential. What matters is your ability to deliver. If you can, then the money will be there. As Freedman told authors Alex Fynn and H. Davidson in their book on Spurs, *Dream On*, there is one key reason that United built on all of this to achieve preeminence over teams like Arsenal and Liverpool:

Well, there is a factor called investment. Without investment, you can't get a return.

Money well spent

To understand the investment factor at United, you only have to visit Old Trafford. Nearly £50 million has been spent on developing the stadium since 1990; enough to build two or three brand new grounds for most clubs. The club is not finished yet, because there are now concerns that it is turning away fans and no business likes to lose customers. United is considering adding another 10,000 seats, although any move is years away. Apart from the stands, United has upgraded its conference facilities and opened its Red Café theme restaurant as well as greatly expanding its capacity for the dreaded corporate hospitality – Club Class seats now occupy an area where once the local masses swayed on the Stretford End.

When the club presents its half-year and annual financial results to City analysts, finance director David Gill always proudly flourishes a list of United's capital expenditure since flotation in 1991. Its most recent manifestation showed that up until 31 January 1998 the club had spent £80,632,000 on a variety of projects, including rebuilding, land acquisition and the purchase of plant and machinery. It also included an estimate of £26 million for future capital spending (excluding player acquisitions), adding up to a grand total of £106,632,000. Gill's next trick was to point out that the club has only raised £23,425,000 of the total from the City. Some £6,685,000 was received on flotation and another £16,740,000 via a later share placing. The message from the figures is that, of course, the other £83,207,000 came from United's business.

Finally, in a very abbreviated list, United sought planning permission in March 1998 on a new £14.3 million training complex, about four miles from Old Trafford at Carrington. The initial cost was to have been £10 million, but planning and environmental requirements plus United's own high standards boosted the cost. Apart from changing rooms and offices, it will include nine full-size pitches and one extended pitch with undersoil heating, which in the planning application adds up to 10.5 pitches. There will be four junior pitches, training areas and what is described as a 'rehabilitation area'. There will be a gym and a pool. In a move with almost Arsène Wengeresque dietary echoes, 30 of the 100 acres will be leased to an organic farmer. The club would like the facility to be up and running by July 2000. Edwards says:

> *It will be a state-of-the-art facility which will take us into the next century. We hope it will help attract foreign players and youngsters to the club.*

Has someone been left out?

Of course, that word 'training' would seem to bring some other crucial elements into the equation which have been ignored until now. Foremost among these factors are, in no particular order, Alex Ferguson, Brian Kidd, Ryan Giggs, David Beckham, Peter Schmeichel, Roy Keane, Paul Scholes, Gary Neville, Phil Neville, Teddy Sheringham, Nicky Butt, Denis Irwin, Henning Berg, Andy Cole, Ronny Johnsen, David May and new arrivals Stam, Yorke and Blomqvist.

Manchester United has 105,000 members and 40,000 season-ticket holders. To them, the selection of 11 men that manager Alex Ferguson fields in each game and that those lucky few secure victory are all that really matters. The business side of the club is only important in as much as it affects admission and megastore prices, the club's ability and willingness to buy or sell certain players and, most recently, the supporters' preference as to whether they would rather stand up in their seats or be forced to remain sitting throughout the game. However, United's current position in sport is as much a matter of business as sporting performance. The two go hand in hand.

In terms of that commercial performance, United is, as said before, not just a well-run football club but a well-run company, full stop. And it is further evidence of the quality of that off-the-pitch management that there is more of a synthesis than a collision involving the beautiful game and big business. That is not to say that there is not an inevitable tension between the two. In particular, it comes down to the issue of cost control.

Over the three seasons between 1995 and 1998, United has been linked with a number of world-class players, in particular South

American strikers Ronaldo, Gabriele Batistuta and Marcelo Salas. In each case the club has been able to afford the transfer fees involved, but deals were not concluded because the club was unwilling to meet the salary demands made by the players' agents. The rationale behind its withdrawals, once set out significantly by Ferguson rather than Edwards or another board member, has been that 'we were unwilling to upset the internal salary structure for football reasons, not just because of the plc'. In the case of Salas, Edwards is adamant about who took the decision:

> *The board would have supported the purchase of Salas, but just at that time Andy Cole was knocking goals in for fun and it was a case of either Cole or Salas because you couldn't play both. We had to say to Alex Ferguson who did you want. It was in the end a manager's decision. Player costs are going up as more income is coming into the game. Players are looking for their share of it. Wage inflation will continue to rise. Wage inflation is a fact of life. It is a question of how you negotiate and we are quite prepared to negotiate.*

However, finance director David Gill proudly points out that at Man United wage costs at around £27 million a year are roughly 26 per cent of turnover. He notes: 'This is the lowest proportion in football within the UK and probably within Europe.'

Alex Ferguson appears to regard the wage inflation issue as secondary, but nonetheless important, when compared to harmony in his dressing room. On one level, he is aware that the board will not sanction across-the-board wage increases, and is tied anyway to several player contracts, specifically for Beckham and Sheringham, that stipulate that the individual may not be subject to a differential to any of his colleagues beyond a certain level. On another, however, he does not want to breed discontent by creating a position where all his superstars are equal but some are more equal than others. And he's right. Where similar positions have arisen at other clubs – notably Chelsea and Middlesbrough – the results have been the collapse of a championship bid or even relegation.

Ferguson made his position explicit in comments following the club's decision in August 1997 to pull out of a deal for another player, German defender Markus Babbel, over wage conditions again:

> *We have five international defenders [the Nevilles, Irwin, Johnsen and the subsequently transferred Gary Pallister] and Babbel would have been earning substantially more than them. What would those players have thought, because the media would have been sure to tell them somehow how much Babbel was getting?*

Instead, he signed Henning Berg from Blackburn Rovers.

The team has many superstar players. It provides the backbone of the English national side and also contains key figures in the Danish, Norwegian, Dutch, Republic of Ireland and Welsh lineups. Ferguson's ability to balance and assess the various no-doubt (and justifiably) considerable egos involved is but one example of what makes him the keystone in the United miracle. Because while business and sport appear to be in sync, if not perfect harmony, the business side could not thrive without the success of the team on the pitch, even at this level. All the club's commercial skills essentially underwrite its footballing performance.

The evidence for this is easy to find. While analysts rightly praise United as well run and note a similarity in its professionalism with traditional businesses, buying and selling of the club's stock seems closely allied to results. In October 1996, the club went down to a shock 5–0 defeat by its then main rivals, Newcastle United. When trading resumed on Monday, the share price fell by 18.5p. This was at a time when there was considerable takeover speculation concerning the club, so investors would be expected to hold tight. When midfield, and martial, artist Eric Cantona retired in May 1997, another dip of 8.5p occurred – and this was just after the club had won the championship and had a new season of European Champion's League football ahead. In 1998, elimination from Europe by French side Monaco and both the home and away defeats to its then chief rival Arsenal had similar impacts. In each case small, penny-sized slides knocked millions off the club's value.

Even Hawkins admits that the one thing about United that could genuinely send serious jitters right through its pack of major institutional investors would be 'Ferguson's resignation'.

The Fergie factor

No man is bigger than his club, but Ferguson comes closer to that than anyone else in British and, arguably, European football. His skills as a manager and as a developer of new talent are widely recognized. The Old Trafford academy has produced Giggs and Beckham, Butt and Scholes, and the two Nevilles. Ferguson's willingness to involve himself in this setup, personally meeting all the parents of prospective youth squad members and maintaining those links as well as his full involvement with youth coaching, are rare commitments from a top-flight manager. With the exception of Dutch side Ajax, no other major European club can point to such an array of self-developed players. And yet this is at first glance a relatively late addition to the United battleplan, albeit one that it intends to take further, as shown by its plans for the new training ground. Most of these players did not seep through to the first team on a regular basis until the 1995–6 season, nine years after Ferguson had first been appointed.

The reality is that Ferguson started working to this objective virtually from his first day in charge. For the club's part, it is now reaping the benefits because it did not merely invest money in its manager but also in the one commodity such men can rarely count on – time. During Ferguson's first four years at Old Trafford, United won nothing of significance and even flirted with relegation in some seasons. At a club of this size anywhere else, Ferguson would have been shown the door long before he crossed his supposed Rubicon with an FA Cup win in 1990. While much has been written about the axe hanging over Ferguson during an earlier tie in the competition at Nottingham Forest, which his team sneaked 1–0, the four years he had already had was twice as long as the average tenure of a Premier League or First Division manager. United had already made the decision to give its man the resources he needed to reshape the club.

The youth policy is also a genuine financial success story, as United's most recent financial results show. Buried among the details is the club's transfer dealing record for the six months to 31 January 1998. It shows that the main spending was £5.5 million on Henning Berg and anticipated income was £2 million from the sale of Karel Poborsky. However, the club also raised £850,000 from the sale of Simon Davies, Michael Appleton and John O'Kane. None of these three is yet a household name, but they still commanded reasonable fees. They are all, of course, products of the youth policy who have become good footballers but are not rated as quite good enough for Man United. Finance director Gill makes the point in accountant speak:

> *We do realize significant sums from home-grown players who don't make it into United teams but are still very marketable commodities.*

Wannabes

Slowly but surely, other clubs are trying to learn the same lesson. Former Leeds Sporting chairman Chris Akers recognizes the difficulties:

> *Luck has undoubtedly played its part in Ferguson's success. We may even look back and discover that he just happened to be at the right place at the right time when a whole group of exceptionally talented players just happened to be at his club. But I somehow doubt that. Man United have worked hard and waited, and waiting is very difficult in football. Fans want success, so do investors. Whatever you do, you are judged on your results week by week. The Premier League and the money involved have also intensified those pressures.*

In the long term, Leeds, for which Akers remains a consultant, has given its backing to George Graham, the former Arsenal manager, and while in charge Akers sought him out, despite his involvement in the transfer bungs scandals, for very specific reasons:

> *We wanted George because of his track record. I like statistics and in recent times, he is one of only three managers who has consistently won things – the others being Dalglish and Ferguson. He knows how to build a winning side. We said to George: 'We will give you the resources, including the time, you give us the team.' After what*

happened, he feels he has something to prove, so that is on Leeds' side as well.

Over the time it takes to Graham to fulfil that objective, Akers is aware, however, that Leeds as a business must do something to satisfy its shareholders:

The club obviously has to look at other aspects of what Man United have done – the merchandising, the museums and all that – but they are so far ahead of everyone else that even if you put all the right people in all the right jobs today, it could still take you several years to catch up or, at least, be doing things that investors will notice in comparison with what they have achieved. The rest of the game neglected the business side while Man United kept plodding ahead, and then, one day, everybody suddenly woke up.

In Leeds' case, this made the club an early pioneer in different aspects of Internet marketing. It launched its away strip for 1997–8 on the Web before it was in the shops and has run Real Audio webcasts with live commentaries:

Computers are potentially a big opportunity. Leeds and Yorkshire has per head one of the highest concentrations of PCs in the country. But it is not just that. Leeds had a lot of ex-pat supporters, and by ex-pat you can be talking as easily about London as LA or the Costa del Sol. The Internet is, again, a very efficient way of reaching out to this market.

A second part of Leeds' strategy is the construction of a 20,000-seat arena next to its Elland Road stadium, although the project has proved problematic:

When we took over the club, one of the main attractions was that it was a single-city club, like Newcastle. If someone comes from Leeds, then they are a Leeds fan, not to mention thousands more in Yorkshire. That was what attracted the club to the stadium project; there are no other similar-sized cities in England that are not already served both by a stadium and an arena. Man United can't do that, because they live next to the Arena and the G-Mex centre.

According to Akers, United has reached so dominant a position that to begin to catch up it is incumbent on Leeds and others to seek out areas that United has not explored, to beat it not at its own but at a new game. In the circumstances, these are not bad business objectives, but there is the suspicion – although Akers is not explicit about it – that in terms of the fundamental football business, they are also buying time. Another of his comments suggests that more clearly:

> *There's a lot of management theory around on this but, frankly, a football club is a very easy thing to run, as long as you're winning. Get it right on the pitch and everything else falls into place.*

This brings everything immediately back to a simple fact. United is the benchmark for the UK's biggest teams, and also for Europe. The magnificent German player Franz Beckenbauer, now president of Bayern Munich, is but one of many top executives who sees things that way. He told German reporters shortly after announcing his club's flotation plans:

> *Manchester is the business objective. Control of the stadium, management of the asset, and exploitation of the name are the three things they have got completely right.*

It is not too surprising that a former West German captain appears to hold back before praising the players, yet Kaiser Franz later said:

> *United has developed a group of young players who can win everything at home and yet whom, I do not think, have reached their peak yet. If commercial skill has helped Manchester to produce a team like that, then the rest of us do need to start to equal that today.*

Barcelona, for so long the biggest club in the world, is also looking over its shoulder. One adviser to the Catalans is open about their worries:

> *Manchester United have been very successful in developing the football business. I am not sure that everything they have done will*

*translate into Spain or elsewhere in Europe, but the fundamental
ideas appear to work very well.*

In the 1997–8 season, Barcelona replaced Englishman Bobby Robson with former Ajax boss Louis van Gaal as its chief coach. The consultant acknowledged that it was a choice based not just on his track record but, 'like Ferguson', on his ability to develop young talent. At a club where sackings are like Number 9 buses – miss one and there's another in a few minutes – one of van Gaal's opening comments at an early press conference was also worth noting:

> *I have come here to do a job, and that is to deliver a system that will operate over the long term. We will be looking to win trophies from the very start, but to complete the project* **may take several years***.*
> (our bold)

Your basic Man United model – big, expensive and a classic design

United has simply reshaped the top level of football, although its ability to do so is heavily dependent on two factors. First, it was always big and has grown from a position of strength. The history of the club, with the Busby Babes, Munich, George Best and Sir Bobby Charlton, has been important but it does not particularly single the club out. When United began to grow rapidly from 1993 onwards, others had similar histories and balance sheets – Arsenal, Tottenham Hotspur, Liverpool and Everton in England and Rangers and Celtic in Scotland. All of these other clubs have glorious histories and dark days on which to build legends. Any football fan can come up with phrases to match any one of these clubs. Yet in only five years, Man United has left them looking like commercial also-rans, although Arsenal and Rangers are making up lost ground.

Secondly, there is the imponderable and ultimately unanswerable factor: United was in the right place at the right time. The happy accident that has boosted all of football has boosted Man United more than most. Its years of being an also-ran which never won the league despite many brave efforts ended just as the Premier League deal started with its multimillion-pound rewards for success. The impositions of the Taylor report also greatly helped the club, by making it rebuild and restructure at a time when its owner was willing to sell out for just £10 million.

Now that owner is not really the owner and is worrying about the effects of his club's overweening influence on the game in England. Martin Edwards is genuinely concerned that United's dominance of the Premiership could harm interest in the game and ultimately damage the business that he heads. While chairman Professor Sir Roland Smith dismisses queries about these concerns with 'That is for the other clubs to worry about', Edwards takes a more conciliatory line:

> *I can see the worry about the competition in the league when you look at Rangers in Scotland winning the championship nine times in a row with some of these championships virtually secured by Christmas. That does prompt concern about whether people will still be interested. It is genuinely different for us.*
>
> *Even though we have won the Premiership in four out of the six times it has been contested, it has always been close most of the time. While we have got interest and a challenge going right to the end, people are not going to lose interest in the game. We don't sit back and think we have got it all made and think we are superior to everyone else. It is a tough league and it is a close league. You have to remember that there have been years where we didn't win anything. In 1995 we could have done the double but in the end it came down to the last day of the season in the championship and we lost out and then we lost in the FA Cup final as well, so we ended up empty-handed. It is that close and sometimes we don't know whether we are going to win anything until the last 90 minutes.*

But what of that opening comparison with the Dallas Cowboys? The atmosphere-numbing corporate hospitality and brand exploitation appear identical. Also, below a certain level of 'big' club, it does appear that United is behaving in an exclusive manner. West Brom chief executive John Wile comments:

There is something that bothers me about the idea that United is the model for every other club. They are a club with international support, and have achieved a certain level of success which allows them to build further and further on that. If smaller clubs like ours start trying to copy United, I have no doubt that they will get overstretched. You cannot build that kind of image overnight. Look at Blackburn Rovers. They spent big. They won the championship. But what has it really got them since? At the same time, it does little good for competition if United and a handful of others pull away from everybody else, if a Blackburn or a West Brom cannot have a shot every once in a while.

Yet it is important that United itself is beginning to reach a similar, if not quite identical point of view. City of London analysts have long detected what they would term a reticence or conservatism in United's business approach. As Brian Sturgess of ING Barings views it:

If you think how far they could go, they are surprisingly restrained. It is almost as though they go along but are always thinking: 'So much and no more.' That is a very difficult one to judge – it can leave you vulnerable.

As Monaco proved in the 1997–8 European Champions' League, United is not invincible. The Manchester side made the mistake, in the view of football experts, of only playing so as not to concede a goal in the away leg and then could only draw at home. That meant that it went out on the unsatisfactory away-goals rule. The Cowboys would never do that. They always go straight for the jugular, although reports of a nicer, cuddlier Man U are also probably overstated.

CHAPTER SEVEN

WHO RUNS FOOTBALL?

Football's a business and it's not going to be run by the blazer brigade any more. It needs to be run as a business by businessmen.
Sir John Hall, former Newcastle United chairman, 1995

THE ENGLISH FOOTBALL ASSOCIATION IS THE OLDEST FOOTBALLING administrative body in the world and arguably still one of the most important. It has draconian powers over clubs, players and managers. It can ban and fine them all – a factor, indeed, that led several of our interview subjects to seek anonymity. Anyone concerned about football has to look to the FA. The organization has successfully maintained much of its status throughout the convulsions that English football has suffered. Through skilful political manoeuvring, the emergence of the breakaway Premier League that might have been a mortal challenge to the preeminence of Lancaster Gate ended up apparently enhancing the FA's historical position at the head of the game.

Bryon Butler, the author of the FA's official history, can write admiringly about it without being laughed at too much. His description of the FA is still accepted by many in the game and by outsiders. He wrote:

It has been the game's pole star. It has made mistakes and enemies but its eminence and authority have remained constant; and in the huge family of FIFA, from Afghanistan to Zimbabwe, it is the one national association which does not require an identity tag.

The confidence of the FA has long historical roots. It only joined football's world governing body FIFA in 1905 – a year after its foundation – on the proviso that it would teach the world how to run football. At the time, the FA's delegation to a FIFA conference in Berne said:

> *Therefore it is important to the FA and other European Associations that a properly constituted Federation should be established, and the Football Association should use its influence to regulate football on the Continent as a pure sport and give all Continental Associations the full benefit of the many years' experience.*

By that point the FA had plenty of experience, having founded the International Board in 1886 with Ireland, Scotland and Wales, when the British reckoned that the rest of the world was not good enough at football to bother with. Things have changed and the rest have caught up, but there still remains a hint of imperial splendour about the organization.

And yet any examination of who runs football can no longer conclude that it is the mandarins of Lancaster Gate in England or their counterparts at the Scottish Football Association in Glasgow's Park Gardens, or even the bosses of the international organizations UEFA and FIFA. They are certainly a part of the answer to the question of who controls the beautiful game. But in a big-money sport they are no longer the omnipotent overlords.

Administrators have demonstrated growing commercial skills and have always been reasonably adept at the game's politics. However, personality and strength of will increasingly count for more in a game where huge amounts of money are at stake. And, of course, it is money that matters more than anything else, as clubs and the new investors attracted to the game are showing.

Clubbing the administrators

The power and lure of money and the influence of clubs were graphically illustrated during the 1997–8 season as Scottish football realized that its cosy old structure of 40 professional and semiprofessional clubs coexisting under the umbrella of the Scottish FA and the Scottish League no longer worked.

The 10 Premier Division clubs announced in 1997 that they intended to retire from their domestic league and go their own way in a league that was commercially separate. The league was to negotiate its own TV and other commercial deals and keep the proceeds for the top 10 and not, as before, share them in a graduated manner with the other 30 clubs. As a sop, these clubs conceded that some form of lump-sum payment would be guaranteed to the outsiders each season. It was a move that underlined the shift in the power base across football as a whole. Top clubs in France, Spain and Italy have flirted both with a European Super League and with their own domestic breakaways. BSkyB, with rare prescience, already calls Spain's first division a Primera Liga.

The Scottish split followed dark rumours of a unilateral split by the Scottish league's Glaswegian powerhouse, the Old Firm of Rangers and Celtic. Both Rangers chairman David Murray and his opposite number at Celtic, Fergus McCann, had dropped vague and not so vague hints about quitting the domestic game to join the English Premiership. And so it was that over the next few months, they went through many of the same arguments that their English counterparts had debated in 1991 and 1992.

Why, it was asked, should Rangers have to receive the same TV cash as, for instance, Stranraer? How could it be that Scottish football had seen a proud record in European competitions replaced by the ignominy of first-round and preliminary-round elimination by part-time opposition? Even more irritating for the big Scottish clubs, how could it be that the teams which were relegated from the English Premiership could still pocket more TV money for their failed seasons than all of Scottish football put together? When the plan was unveiled, Hibernian's chairman Lex Gold, one of its early driving forces (but who fell by the wayside when ironically his club was relegated), said:

Commercial opportunities and in particular TV rights are currently underexploited. This leads to a loss of cash that is urgently needed to improve the game. This new proposal will significantly increase the resources within the Scottish game. The vast majority of supporters and those involved directly in the game realize that major steps forward must be taken if we are to put Scottish football back on the map.

This all sounds very familiar, and the rest of the tale does not deviate greatly from the original script of England's Premiership. Powerful clubs had grown tired of having their agenda for growth and development set by administrators who necessarily had to act for the good of all Scottish teams. Essentially, the argument was over who runs football. And the administrators were simply swept aside.

Celtic's finance director Eric Riley is explicit that the split owed its roots to money and politics. He says that the restructuring idea grew from failed talks involving all the clubs in the Scottish League management committee about improving the domestic game. They agreed that Scottish football had problems, particularly concerning the standard of competition. But they struggled to come up with ways of putting them right. The leading clubs became frustrated at the small clubs' inability, in their view, to see the bigger picture. They had immense respect for the Scottish football administrators in private as well as in public, but were adamant that they were not going to be held back by them.

The bickering did not impress Mr Riley, an accountant by training who describes himself as a 'sports fan' rather than a Celtic fan:

We had people saying, 'Let's appoint outside advisers' and the other side saying, 'No, we can't do that. That's a waste of money.' The ultimate conclusion from that, we felt, being that 'They will tell us things we don't like'. The clubs in the lower league tried to push through a reconstruction that would have expanded the Premier League. That was nonsense and a non-starter. Realizing that we were not making any progress we got together with the other Premier League teams.

Outside consultants from accountants Deloitte & Touche and sports management experts IMG were appointed to canvass the views of everyone in Scottish football, ranging from the clubs through to supporters and the media. Riley admits, however, that they were working to a specific brief from the breakaway clubs:

Essentially, the interests of a club in the Scottish Third Division are so different from the interests of a Celtic or a Rangers. One of the major reasons for the breakaway was to increase autonomy and take control of our own destinies. It is much easier to get agreement within an environment of 10 than within an environment of 40.

And he is open about the fact that money as well as the good of the game was at the root of the argument:

Previously revenue was spread among 40 clubs, and we are willing to let them keep what they already get. Once you get a stronger Premier Division you can then look at the First, Second and Third Divisions, but you need to deal with the Premier Division first. One of the big stumbling blocks was how to divide up the revenues of the 10 within the Premier Division. Celtic and Rangers were prepared to not take as much of the commercial revenue as we might be entitled to – after all, why do television companies want Scottish football? It's for Old Firm games largely – but we are prepared to invest to make the game up here better.

He has no doubt that the top sides in Scottish football have had a bad deal from administrators and TV companies so far:

We must be able to make more money. If you go back to 1996 when Bolton Wanderers were relegated from the English Premiership, they got more from television than Celtic and Rangers got. I think that is very strange. We should be looking at a sizeable uplift. I'm not saying that Old Firm games are as big as the prime English matches, but we're up there. The market value of an Old Firm game is worth upwards of £1 million. Everything that applies to the English Premiership will not apply to Scotland, but I feel we have got a better chance going forward this way than with the current setup in Scotland. I don't think you can stick your head in the sand because the status quo is not acceptable. Pressure will be exerted not to have any change, but that is no longer acceptable.

Club power and the new breed of owners are driving the revolution and calling the tune. This reflects the fact that in Scotland as elsewhere, the people running the game have changed. People such as Fergus McCann and David Murray are businessmen on a different scale from the men they replaced at their clubs. McCann inherited a sleeping giant dominated by warring families and floated Celtic on the stock market. Murray replaced businessmen with relatively limited ambitions who had seen Rangers decline and has now hooked up with one of Britain's richest men in the shape of Bahamas-based Joe Lewis and his ENIC trust.

The 1997–8 Scottish Cup winners Heart of Midlothian are floated on the stock market and run by a company called, without any apparent sense of irony, New Hearts. It is controlled by solicitor Leslie Deans and catering tycoon Chris Robinson. More financially aware managements are in control at clubs such as Aberdeen and Dundee United. However, the presence of multimillionaire Tom Farmer, the founder of car repair group Kwik-Fit who only started that business after retiring at the age of 28 when he made his first fortune, did not save Edinburgh's other team Hibernian from its 1998 relegation.

In this environment, ask yourself how long it will be before similar things happen in France. There, a Communist sports minister is stripping away rules which forced clubs to be run on a not-for-profit basis and which have consequently seen most of the country's top talent heading for overseas clubs. In Italy and Spain, meanwhile, relaxations on stock-exchange regulations and once strict member-ownership schemes are also attracting more commercially savvy investors with new ideas on how football should be structured.

It is a moot point whether these people are using their power well. Judgement on the Scottish breakaway will be reserved until the wider football community sees how it affects the lower three divisions, despite protestations from the country's big clubs that they are not about to make England's mistakes. But the fact that they have pushed through their plan, despite disturbing evidence from south of the border and the reluctance of the local authorities, shows that a very determined mindset dominates the boardrooms and, more importantly, that local administrators have only a Canute-like influence over the prevailing tide.

Riley acknowledges the shift that has occurred as men with more traditional business objectives take on more and more power:

You can see examples of individuals coming into football who are more commercially minded. Football is now very much a business and you have got to think like that. In the past, directorships of football clubs might have been passed down in families and they tended to be absentee managers. Now the thing has become much bigger and specialist staff have been hired in from outside. It is a business, after all.

In the early stages, the men in suits have been able to set out their case in ways that could even be said to reflect the majority of fans' ambitions and desires. More people support the big clubs than the small. Why do the strong have to support the weak when the weak are dragging the strong down? Developing a better national game and competing in Europe and in the World Cup means building clubs that will be centres of excellence. Winning in Europe requires teams that have a tough domestic competition to prepare them for the ultimate challenge. What does it profit a team to conquer Scotland and still get stuffed at home by a bunch of Scandinavians, as Rangers does? More prosaically, is it better to have a limited number of strong teams rather than a wide selection of reasonable teams and a vast array of duds? It all sounds perfectly intelligent and knocks forever the idea that administrators are all-powerful. Clubs and tycoons beat administrators every time.

The Scottish breakaway is the latest example of a trend. Clubs across Europe have always been powerful in the game's hierarchy. No matter what the administrators have said, they have always had to tread a fine line when dealing with the owners of the teams that actually make the game happen. And these owners are today much more aggressive and dynamic than they were in the past.

Rich men have always been attracted to football across the Continent. But today's club owners, who largely came into the game in the late 1980s and early 1990s, are a different breed of rich men. In England, the likes of Newcastle United's Sir John Hall, who despite his recent retirement as club chairman still owns a majority of the Geordie side, and Spurs' Alan Sugar are not the same as old-style local boys made good. Sir John, whose fortune comes from property development at Gateshead's Metro Centre, has regularly blasted the 'blazer brigade' at the top of football. Sugar, who succeeded with computer and electrical goods giant Amstrad, took the FA to court and won over its decision to dock his club league points and to ban it from the FA Cup because of 'offences' committed by previous directors. The owners do not sit there and do what they are told any more.

Above and below them are other extremely wealthy businesspeople attracted to the game as much by the chance to make money from the next big growth leisure industry as by love of the sport. Everton's Peter Johnson has not made as much of a success of the Merseyside club as he has of his other businesses, Christmas hamper firm Park Foods and parcels company Nightfreight. Arsenal is dominated by commodities trader David Dein and diamond merchant Danny Fiszman. Chelsea's Ken Bates has survived numerous boardroom battles at his club. Blackburn's Jack Walker, like David Murray a steel tycoon, has bought numerous players for his club. Aston Villa's Doug Ellis has made a fortune from holiday businesses, claiming to be one of the first to launch package tours with his wife buttering the sandwiches for holidaymakers. Lionel Pickering has traded a fortune from free newspapers for control at Derby County.

On the Continent, a similar process has taken place although the other Europeans were ahead of the game compared to the British. Former Italian Prime Minister Silvio Berlusconi was the pioneer in Italy. He has been openly contemptuous of the administrators, once telling Italy's main sports daily, *La Gazetta dello Sport*:

> *I see no great amount of business skills in these organizations, and therefore I do not think that they are of any real importance.*

In Germany, the Soccer Federation has suffered a court defeat at the hands of its bigger clubs over TV rights. The German Federal Court rejected its claim to exclusive rights to sell matches involving Bundesliga clubs in European competition. That has meant that the Federation has to sanction a free-for-all in which the big clubs sell their own rights and ditch an arrangement under which clubs which were not competing in Europe received some of the revenue.

The reality is that already many of the big clubs are thinking of breaking off from their local and regional administrators. The idea for a European Super League has not come from the mandarins of the game. It is the big clubs across the Continent who want to see a Super League. Even those at major clubs who have a good word for the various FAs say that things must change. Mike Edelson, the man behind the flotations of Sheffield United and Leicester City and also a Manchester United FC director, notes:

To be more effective, the people at the top of the FA need to be put in positions where they can act more like executives rather than the Council's factotums. The rubber stamping remains a frustrating process, although it is improving.

The entrepreneurs have pressing reasons for being concerned with the administration of the sport and for wanting to influence it. It would be unfair to say simply that their interest is financial, as the new breed does have an interest in the development of the sport and has come up with ideas which have improved numerous aspects of football. They are the people behind the TV deals which have enriched the sport and have helped fund the mammoth influx of world superstars to the British game. A tenth of the players on show at the 1998 World Cup were employed in the UK, which is at least part of an argument to show that the quality of the football on British pitches has improved.

However, they do have a lot of money riding on the success of football and many have become much richer on the back of the game. Flitting briefly through the shareholdings of British clubs shows many people with sizeable fortunes at stake in their clubs. The power behind Arsenal, English football's 1997–8 League and Cup winner, is David Dein. He is described by Wimbledon's boss Sam Hammam as the 'most influential figure in the modern game' and is a member of the FA executive. He paid £290,250 for his initial stake in the club back in 1983. The chairman, Peter Hill-Wood, said at the time:

Some rich men like to buy fast cars, yachts or racehorses. But David is more interested in football. I'm delighted he is but I still think he's crazy. To all intents and purposes it is dead money.

Mr Hill-Wood was dead wrong, as Dein's stake is now worth £35 million. Alan Sugar invested around £8 million in Spurs, an investment which is now worth around four times that despite the team's erratic on-field performance. The Halls paid around £2 million for a controlling stake in Newcastle and are now sitting on nearly £100 million from their investment – no wonder that the miscreant Douglas was soon invited back 'on board'. Many of the club owners are genuine football fans who love their clubs and it would be unfair to accuse them of only being interested in money. But then again, they have shareholders, personal ambitions and other duties to fulfil.

Playing the City

The people who have changed the game have not done it all by themselves. While the majority of clubs are still private companies, a substantial minority are stock-market quoted. Being on the stock market means attracting institutional investment from pension funds and City firms, who then take a stake in the club and accept part of the risk of owning shares.

Merchant banker Tony Fraher is among the most prominent of City investors in football via Singer & Friedlander's Football Fund. He forcefully expresses the view that the City relationship with the game has now changed:

Fans moan nowadays about the City running football because clubs are floating on the stock market. It's rubbish and people just don't understand what has happened. The City has always run football through bank loans. Do people think that when a bank decides to give a multimillion-pound loan the decision is taken by the local branch manager in wherever it is? Of course it isn't. Big loan decisions are taken in London at the head office, not by some branch manager deciding to dole out a couple of million. The City is now

changing its relationship by investing in clubs, by buying shares.
Before, if banks had a loan they could threaten to shut a club down.
Now, if they own shares they have to accept the risk, but they will
want dividends and profits in return. And they will definitely want
a return for their money.

Fraher's robust view about the City coming in as a partner will not
find favour with many football fans, who reckon that the moneymen are all-powerful and run everything in a malign way from
the shadows. They will cite the case of Newcastle United's £193
million stock-market launch and its role in the departure of manager Kevin Keegan. He makes it clear in his recent autobiography
that he left so abruptly in January 1997 partly because of the
stock-market launch. He wanted to stay until the end of the season, but was told he had to go immediately because of the flotation. The club could not go to the City without a manager on
board, Keegan was told. But the Newcastle example is as yet an isolated one and Keegan was going anyway. The City's role in that
affair simply hastened his departure by four months.

Yet fans are right that Fraher's comments about wanting a
return means that the moneymen play an important role. They are
right that the institutions will worry about the effects of administrators' rulings on the game. These investors will not be happy
about a club meekly accepting decisions by administrators which
hurt their investments. If Spurs or any other publicly quoted team
were in the future to be docked points by the FA, the institutions
would want to hear what the club was going to do about it. Relegation from the Premiership is very costly, after all, and will hit the
share price.

One anonymous but deeply disenchanted Northern exile in the
City after Bolton Wanderers' most recent relegation in 1998 even
argued the case for suing the referee of an earlier game against the
team that escaped the drop, Everton. In that match, television had
clearly shown that a Bolton shot had crossed the line, although the
official refused to give the goal. That goal ended up costing the club
millions, because if it had been given Bolton would have won
rather than drawn the match and ended up three points ahead of
Everton, rather than being equal then dropping on goal difference.

It was an incompetent decision, argued the exiled broker, so sue the ref. This is not quite as foolish or implausible as it sounds, although generally City investors do accept the decisions in the game. Suing a ref on these grounds is less likely than, say, seeking legal redress if a star seven- or eight-figure player receives a 90-minute kicking, resulting in a broken leg and a long layoff. Has the ref failed to spot fouls and caution or send off opposition players? Has he therefore failed in what lawyers call his 'duty of care'? A similar case has been tried in rugby union and the referee was initially judged culpable. Is even the ref's decision final given the new balance of power?

The City is under an obligation to play an important role. Its own regulators will make sure that it does. Once clubs are floated on the stock market, they come under the influence of the Financial Services Authority and the Stock Exchange in the UK. Stock-exchange rules can have an impact on matters such as the appointment of a manager or buying a player. Clubs have to report information to the Stock Exchange which could affect the share price. That can mean major deals being revealed first on City news wires rather than to fans or even employees.

But the markets' role is really an issue for the future of the game. Tony Fraher expresses a truth, but only a partial one. The City is a growing force, but not a major influence. Institutions have taken a stake in the game, but the majority of the 21 English and Scottish stock-market-quoted clubs still have dominant individual investors. These individuals call the shots at their clubs. The farce of Newcastle United's boardroom shenanigans, which led to multiple departures in 1998 in the wake of the row over the antics of Douglas Hall and Freddie Shepherd, demonstrates that point. All of the rage and fury ran up against the simple fact that the Hall family controlled 58 per cent of the shares through their Cameron Hall Developments firm and the Shepherd family could chip in another 10 per cent. Despite the row, they still do. And so Doug and Fred are back in the directors' box.

The argument does not end there, as institutions can still bring pressure to bear and in the Newcastle case notably have, with boardroom bustups which saw the departure of chairman Sir Terence Harrison. Douglas Hall and Freddie Shepherd did have to stand down for a time. Institutions and City analysts are now more vociferous in demanding change at football clubs. They are regularly quoted giving their views on what should happen. While they have not quite gone as far as trying to influence transfers and managers, it cannot be too far off. For all that, however, the City's role at present is limited at all but a few clubs where there is genuine widespread share ownership.

In England these include Man United and Tottenham, where the institutional investors are important and when push comes to shove there is not a single investor who can veto everyone else. United is no longer dominated by the Edwards family, who only control around 14 per cent of the shares today. At Tottenham Alan Sugar owns a 40 per cent stake. These are both important shareholdings, but mean that as the club is not reliant on one investor it can be bought out without that investor's consent. Leeds Sporting, which owns Leeds United, is another where there is no majority investor.

That simple point illustrates just where the City sits in the 'who runs football' debate. It is a source of finance for clubs, but must also be a source of trouble for the administrators in the future. What would the FA do if a major international media company were to take over a football club? How would Graham Kelly measure up to Ted Turner, for instance?

Faceless administrators

Football's administrators do not do themselves very many favours by their actions and invariably stumbling performances in front of the cameras. They are very easy targets who are often made the whipping boys for all the supposed ills of the game. In England, figures such as Football Association chief executive Graham Kelly and Premier League supremo Peter Leaver are regarded as faceless, charm-free individuals. In Scotland, the SFA's Jim Farry was turned into a hate figure and dubbed the Ayatollah for banning players at the Scottish Cup Final from celebrating too much, and attacked by government ministers for not mourning enough on the day of Princess Diana's funeral.

On the wider stage, former UEFA chief Lennart Johannsen and the also departed FIFA head Joao Havelange have substantial own-goal tallies.

In one infamous incident, the UEFA man was caught talking, apparently seriously, about 'darkies'. This is not diplomatic language. He then earned instant loathing in Scotland when he decided that the famous Estonia v Scotland game had to be replayed after the so-called 'one team in Tallin' farce when Scotland turned up to play and its hosts did not because of a spat over floodlights. Johannsen, a Swede, helped take the decision to replay the game rather than award Scotland a walkover, even though it benefited his own country which was vying for the same World Cup qualification spot.

Among the favourites to replace Johannsen was David Will of the Scottish Football Association. Mr Will is highly regarded in UEFA's corridors of power, but his club experience is with the not particularly highly regarded Brechin City of the Scottish Third Division. Many people will question why someone from Brechin could become the most powerful man in European football.

Johannsen could, however, have had sympathy for Mr Havelange, who suffered much worse because of his autocratic political nature which frequently put his dealings under the spotlight of investigative rather than sporting journalists. Joao's interference in domestic Brazilian soccer – once run by his son-in-law – and generally haughty demeanour did him few favours. This is the man who banned Pele – yes, that Pele – from the 1994 World Cup draw for criticizing corruption in the Brazilian game, even though the dispute had nothing to do with FIFA.

The unavoidable fact, nevertheless, is that these men preside over a sport that is growing internationally at a phenomenal rate, and, as far as the business side is concerned, they generally appear to be doing fine. While much of football's financial success has sprung from a happy accident rather than leaping straight from a brilliant master plan, the central administrators have built well on the foundations. They can be proud and point to unalloyed achievements. The biggest stages on which they perform, and arguably the best examples, are the international tournaments, which they run very successfully. As Aston Villa's commercial director Abdul Rashid points out:

The FA and the Premier League have serious commercial skills of their own, outside what we are doing as individual clubs. Euro 96 was an extremely well-organized and profitable event – it raised the standards for how to manage this kind of major tournament even beyond what the Americans achieved with the '94 World Cup. Until 1994, you had never seen a World Cup or a European Championship make a sizeable profit for UEFA, FIFA or the host nation. The Americans broke even and made a handsome profit, but with Euro 96, England delivered serious returns from a smaller event for the game and for the economy as a whole. The FA takes much of the credit for that.

Mark McCormack's IMG Group has experience of working with both the FA and SFA on their commercial programmes and its football chief Andrew Croker is impressed with the administrators with whom he has dealt:

If you look back at the history of the Premier League, the best thing they managed to achieve, amazingly, right up front was how to split the money among the clubs, how to split the sponsorship money, the television money. All the subsequent issues weren't clouded by them thinking how it is going to affect them financially. The key thing in Scotland, which I think they have achieved, is how to split the money up. Once you have agreed that, the only thing is how you make the pot bigger. It was very clever in England the way football fans believed the Premier League was something new and exciting. Suddenly it was the Carling Premiership and Sky and it was all smoke and people coming up in helicopters and there was a new logo and it was exciting and sexy. It was commercially very impressive.

We have worked with the FA on their commercial programme. At the FA we have a core group of eight sponsors – Littlewoods, Green Flag, Umbro, Carlsberg, Agfa, One-2-One, Burton and Walkers – and around the England team you have got Green Flag, Mars, Coke and Umbro. That is quite a manageable size, after that it gets too messy. It all works pretty well and the FA are good to deal with.

Businesspeople have no trouble dealing with the FA and SFA and the same applies to the international bodies. Summer 1998 saw the World Cup in France which, thanks to TV rights sales and sponsorship from the likes of Hewlett-Packard and adidas, had already broken even and was indeed well in the black for FIFA, which organized the key commercial deals, before a ball was kicked or a ticket sold. Havelange has just left FIFA, crowning his 20-year presidency with a competition that may well be shown to have earned £600 million for the world governing body when the final accounts appear in early 1999 (although, unlike England with Euro 96, France itself could still end up losing a great deal of money, even if the team took the trophy). Havelange's aggressive pursuit of high-profile partners is little different from the commercial techniques applied at continental and national level by individual associations and leagues, but he has been particularly tenacious.

UEFA, for its part, has taken the Champions' Cup, turned it into the Champions' League and created a huge money-making machine. The vast sums available to participants and the startling amounts that broadcasters are willing to pay are only part of the equation. Beyond that there is sponsorship and merchandising income worth another £5 million to £7 million a season.

These examples do not represent the work of what are traditionally thought of as sporting administrators. Old buffers in blazers are not up to the demands of the commercial wheeling and dealing in which administrators now have to become involved. The FA's staff are as adept at the business side now as are their counterparts in other sports. The deals struck around events such as the Olympic Games, major tennis tournaments such as Wimbledon and Formula One motor racing require high levels of business skills. To some extent, football lagged behind all these competitions during the 1980s and is only now re-establishing its preeminence. Football's mandarins have had to change step to keep in time with the world of sport as a whole.

That, at least, is the official view. The reality is that the FA, SFA, UEFA, FIFA and almost all of football's other administrative bodies remain not-for-profit organizations. Where they have been successful, they can claim that much of the income goes back into improving the sport. In FIFA's case particularly, its marketing has played a key role in the growth of African football, to a point where the 1998 World Cup included five teams from that continent – Cameroon, former Olympic champions Nigeria, the resurgent South Africa, Morocco and Tunisia – that could not simply be considered makeweights.

Even in the traditionally political sphere of the administrator, things have generally been going well at national levels, although conflict remains within the continental and international bodies. Mike Edelson says:

> *I genuinely feel that the FA today is a far more effective representative of the game than at any other time. There will always be individual conflicts between individual clubs themselves or between them and the FA, but generally they are efficiently and I wouldn't quite say harmoniously but fairly happily resolved. But the more important aspect is that the FA has created a consensus in the game that we have not had before and it has built up the image, the brand if you like, of football in the UK.*
>
> *Where it is mutually beneficial, clubs are now more willing to exchange commercial information, to cooperate on centralized marketing plans and so on. I think you had the famous Rick Parry quote about him running a 22-headed monster. Well, it is largely to his credit that after he left the FA and the Premier League, you would not say that any more. We have some mavericks, but everyone is now basically pulling in the same direction.*

Parry, the first Premier League chief executive who is now running Liverpool FC, even has admirers among people outside the game who are not enamoured of the commercialization of the sport. John Williams, of the Sir Norman Chester Centre for Football Research, comments:

> *Rick Parry at the Premier League performed a considerable balancing act very successfully in the first five years. He kept all of the clubs on board. In the main, he managed the individual ambitions of Man United to become a huge multinational company of major proportions on the one hand but a member of a league on another, kept the television deal intact and managed a reasonably equitable distribution of resources from television among the larger clubs. How long that is going to last is a moot point.*

Farewell then to the halcyon days when the only thing a gathering of British club chairmen could ever agree on was the timing of the coffee break. Even at the basic level of the implementation of all-seat stadia following the Taylor report, the English FA has behaved intelligently and achieved results. Cooperation between the different associations across Europe has done much to reduce hooliganism, with often overly energetic policing now proving the bigger problem.

On the downside, there have been unseemly spats in recent times at UEFA, over Germany and England's competing bids for the 2006 World Cup, and at FIFA, as UEFA president Johannsen and FIFA general secretary Sepp Blatter battled to be elected as Havelange's successor, with Blatter, the continuity candidate, emerging victorious. However, such events tend to be characterized by a battle between two groups of reasonably similar views as to where football should be going and how it should be led there. They are never battles between two diametrically opposed views of the way ahead, as has happened in other sports such as rugby union and rugby league.

Charge of the blazer brigade

Everyone should really unite in giving some overdue kudos to the football administrators. Fans should admit, just this once and very quietly, that the administrators have got a lot of it right, that in many respects they do know what they're doing.

But the limits to their powers should also be acknowledged, because if there are questions to be raised here, they concern the extent to which the FAs have adapted to the new age while performing their traditional custodial duties towards the game. It is the clubs, club owners and the growing influence of the City who now run football, while administrators often appear just to be going with the flow.

The various associations must stand accused of not addressing issues such as the financial power of the teams at the top, the fears about a dearth of business probity, the worries about fans being priced out of the game, the belief that they are in thrall to the big clubs and the view that they are failing to promote grass-roots football.

The English FA, as one of the most prominent associations, is one of the biggest targets. It is attacked for not doing enough about the growing income gap among clubs. It is seen as having encouraged the setting up of the breakaway Premier League to neuter its political rivals for power over the game at the Football League, without proper consideration of the general consequences for the 72 excluded teams. In response, the organization has a tendency to hide behind the fact that the Premier League is a separate commercial operation which even works out of separate offices, and then blurt out the old chestnut that nobody expected the damn thing to get so rich and so powerful.

This attitude suggests that the FA, or indeed any administrator, cannot any longer be held responsible for the financial development of the game. Its own spokespersons acknowledge the power of the clubs and even hold up the successful clubs as the models to follow. Similarly, the FA's powers are limited when it comes to dealing with the corruption that exists in the game. Experts say that the FA has consistently failed to attack corruption with suitable and sufficient vigour. The bung inquiry over under-the-table cash payments to managers and the FA's own follow-up to the 1997 English match-fixing trial ultimately resulted in only feeble penalties against wrongdoers. In the bung case, there was merely a one-year ban on former Arsenal manager George Graham when in some people's view it should have been life, and there has only been the subsequent investigation of soft targets such as retired manager Brian Clough and two other junior figures.

However, given that the investigation took place in a climate where the FA came very close to being both a criminal court and a criminal investigator, it is perhaps not surprising that it has appeared to tread lightly. Legal advisers were telling it that it would have to be absolutely sure of its facts before handing out any long bans, or face extremely costly court actions itself for depriving individuals of their livelihoods.

Court challenges can easily upset the best-laid plans of football men, as was seen in the case of Jean-Marc Bosman which has resulted in predictions of the end of the transfer market. Similarly, one could upset any attempt by the FA under present legislation to get too tough on transgressors. But the FA is seen as having some influence on how fans are treated and is generally believed to have a poor record. Critics claim that it has wantonly ignored the needs, wishes and views of supporters and is actively excluding real fans through its pursuit of corporate hospitality targets and other commercial goals. They point to empty stadia early on in Euro 96 and recall that a seventh of the crowd at the tournament's final were there on freebies.

The FA admits that it has had a poor relationship with supporters, although bridges have been built by cooperation over facilities at Euro 96 and the strong line the association took after English supporters were attacked at a World Cup qualifying game in Rome. The FA is doing its best, but has acknowledged its limited role in dealing with fans. It only really comes into contact with them when there are England games or FA Cup matches. The rest of the time fans, it would appear, have to rely on clubs and club owners.

Amid the criticism, the FA's executive lineup has finally begun to adapt to the times. Former BBC journalist David Davies's appointment as its public affairs director was one small step forward. At last the association has someone who can walk the walk and, even more importantly, talk the talk, rather than looking like a rabbit staring down an artic (although his role in fobbing off and ignoring requests from national journalists to interview Glenn Hoddle while co-authoring a 'kick-and-tell' World Cup diary has blunted his reputation).

Other recent additions include the commercial director Phillip Carling, who has been in charge of the FA's sponsorship programme. The big issue for him recently has been the new England kit deal. That attracted bids from firms such as Umbro, Reebok, Nike, adidas and Hay & Robertson's Admiral, all keen to do the deal which is regarded as one of the major prizes of the football strip world. Umbro won. But the FA's negotiators had the commercial sense while weighing up the bids to spot the potential for another moneyspinner and have signed with Admiral to produce a range of England leisurewear from the summer of 1999 using the Three Lions imagery. Hay & Robertson's chief executive Lance Yates reck-

ons that it could be a £20-million-a-year business which will gen-
erate royalties for the FA on top of a sizeable upfront payment.

And yet for all the praise that can rightly be given, there is a
sense that the FA and other administrators have lost their main role
and are creating another one. There are even suggestions that the
FA and its rival organizations are split over how to move forward.

Who really does run football?

The administrators head organizations that once were powerful,
still seem powerful and yet also are regarded with growing contempt and/or disregard. How can this have happened?

Sports lawyer and former Wigan Athletic owner Nick Bitel sees
it like this:

> *The FA's big problem is that its role has been rewritten without those
> changes being explicitly acknowledged within its constitution, its
> regulations or its structure. To use a cliché straight from the psychi-
> atrist's couch, it's undergoing an identity crisis.*
>
> *The FA is supposed to be football's governing body. It is sup-
> posed to be the law, the final arbiter. And up until now, it pretty
> much has been, with its catchall laws about 'bringing the game into
> disrepute'. But today, if a club has gone public by floating on the
> stock market, it automatically has a legal duty to put its commer-
> cial responsibilities above whatever the FA rulebooks say. So, think
> back to when Man United wanted to extend the season and ask
> yourselves this question. Even if the club had not wanted to wind up
> the Pooh-Bahs of Lancaster Gate for footballing reasons, how was it
> supposed to face its shareholders if fixture congestion had led to it
> not winning the league and not qualifying for the Champions'
> League? Would United have failed in its duty because it did not
> make an attempt to get things changed?*
>
> *It's a difficult one to prove but, one day, somebody will take
> this kind of thing to a judicial review, and the reason will be that
> the business side of the club must come first. In fact, Alan Sugar has
> already done that when he brought the courts in over the fine and
> the FA points deduction for some alleged irregularities at Spurs –*

*but, compared to what might happen, I think that is small scale.
Even if the directors say that they are terribly sorry to be under-
mining the FA's authority, they'll still do it. They'll have their solic-
itors telling them that they have to do it.*

Bitel argues that the various associations are already tussling none
too well with this problem in the wake of the European Court's
ruling in the Bosman case:

*To soccer's bureaucrats, Bosman was a watershed for two reasons.
First, it showed that the draconian powers vested in a UEFA or even
a FIFA were not as great as was once thought. Everyone talks about
these being autocratic bodies, but UEFA was brushed aside with very
little difficulty. It found out, to its horror, that it was not above the
law. The second critical issue is that it only took one man, a pretty
tenacious one and understandably so, but still only one man and not
even one of the great players, to basically turn the whole European
transfer system inside out. So, again, the UEFAs and FAs can talk
all they want about consensus and majority views, but it potentially only takes one maverick to sweep all that away.*

Bitel believes that the FA may be facing one such maverick very
soon, because of the system introduced to deliver Bosman into
English football while still allowing clubs to benefit from developing young players. The agreement, also backed by the Professional
Footballers' Association, states that clubs can continue to retain
registrations on players under 24 years old and use the traditional
transfer system, but that those above such an age will become free
agents once their contracts expire:

*I can understand the logic in this. You do not want to give a 17- or
18-year-old a six- or seven-year contract on a high wage. He has
not proved himself as a fully fledged professional and, for smaller,
poorer clubs, it means that you are making an onerous long-term
financial commitment with very little security. So, the FA and the
PFA sit down and strike this sort of gentleman's agreement.
    But what happens when you have someone who has just turned
20, is obviously of the standard of a Ryan Giggs or a Michael Owen*

and is with a small club? His first two-year contract expires and he wants to move up to the big leagues, but either the club won't let him or they stick a ludicrously high price on him. Added to that, they are still only offering him a small wage increase. His agent is going to go 'Bugger that', head to the court, make an application under the same article of EU law and – guess what – the whole system will collapse. Just like that. This is an issue of basic employment law. You cannot differentiate on age. I cannot believe that no one in the FA or the PFA has thought of this. Where are the foundations?

The upshot, according to Bitel, is that the various associations run the risk of 'becoming irrelevant':

You are actually reaching a point, not just in Britain but through-out Europe, where club owners are asking themselves just what exactly does a football association do? Why does it matter?

Is it a governing body? How can it govern if its laws keep being overturned? Is it a trade association? Well, in that case it should have very little to do with discipline and commercializa-tion, and concentrate on the image of the game. Is it a commer-cial organization? Well, if it is drawing in large amounts of cash from tournaments and sponsorship, it is doing so in competition with the clubs it supposedly represents. There's only so much in the pot, and who actually provides the teams for these competi-tions? What organizations are also trying to find high-profile partners? What was the Premier League if not an attempt by the biggest to control their own destinies independent of the Football League? So, they now want the FA to be in charge? And so on and on and on.

Clubs have perfectly legitimate reasons to challenge the adminis-trators without going the whole hog of actively opting out. Lawyers can see the scope for challenging the administrators' reg-ulations and point to successful challenges to central tenets of foot-ball law. But the legal challenge is not the only problem.

For John Williams, the challenges ahead for the administrators are all going to be financial. He says:

There's going to be quite a struggle, quite a tussle here between com-
peting brands and competing economic interests. On the one hand
there is the one brand, namely the Premier League, the whole interest
of the Premier League to sell its brand across the world just as the
NFL and the NBA do in American sport. No one is really interested in
a large sense in the NFL in the UK as a sport, but they are interested
in the products – the shirts, the hats, the gloves, the shoes and so on.
The vast majority of people have never seen Michael Jordan play
basketball and yet everybody knows who Michael Jordan is and will
buy his products. The Premier League's view is that there is no reason
why it cannot become the NBA or the NFL of the twenty-first century
selling its products across the world. The problem is that Man United
and other clubs are also brands and they think they are bigger brands
than the Premier League is. So there is going to be tension between the
leagues and the clubs over brands and markets.

Commercialization provides the battleground for a war over markets. Administrators may run the competitions, but who provides
the teams for those competitions? Clubs provide the teams, of
course. But then again, clubs rely on players – and who runs the
players?

Williams believes that the role of players will change, providing
yet another twist to the debate:

There are also going to be increasing tensions between leagues, clubs,
players and sponsors. There is already debate about who owns what.
Who owns players? Is it the player himself or the club or his spon-
sors? You have already had the intervention of sponsors in the trans-
fer of Ronaldo to Inter Milan trying to direct their player to a specific
club so they can sell products. The joke used to be at Arsenal that
you couldn't talk to a player unless you went through George Gra-
ham. It couldn't happen now. Even at Man United where Ferguson
rules with a rod of iron, he cannot always control Giggs or Beckham.
Somebody else has a call on the time of the players and they are the
various players' individual sponsors. If clubs cannot control them,
how can the FA?

Take the example of the Premier League's deal with model firm
Corinthians to make small model players. They sell massively, but

around a quarter of the sales are of Man United players. Eventually the clubs are going to wake up and smell the coffee and decide to do it themselves. But then again, a third of the United model sales were previously of Eric Cantona. Eventually the players will work out they can sell the products themselves. Michael Jordan sells his Air Jordan stuff separately from the Chicago Bulls through Nike, after all.

The increasing commercialization of football associations is a response to this problem, although hardly a perfect one. Controlling and administering large tournaments or umbrella commercial deals for local leagues gives the administrators back some of the influence that has undoubtedly been reduced. Havelange ran world football, but all that most countries appeared to want from him as he reached the end of his tenure was his support for their preferred World Cup 2006 bid, with England ultimately winning his blessing. The event was all. Even side decisions such as the ban on tackling from behind were intended to increase the 'entertainment' value of the spectacle and thus make it more marketable. In 1994, FIFA even briefly and embarrassingly flirted with the idea of turning games into four 20-minute quarters so that they would appear more familiar to the US audience.

However, as football stumbles through its financial revolution, this shift leaves a distinct power vacuum. Who exactly is governing the sport at all its different levels? It is probably right to take FA claims about the UK bung inquiry at face value. On the basis of the evidence, it may well have acted to the limit of its powers. But the comments of more than a few conspiracy theorists also spoke volumes. They argued that the FA had held back because it did not want to upset the financial image of the game, particularly since the UK's quoted clubs were already having a generally tough time on the various stock markets. They spied a commercial cover-up, and the FA's own increasingly commercial role only served to feed their doubts.

Even players regard the FA with ambivalence. Rather like their own clubs, they know that when salaries of £10,000 a week are the norm, a £2500 fine – pretty much the steepest the FA will offer short of conduct requiring a ban – is a drop in the ocean. Moreover, as one agent explains:

Unless you are dealing with something like the Cantona thing or a failed drugs test, the FA is always going to play it fairly safe. It is obsessed with the image of the game these days.

And then there are the supporters, a lobby that has always had at best a hesitant relationship with the FA. One senior FSA member says:

The FA is always in a position where it can do more harm than good for supporters, although it has improved. The way that it rapidly backed English fans when they were attacked by the Italian police during a 1997 World Cup qualifier was really positive. Before, they had always sided against their own supporters. But it remains an isolated case. We do not see the FA as a representative of those who support the game but as a pressure group for a different view. So, personally, I would not say that it was a governing body.

When English football created a Football Task Force bringing together all the different football interest groups, some observers thought that this might be the first step towards creating a new framework for the game in its new financially driven environment.

One Premier League chairman still thinks that the FA should take this role, but in a heavily changed form:

I think you need to see the FA thoroughly streamlined and, possibly, broken up to perform different tasks – regulation, international tournaments, the grass roots – so that everyone has a clear idea of what is going on and everything is organized. The money in the professional game today does place tremendous strains on the structure while also opening up many positive opportunities. The clubs, however, can look after the opportunities themselves; the strains, the disagreements and the breaking points are where you need an organization that can intervene.

In that respect, I think you need a more executive FA for the professional game, run by fewer people and no longer answerable to an outdated Council. The current situation is that the armed forces still have as many votes on the FA's ruling body as the Premier League, and that just doesn't work any more.

Below this level he also proposes more 'targeted' organizations looking at amateur football, schools football and various other levels: 'Everything in its place, and run by people who can do things.'

Nevertheless, existing vested interests do tend to militate against such proposals. As the chairman has it:

> *Will Carling was talking about 50-odd old farts in rugby. Well, he should go to the FA Council, they've got about 150. This existing structure with Graham Kelly et al. answerable to a council that gives a seat to every branch of the game does seem foolish, and if anything may have contributed further to the FA becoming a commercial rather than a governing organization – commerciality is the kind of fringe activity which, according to one source, 'goes flying over the Council's head'. However, only those old farts can vote themselves out of existence and let's be honest, how many of these guys are going to say that they should not get free tickets for every final, every Wembley game, and the World Cup? It's a very nice life.*

A similar situation exists at the Scottish Football Association, where 60 part-time people work on eight standing committees. Very few Scottish football fans will be able to name even one of the committees with their representatives drawn from the divisions, the affiliated associations, the Scottish Football League and affiliated national associations. The SFA has 84 employees spread across the organization and an annual income of £10.6 million, of which around a third goes back into the game north of the border and most of the rest is spent on the Scottish national team. It is difficult to see how an organization structured in that way can control the ambitions of multinational plcs such as Rangers and Celtic.

The greatest challenge

With traditional governing bodies already fearing that they may become irrelevant, the future holds greater threats. Football associations have so far 'gone along' with the financial revolution. The FA backs the Premier League, the SFA backs a Caledonian equivalent, UEFA offers the Champions' League to head off a Super

League and FIFA looks for long-term partnerships with long-term players in New Football, like adidas and media mogul Leo Kirch, who is about to take control of TV rights to the World Cup.

If you can't beat 'em, and if you can't join 'em, strike one of those strategic alliances so beloved of today's business giants. That seems to be the thinking, but it is crucially flawed.

Ignoring – ignoring! – the fact that this approach leaves little room for the game's customers, the FAs need to ask themselves what exactly makes them so important to their business partners that those sponsors will view their relationships as having long-term benefits.

If football's future is to be one where major conglomerates are allowed to come in and control the biggest sides, and if these different groupings can work directly with one another – something that they already appear to find quite easy to do in, say, international media – somebody is going to get left on the sidelines. Guess who?

The situation has gone beyond the point of corporate league and team sides. Under its reputed $250 million deal with Nike, the Brazilian national side already commits itself to international friendly tours arranged not as much through its domestic FA as through the sportswear manufacturer. Wherever Nike had a strong market – in Europe, South America or Asia – Brazil appeared during a phenomenally arduous warm-up tour for the 1998 World Cup, one that domestic fans attacked for including too many meaningless games that obliged the country to put out a substandard side for occasional sporting humiliation. No matter – in global terms Nike is calling the tune, and this from a company that has already effectively moved a player, Ronaldo, from one team to another for its own merchandising objectives.

Moreover, as a number of smaller associations are now seeing, Brazil is being slowly but surely turned into the Manchester United of international football. Why support your own national side when you can easily buy a piece of the massively talented but also massively marketed boys from Rio? Anyone who doubts that this is the case was obviously suffering from temporary colour blindness during the World Cup when, even in 'established' nations like England and Scotland, gold-coloured Pele- and Ronaldoemblazoned kits spread like dandelions the minute that the 'home' sides were knocked out of the tournament.

Adidas, meanwhile, was left to puzzle over the value of its $300 million direct sponsorship contract with FIFA for the World Cup. It was not just that three of the four players chosen to lead its marketing were sent off (Zinedine Zidane, Patrick Kluivert and David Beckham), while the last – Alessandro Del Piero – suddenly lost his scoring touch; it was simply that apart from exclusive exposure of its name for perimeter advertising, Nike, through its deal with not just Brazil but also Italy and Holland, was continuously making a bigger impact in advertising. The World Cup brand is thought to be the most powerful in international sport, but it is the players and teams who come first.

That, then, is just part of the global picture. UEFA is meanwhile wringing its hands about ENIC, the investment trust which controls or has a major stake in four European sides, all in different countries. What will happen if AEK Athens is drawn against Rangers in European competition, for example? UEFA has said that it will do something to stop this happening, but given the facts that at each domestic level ENIC's ownership is perfectly legal and that it is trading largely across borders within the European Union, the sporting organization's room for manoeuvre would seem to be severely limited.

Even 'one man, one club', so long a pillar of control of ownership by associations at national level, may not be enough. The FA was originally able to ensure that it had a seat on the Premier League breakaway bus because the big clubs needed its sanction to be allowed to enter UEFA competitions. So far, so good. But what if UEFA loses the biggest prize, the old European Cup, for it to be replaced by a commercially run, Berlusconi–Murdoch–Kirch–Canal Plus-controlled alternative? If it wanted, each of these groups could buy up four teams in every major football market and create a broadcasting alliance based on the cream of European football without national FAs being able to do a damn thing about it.

The response from Lancaster Gate and its equivalents across the Continent is that this kind of split will not be allowed to happen. Some way of keeping the big clubs on side will be found, almost certainly by ensuring that they have more control over their TV and merchandising rights and thus get even more money than they have already. But this looks like nothing so much as salami tactics from the largest sides, cutting away one thin slice after another, gradually eroding the existing power base and confirming their precedence.

What especially damns the administrators is the fact that they have allowed such changes in the relationships between clubs and sponsors and in the ownership structures that are developing in the game to sneak up on them. They always appear to be left complaining about something after it has happened, rather than having anticipated any of it. And yet, the financial power shifts in football have made the future far easier to foresee than they admit.

It is an ironic fact, but some of the traditional big club owners are among those mounting the most staunch rearguard action to this kind of development. Figures such as David Dein and Martin Edwards have each recently spoken out about devaluing competitions by following the commercial route too far. It is worth asking whether or not these will actually be the people running our clubs, even our national sides, in five or ten years' time.

Football needs to be run by people who are more interested in the good of the game than the health of the balance sheet. This is not a challenge to the profit motive in itself, but more to the worrying impact if the lust for cash continues to go unchecked.

CHAPTER EIGHT

FOUL PLAY

No. We haven't finished with football yet. Not by a long way.
Press spokesman for the Inland Revenue, April 1998

CONTROLLING FOOTBALLERS AND FOOTBALL CLUB OWNERS HAS always been a difficult job, because the game has always been a bit dodgy. The foundation of the sport was partly due to rows over money and underhand payments. Ever since professionalism with cash for players and prizes for owners came into the sport, the temptation has been there to bend the rules and even to break them completely.

It is no surprise that throughout the history of the game there have been worries about corruption. Avid fans would, for instance, instantly be able to give a definite answer when asked to spot the connection among the following giants of European football. They would know straight away that Juventus, Manchester United, Liverpool, Inter Milan, AC Milan, Real Madrid and Borussia Dortmund have all won the European Cup. They might not spot that all have also at some time been seriously accused of match fixing. The previous convictions do admittedly go back a long way and should really be forgiven by now. But football's dark side is there with a long list of fixes and shady dealing which is not easy to dismiss.

Values of the game

Of course, some people will always believe that it is all fixed all of the time with no exceptions. The 1998 World Cup produced the usual crop of rumours about match fixing and drug taking. These beliefs in themselves would not really matter, if New Football were not a reinvented glamour sport reliant on attracting big money into the game and keen to show that it has cleaned up its act. The sport really has to show that it is the beautiful *financial* game if it is to prosper.

Football is seeking a closer relationship with high finance, where business dealings have to be clean and seen to be clean and are conducted in the open. Publicly quoted companies have to be careful about loans to directors and awarding contracts to other companies owned by directors, because the deals have to be made public. Shareholders in stock-market-quoted companies will not tolerate cosy backroom deals and backhanders and will demand action if they find out about them. Corruption is the spectre at the feast that has to be banished.

Match fixing is probably the brand of sporting corruption that is considered most unforgivable by fans. After all, competition and uncertainty of outcome – even if there is only the merest smidgen of a doubt about who is going to win – form the lifeblood of football. There are some very good reasons why wrestling is not the world's most popular sport, quite apart from the ludicrous people in strange costumes involved in it.

But the game's dark side covers much more territory than just simple, straightforward match fixing. In financial terms, these other areas have begun to gain equal and perhaps greater significance. Tales of transfer bungs – payments that some club managers are alleged to have earned from buying or selling players and dealing with agents – and FA investigations into financial malpractice in England, plus the hovering presence of the Inland Revenue and VAT authorities, stoke the worries of the new investors in New Football. The accounts and standards of business probity at many clubs set the paranoia aflame. There are practices such as 'clipping the turnstile', where club owners turn off the counters on part of the gate, take the cash and drop it straight into their own offshore bank accounts or pockets. And there is a wide range of more traditional frauds such as simply not paying the taxman or siphoning funds from a successful club to support an unsuccessful outside business – or, indeed, vice versa.

To the typical supporter, such sins are sometimes regarded with less hostility. The Department of Trade and Industry may have determined that former England coach Terry Venables is unfit to be a company director – a fairly damning judgement on any individual – but that did not prevent Crystal Palace employing him to manage the club. Nor did it stop broadcasters seeking him out as a pundit for the 1998 World Cup or for his opinion on the 'Gazza's been dumped' question as a nation mourned. Venables' business associate Eddie Ashby has been jailed despite a character reference from El Tel. And still Terry Venables is a marketable commodity who, for example, earned an £85,000 upfront payment from clothing company Hay & Robertson to promote its range of Admiral Elite clothes. He will also make royalties from sales of the clothes. The company's chief executive Lance Yates shrugs his shoulders and says: 'Terry's business dealings have been absolutely disastrous but I think he is still respected in football.' Mr Yates is not wrong.

On a broader scale, every supporters' club boasts its share of taproom braggarts who will swear blind that some, most likely all of their team's directors are 'on the make', only to shrug the accusation off just as quickly with: 'But that's how it is, you know.' Fans at all clubs will tell stories about how crooked their directors are and how the club is being run into the ground just to line the pockets in the boardroom. People talk about club bosses living the high life on expenses to the detriment of fans and the team. For the most part it is just talk and nothing can be proved.

But unfortunately, there are plenty of reasons to be afraid about the business standards in football and the recent history should make people very afraid. Football is, after all, a sport which has been described by a former deputy commissioner of the Metropolitan Police as requiring radical and probably enforced change to its entire business culture.

The top cop in question, Sir John Smith, was asked by the Football Association to dig deeper into the issue of corruption in football in the wake of the George Graham affair, plus further allegations about unlawful loans and bungs against Terry Venables dating from his time as chief executive of Tottenham Hotspur and also the 1997 match-fixing trial of three prominent footballers with English clubs accused of arranging results to benefit Far Eastern betting syndicates. He wrote in his 1998 report, *Football, its Values, Finances and Reputation*, that:

> *The extensive media coverage given to the trials of Bruce Grobbelaar, Hans Segers, John Fashanu and Richard Lim has done little to improve the public's perception of a somewhat tarnished game even though the innocence of those mentioned was established. Neither has the sport's image been helped by the revelations in the report of the Football Association Premier League inquiry into irregular payments connected with transfers.*
>
> *Another concern of many has been the mismanagement, which has occurred in some football clubs. It has brought some to the edge of extinction and destroyed others altogether. In such cases football's poor reputation will always cause some to think the worst, believing that greed, profiteering, or corruption has played a part in financial crises at club level.*

The football business is, in other words, not business as practised elsewhere in Europe. Even the City of London, which is for many outsiders a byword for corruption and insider deals, has taken fright at what goes on in football. Senior executives at many publicly limited clubs concede in private that the share-price slump of the football sector on the stock market is in part due to worries about the business standards in the game.

Newcastle United's boardroom shenanigans in 1998 were completely above board in terms of financial probity, but demonstrated the fears that many City experts have about football clubs. After all, the club lost a total of three chairmen in the space of three months as first Douglas Hall quit as club chairman, to be replaced by his father Sir John, who then retired again shortly after the company chairman Sir Terence Harrison resigned. The club also lost a finance director in Josephine Dixon, a non-executive director in John Mayo and a club vice-chairman in Freddy Shepherd. That all happened at a club with City-approved finances. If it can happen there, God alone knows what goes on elsewhere.

Divine intervention is sadly not entirely necessary. Sir John Smith's investigation helped uncover some of the practices deemed acceptable on Planet Football but not elsewhere. But just as careless talk could cost lives according to wartime posters, corruption and even simple shady but legal behaviour can shut teams down.

Brown envelopes and Max Clifford

Second Division Bournemouth went through a near-death experience in the 1996–7 season when crippling debts of £4.8 million and the Inland Revenue almost forced it out of business and out of the leagues. If the club had not organized a rescue via receivership through accountants Arthur Andersen and a fundraising drive, it would not now exist. The current management believes that part of the reason for the club's plight was that previous management were not thinking about the good of the club. They were more interested in their own good, the new men believe.

Chairman Trevor Watkins is adamant there will be no return to the past practices at Bournemouth, which is now run as a community club without the traditional 'sugar daddy' setup of most lower-league clubs. He says:

> *No longer are we going to enter into 'I'll scratch your back, you scratch my back' situations, no longer are we going to have to have people hiding money in odd places so the Customs & Excise don't find it. Money was hidden in beds and wardrobes in the past apparently. We don't want wires cut on turnstiles so that people can get in for free. There were 468 complimentary tickets given out in the past – 10 or 15 per cent of our gates. We just had cash accounting, no proper receipts.*

Watkins' amazement at the practices he heard about is not a product of naivety. Bournemouth may not be one of the giants of English football, but it is still a substantial club with a serious history. As a business it is also reasonably sized. It has an annual turnover of around £1.5 million, and for a firm that size to rely on cash accounting is bizarre.

But the strangeness did not end there, according to Watkins:

We heard lots of stories about brown envelopes. That was the culture here. Everybody who had been involved with this club had been on the make. Basically it was an attitude of: 'He's taken money out of the club, so will I.' The ex-chairman and company secretary spent most of their time in the supporters' club drinking beer and playing the slot machines and taking large sums of money out of the club. What has been going on here is not that unusual. I'm sure it has been going on at every club in the country. There are plenty of clubs in our position and there are plenty of clubs that could go down the pan. I think you will see five or six going soon.

As an example of the mismanagement at Bournemouth, Watkins offers the example of the supporters' club which is just beside the stadium:

The supporters' club took in £180,000 a year but still made a loss of £1500. It was surprising when most of the money was coming in on beer sales and gaming machines. Both of these are high profit margin businesses where you should be making money. You have 1000 members who pay £7 each, you have bar profits which are 54 per cent consistent and you have a gaming machine which returns £800 a week. How does it lose money? You suspect that something else is going on. Everybody has been promised things, everything has been promise, promise and none of it ever came up to scratch.

A solicitor with a major law firm in the City of London, Watkins was thrown in at the deep end when Bournemouth was facing extinction in January 1997. As a fan for nearly 25 years and a lawyer with experience of receiverships, he offered his help to the club shortly before the receiver Alan Lewis, who incidentally is a Crystal Palace fan, was appointed.

Trevor Watkins went to meetings with the remaining directors where he met the men running his club. He was not impressed by the business skills on display. One of them, Roy Pack, a former professional footballer albeit one without much of a record, lived in a hotel, did not have a bank account or a credit card and relied on cash. Another, Norman Hayward, had given a £650,000 personal guarantee to the club and faced losing a lot of money. Watkins says:

> *They were in there with piles of documentation. They said: 'We are here to bring Lloyds Bank down, we are going to completely destroy them.' They were telling me how corrupt everybody was and how everybody had been ripping the club off and how they were going to unravel everything that had happened in the club back until 1991 and it sounded like complete cloud cuckoo land. They already had three firms of lawyers instructed, which also sounded very odd. If I want something done I go to one firm and get them to do everything for me. As a supporter of this football club for 25 years, I recognized that their agenda did not fit with ensuring the survival of the foot-ball club. If they were going to attack the receiver, if they were going to attack Lloyds Bank, those guys had all the cards, they had the whip hand.*

Shortly after the meeting, the receiver moved in and Bournemouth played Bristol City away. Watkins attended meetings with the directors on the morning of the game before they all went to the match. He says:

> *Hayward hadn't been to a game in three years. This sudden care for the football club, I think he sniffed a cheap deal.*

The next day things became decidedly strange:

> *Pack called me Sunday morning saying, 'You've got to come to a meeting mate, you've got to come to a meeting, we're seeing Max Clifford.' I said 'Oh', but I thought I'm not going to pass this oppor-tunity up, I'll go and see what he is doing. So I went to see Pack at his hotel and off we went to the Carlton Hotel where Max Clifford was staying. Max obviously hadn't got a clue about anything, he had been down seeing his family for the weekend. Pack accosted him on the steps of the hotel and said, 'Max, Max, you are going to help*

save Bournemouth Football Club.' Max was going: 'Who are you?'
Pack has this big pile of papers and says, 'You take this. This will
show you, we are going to bring Lloyds Bank down.' Max goes: 'I'm
sorry, but basically you are going to have to agree a fee with me and
secondly I'm not even sure it is my cup of tea.' By this time I'm
thinking there is something very odd here.

The next step was to organize meetings and rally support. The
local council gave the club the use of the Winter Gardens in
Bournemouth for free to hold a mass meeting. More than 3000
people turned up and only 2300 got in. At Bournemouth's previous home game against Rotherham, only 3100 had turned up. The
club raised £33,000 that night for a fighting fund and the receiver
got a standing ovation.

After that, the fun started for Watkins and his colleagues. The
squabbling with the previous directors turned nasty. There were
claims of death threats and accusations that the old board was
more interested in making money than in saving the club. However, Bournemouth survived and went on to a successful season in
1997–8. But nothing will wipe away for Watkins the memory of
what he and his new-broom team found at Bournemouth:

Nothing had been done for the club in years. This club was robbing
Peter to pay Paul all the way through, forever taking out different
loans and doing different deals and dodgy deals to ensure that foot-
ball kept going. The club was on a drip feed, a life support machine.
Basically the Inland Revenue had been told they would get all their
money back by December 1996. It was pipe dreams, it was never
going to happen and that was why the taxman decided to finally
wind the club up. The business plan provided for this club to repay
£250,000 a year of capital on top of interest payments, which if you
consider that the average loss per season at a club like ours is
£275,000, unless you sell players you ain't going to do it.

Against that background, we decided the only way forward
was to try and get the club run by people who love the club, watch
the club, support the club and are business people who can stand
back and run it dispassionately. Someone has to. We are running a
club as a business should be run, which means taking into account

all cross-sections of people who supported it and put money into it. It just means running a business efficiently but injecting into it a human element. That means everybody pulling together, everybody pulling in the same direction and nobody taking something for nothing. Up until now all the directors would have been on freebies. Now all the directors pay for their tickets. It costs us all £763.25 each.

At Bournemouth the club is now run by a trust fund which owns 51 per cent and 17 individual supporters who own the other 49 per cent. The fund paid out £130,000, while the individuals stumped up £400,000 in an attempt to be as democratic as possible. The directors are open about the way they are running the business. Watkins explains:

We go into the supporters' club before games and we tell them what is going on. We tell them quite frankly what is happening on the playing front and how the club is developing. We give detailed statements in the programme, we are accessible. We don't hide from people and from complaints and we are as open as possible with financial figures.

There have been squalls. The club put up basic ticket prices by £1 to £8.50 after saying initially that prices would not rise. It sold a star player against protests from fans. But Watkins is adamant:

Without the strategy there wouldn't be a football club here. The club is now worth £5 million and we only paid £2 million for it. People have put their jobs and their families on the line to save this football club. This club has gone forward more in the last couple of months than in the last 20 years. Forget the emotion of it. It is just a hard, cold business. We need to be distant to an extent. We want to strengthen the playing side and then build a new stadium within three years. At the end of the day we would look at flotation. You have got to get a track record and have a business plan and show to institutions and to investors that this is a proper business that they can have confidence in. That could happen in 1999, which would allow ordinary individuals to buy shares.

We have no choice but to use our heads because we have not got multimillions to throw at the club. We are having to look at every area of the club and make sure everyone is value for money. The chairman and club secretary in the past was taking out £150,000 a year, which is amazing in a club turning over £2 million or so, but everyone now has got to be worth their while. The reason many people get involved is for emotion. For them football is every little boy's dream. That means a lot of clubs are autocratic, controlled by one or two people who have the money. It is amazing how people who are successful in business forget it all when they get inside a football club. That is why we have to be different here.

People here threw money at problems and it did not achieve anything. And it hides problems because money covers things up. Nobody asks questions in football. The previous chairman surrounded himself with a weak board and we assume he just told them everything was all right and let's go and have a drink lads and they said 'Fine, Mr Chairman'.

The Bournemouth problems are undoubtedly replicated at dozens of small clubs around the country. But the problems are on a small scale and do not attract the headlines and scrutiny occasioned by higher-profile nefarious dealings. The serious mud that has been thrown at football relates to big clubs. And football has had plenty of mud off the field. People have long memories and continue to point specifically to the case of former Arsenal manager George Graham as being the biggest stain on the image of the game. It is still seen as an exemplar of the way the game is run. The Graham case is particularly instructive, because it illustrates some of the problems that football still faces on several levels and also because it continues to cast such a long shadow over the game's finances.

The activities for which Graham was censured happened while he was very successfully managing Arsenal between May 1986 and February 1995. During that time, he came into contact with Norwegian agent Rune Hauge, working through him to buy two Scandinavian players for his club: Pal Lydersen from IK Start in September 1991 for £500,000 and John Jensen from Brondby in July 1992 for £1.5 million. Some weeks after each deal was concluded, Graham received cash payments from Hauge, the first, worth £140,500, in December 1991 and the second, worth £285,000, in August 1992. He initially declared these neither to his club nor to the Inland Revenue.

A 1994 investigation into Hauge's tax affairs by the Norwegian authorities raised questions over the two payments. Subsequent inquiries into the £425,500 payments by Arsenal and, later, the Football Association determined that Hauge's gifts were so-called bungs, payoffs from the agent connected to the two transfers. The two bodies were not convinced that Graham had actually solicited the money, and he did alert his employers and repay all the money plus interest to Arsenal soon after he became aware of the Hauge probe. Graham was nevertheless, and understandably, found guilty of misconduct. As a result, he was sacked by the club at a two-and-a-half-minute meeting in February 1995 and, two months later, the FA slapped a year-long ban on his working as a manager. He has since returned fairly successfully to the manager's job at Leeds United, a club which incidentally is quoted on the stock market and is required to be squeaky clean.

Graham has accepted he was 'greedy' to take and not declare the money, but argues that Hauge was rewarding him for his wider contribution to the agent's work, which included an introduction to Manchester United. That club, in turn, purchased players such as Peter Schmeichel and Andrei Kanchelskis through the agent. Graham set out his feelings in his autobiography, *The Glory and the Grief*:

> *I did not feel that I was cheating anybody. Hauge was picking my brains, and so I convinced myself that it was reasonable to accept a gift in return for my time and knowledge … His reputation in Europe as an agent who could get things done was soaring. That was due in no small measure to all the advice I was giving him in our numerous conversations. Now without any prompting from me, he was saying a big thank you. Your scratch my back, I'll scratch yours. How many business deals are carried out on this basis in Arsenal chairman Peter Hill-Wood's beloved City of London? Hundreds, I would guess. Every day.*

But why does the George Graham case continue to stand out? Why weren't more people involved in the investigations? When coupled with the separate match-fixing allegations levelled against Grobbe-laar, Segers, Fashanu and a businessman at almost the same time, it certainly did not help to portray New Football in a favourable light. It is likely, however, that other specific elements in the Arsenal case may have influenced financial observers.

Partly, the case still resonates because of the club it involved. Arsenal is meant to stand for all that is upstanding and honest in English football: Highbury's marbled halls and all that. This is the team that discovered and lured in the middle classes long before Manchester United had even rebuilt Old Trafford. It is also a club run by well-known City of London figures and supposedly shrewd businesspeople, such as the Hill-Wood family, former trader David Dein and diamond merchant Danny Fiszman. Before his fall, Gra-ham, with his 'correct' dress sense and disciplinarian air, fitted the image: the officer class's perfect sergeant major. At about the same time, however, the club suffered a series of scandals, including star players Tony Adams and Paul Merson declaring various addictions. When the bung scandal broke, a feeling began to build that if these kinds of things could happen at Arsenal, again, what might be going on elsewhere?

But a further element is cash and its role in soccer culture. Foot-ball's boardrooms today are full of talk about bond issues, revolving lines of credit and mezzanine finance, but outside the wood-panelled sanctum the sport retains a strong cash-in-hand culture. Some celebrity players still expect to be paid with a brown bag stuffed with fivers when they make a promotional appearance or even give an interview to writers of a book on football finance. Graham's first present from Hauge came in the slightly more modern form of plastic envelopes passed over in the lounge bar of the Park Lane Hotel, but it still followed the traditions. This kind of 'few bob' that can easily be concealed from the Inland Revenue is a hang-over from the days of the maximum wage, when 'boot money' was not a deal with a sports firm but 'bonus' pound notes tucked away amid a player's kit. You have to stretch your imagination to get to almost half a million such hidden goodies, but the funda-mental problem is the principle that underlies the transaction.

And finally, there is the relationship between the boardroom and the playing staff. Graham alludes to it above in his reference to

Hill-Wood's 'beloved' City of London, and his book also refers to the club's history of 'them and us. The Toffs and The Toilers'. While he acknowledges that the situation is today much improved, the same sense of antagonism also lurks when he talks of the £35 million he is believed to have earned for Arsenal during his tenure. His bitterness is open when in his book he describes a meeting to discuss his conduct:

> *Arsenal director Sir Robert Bellinger, former Lord Mayor of London, does much of the talking at the board meeting. He said that the sum involved was substantial, and he questioned whether the payments were unsolicited gifts. I know it is hard for anybody to believe, but I did not ask for the money. When I pointed out that few people would have been able to refuse, Sir Robert said that he had been offered gifts in the past but had said 'no'. Bully for Sir Robert. I told him that his financial situation was probably different to mine.*

Graham's views have echoes elsewhere in the subtle switch of emphasis from class to money. No player or agent will personally criticize directors, except in the most extreme circumstances – they negotiate wages these days. However, there is private resentment even now of the big six- and sometimes seven-figure salaries that boardroom fat cats are 'unfairly' drawing thanks to other people's efforts. After all, the players and the managers do all the work which makes money for the club. As one agent says:

> *You are dealing with a situation where players can see directors earning millions from going public and a young man might well start to think: 'I should be getting a lot more of that. Who does the graft around here?' As long as that is just part of how we approach wage or bonus negotiations, well, all's fair. But you can see how other temptations might start to arise.*

The game's increasing moves towards an all-or-nothing financial culture pile on more pressure and raise the problem of match fixing. This is a potentially lucrative vice. In September 1997, the UK's largest bookmaker, William Hill, published a survey showing that 54 per cent of its clients regularly bet on football matches, making it the company's second largest business after the 90 per cent that bet on horse racing. Growth in the market is continuing, and not just in Britain. Gambling on Premier League results is big business in the Far East, and it was on this source that the original accusations against Segers, Grobbelaar and Fashanu were based. They had, it was claimed, fixed certain games, although the court accepted the three men's defence that they had only, in fact, been involved with a Malaysian betting syndicate to forecast the result of Premiership games.

The 'not guilty' verdict after two separate trials was undoubtedly a relief for Lancaster Gate, which had felt as though it was about to face 'a wholly unexpected scandal of Italian proportions', in a reference to the country where match fixing has historically been most prevalent. Instead, the English game was given a clean bill of health, although the FA still went ahead with charges against the players for their forecasting work, which also contravenes FA regulations.

Graham Sharpe, William Hill's media relations manager, has argued for some time that match fixing by gamblers is nowhere near as prevalent or as likely to become so as some fear. In his book *Gambling on Goals*, he says:

> *For over one hundred years, football has tried to distance itself from the idea that people should enjoy a harmless flutter, or even a serious wager, on the outcome of football matches and the various competitions of which they are a part. The justification for this has always been that such activities lead to pressures being exerted on those involved in the game to resort to underhand or even criminal activities in order to influence the results of matches. In a century and more of the organised history of football there have been a tiny number of occasions when such skulduggery has been proved conclusively to have taken place.*

However, there are those who fear that it is not only gambling that provokes match fixing. There have been a number of high-profile attempts to fix games in European competitions and also other domestic leagues to ensure that qualification for lucrative pan-continental tournaments is secured. As Sharpe again notes:

The football authorities have been singularly unable to prevent a far greater number of scandals and match-influencing incidents, which have had nothing whatsoever to do with betting. These involve attempting to 'buy' success for clubs – either by trying to bribe referees and linesmen or opposing club's officials.

The most famous example in recent times involved former French government minister and owner of Olympique Marseilles, Bernard Tapie. In 1993, Tapie sought to guarantee that his team would secure the domestic title by bribing two players on an opposing team, Valenciennes, with FFr250,000 apiece (about £25,000). At the same time, allegations emerged from the coach of CSKA Moscow, one of Marseilles' opponents in the previous year's European Cup, that players there had also been offered cash to smooth the French side's ultimately victorious progress to Europe's premier trophy. There is no evidence that the team tried to bribe Rangers in the European Cup semi-final, but then again, why bother? Marseilles was stripped of its various honours, ejected from the following year's European Cup and relegated from the French First Division following investigations by the local FA and UEFA. Tapie, for his part, went from confidant to French President François Mitterand to convict in a French prison in two years.

The cautionary part of the tale revolves around Tapie's ambitions for Marseilles. With Silvio Berlusconi, his popular pre-1993 image placed him at the vanguard of Europe's New Football. Here was one of the men building a super team for the forthcoming super league. His methods in going about this were to shock the entire game. Again, with so much now at stake, it was seen how far not merely some players but some owners would go to get their snouts in the trough, even if, particularly in Tapie's case, they had public images that put them at the heart of society.

UEFA, the European association, has woken up to the threat to the integrity of its tournaments. In 1998, officials due to oversee the European Cup Winners' Cup quarter final between England's Chelsea and Spain's Real Betis were spotted accepting hospitality at the Spanish club's stadium two weeks before the game. The referee and linesmen argued that they were with Scandinavian clubs that were playing near to Betis's Seville home during their mid-winter break, and no payments or any form of corruption were ultimately proven. However, UEFA nevertheless quickly decided that it would be prudent to assign other officials to look after the game. Previously, the administrators had been seen as taking a more *laissez faire* attitude to such incidents.

One senior source close to Chelsea describes why UEFA decided to act:

> *I think that [Chelsea chairman] Ken Bates put it to UEFA in no uncertain terms that not only would this potentially cast a shadow over the game, but also that as it is a quoted company, it would take the strongest action if it felt something had gone wrong. In the past, clubs were expected to take these things through UEFA. With Chelsea's duties to its shareholders, however, it was saying that it might go straight to the courts. UEFA did not like that, but the way things are today they will just have to put up with it, because Chelsea won't be the only club that now takes this view.*

The significance of all these instances of corruption lies not so much in what was done but in the culture it appears to expose, even at the summit of the game. At worst, it is a culture of envy and backhanders; at best, it still falls a long way short of 'standard business practice'. And at any rate, it produces circumstances in which corruption can thrive.

Interesting times

And yet senior football figures believe that the corruption problems are overrated and that the rules of the financial football game are now different from the dark days of the bung inquiry. West Ham's managing director Peter Storrie is a highly experienced football executive. He says:

> *It has changed now. Clubs are employing chief executives or people like myself. We're the people who now deal with the players' wages or the transfer amounts. That old-style situation on supposed bungs is tending to go out of the game now. The bung, or whatever it was,*

happened three to three-and-a-half years ago. Most Premier Division sides have chief executives who now deal with that side of the business. Managers now are coaches. They decide the players they want to buy and sell. Obviously, the chief executive has to then agree on the valuation of the player, but then it is up to the chief executive to deal and conclude with the player on the wages. No one has ever offered me a bung or a big Christmas present. This is one other area where the game has become like big business. These sorts of things that people allege, and they are still just things that people allege, I am not aware of them happening.

At the top of the game, the reality is that corruption has receded significantly, in the past decade at least. In the UK, football's post-Taylor dash for cash forced clubs to clean up their accounts and their financial management, as one senior City figure who has read through his fair share of financial footballing figures from before and after 1989 testifies:

Traditionally, clubs would only present even the most basic information to their bankers, never mind what they would send to Companies House. Some chairmen would bluff their way along on the basis that a bank would not dare to foreclose on a club because of the potential PR backlash. While that did not always work, quite a few loans did go through on the nod. Taylor changed the circumstances because the sums involved went from, perhaps, several tens or hundreds of thousands of pounds, up into millions due to the work involved. At that point, even the most – what should I say? – taciturn clubs realized that things would have to change and that there would have to be fuller disclosure and some more transparent housekeeping.

His anonymous view is backed by merchant banker Tony Fraher of Singer & Friedlander, who runs his firm's Football Fund investing in the sport. Fraher has met and spoken to many of the top clubs plus sides in the lower divisions and endorses the view that the business side of the game has changed, and for the better, in the Premiership:

The management of clubs is improving definitely and certainly in the Premiership, and beginning to improve in the First Division. Clubs have got in professional management, professional business managers right throughout the business who don't get involved with what is happening on the pitch. The City does not want them to interfere with it. You used to have the manager who did everything. He coached the team, washed the kit and when he had nothing else to do, they shoved a broom up his backside and he swept the floor. He just did everything and it is completely wrong. There should be a coach who should not be interrupted by business aspects. He should just focus on the team. Then there should be a board of directors which looks after the business. That way temptation is removed.

But while the lessons have been, and are being, learned at the top of the game, the implications of the new financial status have not quite sunk in lower down the scale. Fraher believes that many clubs have not grasped the lesson that being a proper business benefits the football club and its financial reputation. He takes the view that the various financial crises that have hit a number of clubs owe as much to unusual business practices as they do to the income gap that has grown and grown in British football. His case is that football clubs need to be businesses in order to succeed as football clubs. It is an argument that is hard to refute when you contemplate the chaos at several English and Scottish league clubs. The few remaining supporters of Doncaster Rovers, demoted from the League at the end of the 1997–8 season, would presumably have traded any amount of cold business logic for survival.

Fraher says:

As you go further down the leagues, clubs are run by a lot of guys who can spend a bit of time with the club but not a lot. Many small clubs have no financial planning, they often don't even have an accountant. Many clubs have been in trouble with the taxman. The guy they always leave out is the guy who can crucify them. If you are going to pay anyone pay the taxman or the VATman. To hell with the banks, because the taxman and the VATman won't show you any mercy. If you owe it, you owe it and if you owe it, you pay it and if you can't pay it they'll take it out of your hide. You can to an extent have the bank over a barrel because if it is the big bank in your area and you go bust it is very bad publicity for that bank. When a company goes bust, into liquidation, the shareholders receive nothing; they are bottom of the list. Top of the list is the taxman, then secured creditors.

The rush of City flotations in 1996 and 1997 forced along the trend for more honesty. A combination of analysts' demands and reporting regulations has obliged clubs to provide more information in their share offer prospectuses, at briefings and in their results statements. The fact that many UK clubs, listed or not, have increasingly looked to recruit senior staff from mainstream business sectors has also had a positive impact. People coming from other businesses where traditional standards apply expect to see the same standards in their new jobs. This pattern is now increasingly apparent outside Britain, as clubs such as Bayern Munich, Atletico Madrid and Benfica also look at taking the stock-market route. Clubs such as Vicenza in Italy, whose previous owners were often in trouble with the law, are now part of the English National Investment Company.

And yet football has not wholly rid itself of the stigma, largely because corruption has never entirely gone away. Moreover, when it is uncovered, the game remains under such intense media scrutiny that each slip receives far more attention than a similar incident in any other industry, with the possible exception of politics. Football is subjected to saturation media coverage and the smallest incidents involving players are blown up into sensations. If unsavoury business practices by directors are exposed, the culprits will face intense pressure. It is a situation that is bothering many directors, and herein lies the problem with what fans consider the lesser types of corruption or dodgy dealing.

One Premiership club's financial director says that he was 'convinced' that potential investors' suspicions about illegalities and unlawful payments were an 'underrated factor' in the almost universally poor performance of UK football shares on the stock market, after the very brief euphoria of 1997 and the difficulties faced by clubs that only now feel ready to tap into new sources of finance.

Sir John to the rescue

Retired policeman Sir John Smith is adamant that football must tackle corruption. He writes:

> *Any company or business, which hopes to remain successful, has to tackle areas of concern about its integrity. Football is no different. I believe that football can continue on its upward path only by recognising that its immense hold on the public imagination carries with it the responsibility to demonstrate that it is run according to the highest standards off the field as well as on. I believe that a significant majority of people inside football recognise and accept that responsibility.*

He calls for the setting up of a specialist compliance unit staffed by accountants, lawyers and investigators that should take the lead in making sure that clubs stay within acceptable financial boundaries. He wants the Football Association to take a stronger role in policing the game, by setting down guidelines or, at least, enforcing and promoting those that exist more actively. Sir John urges the game to copy the corporate world it is so eager to embrace by adopting a code of conduct. He writes:

> *It is unfortunately true that football does not have a good ethical reputation. Having a code of conduct is not a cure-all. We live in an age where people are inclined to be cynical about fine words and large promises. Football does not start with a clean sheet but with a public perception that standards of conduct are not high.*

Sir John suggests a code of conduct which focuses on the community role of clubs, anti-discrimination, supporter involvement, a positive attitude to youth, high levels of propriety, trust and respect between clubs, opposition to violence by players and spectators, and discipline. However, he is explicit in his view that only the Football Association can transform football:

> *I really believe self-regulation can work if there is a will to make it work. Football must put its own house in order, if for no other rea-*

son than to obviate the prospect of public authorities stepping in to regulate football from outside. That would be a step too far. It would be too distanced from football and not supported.

The Football Association's chief executive Graham Kelly said at the time of the report's publication in January 1998:

We have always said that the FA are not a police force, but I don't think that's good enough. We have to be proactive in these issues if we are to be seen as a credible governing body.

Sir John's thoughtful and well-written report and Mr Kelly's sensible words aside, there must, however, be real doubts about the ability of Lancaster Gate to take on this role. Following on from its inquiry into George Graham, the FA has so far only brought similar bung charges against three men. In turn, only one of those, former Nottingham Forest manager Brian Clough, could be said to have a high profile in the game, and Mr Clough retired from football in 1994. And here, the investigation has finally been dropped because Clough is not a well man. Even in the game itself, there are many who think that the FA has only gone for soft targets because it finds it hard to reconcile its duty to hand out judgement with that of preserving the sport's image.

As noted before, the FA's disciplinary judgements tread a fine line. The organization does not want an embarrassing repeat of Alan Sugar's High Court judicial review that struck down its original points deduction and fine against Spurs, nor does it want to find itself investigating issues at the same time as the police and accused of interfering with the correct legal process. This demonstrates the weakness of the FA and self-regulation when the law becomes involved. An argument also remains that Sir John Smith's findings still leave open the option of promoting a new culture. Instead, the new game runs the risk of adding further vices while failing to deal with those already there.

For example, players' representative Gordon Taylor of the PFA draws a stark comparison between the pressures on today's players and those during his own time as a player for teams like Bolton and Birmingham City, today two of England's quoted clubs:

Winning has always been the main thing, but with so much money now at stake and with such a dogfight in the Football League, a young player is under far greater pressure to perform. He is certainly far better paid, but what is being asked in return is enormous. You have people talking about single games worth tens of millions of pounds because relegation or a championship or just a place in Europe is at stake. And yet, you are talking about the central figures – the players – being people who are taught very little about what is at stake beyond sporting achievement. It isn't going to help.

The money at stake can, however, work a more positive influence, where clubs are subject to strong regulation and prudent financial conduct. Big money creates the problem by putting so much at stake in one game, but then helps to provide the solution by giving clubs an incentive to ensure that the game is clean. Nevertheless, there is an inevitable tension between this attitude and those who want to build big clubs at any cost to board the gravy train.

The issue of who polices the game needs to be addressed more closely at all levels. Aston Villa chairman Doug Ellis has been around a long time and made his own fortune before he got involved in the beautiful game. He perhaps can afford to take the long view, but is still acutely aware that it could all be lost by one moment of financial madness. He says:

There are tremendous rewards available today by playing the game straight. That is not a reason for saying that the majority of clubs were not doing so in the past, but what it does highlight is that anybody who is tempted to go over to the wrong side should look closely at just how much they stand to lose. I do think that we need to encourage more of that thinking in the game.

CHAPTER 9

LOSING SUPPORT

Without supporters, there would be FA left.
      Slogan on Football Supporters' Association t-shirt, 1998

ACADEMIC JOHN WILLIAMS OF THE SIR NORMAN CHESTER Centre for Football Research remembers football past and how the game gradually began to change. For him, it is summed up in the attitude displayed towards supporters during a match in the 1980s long forgotten by most people. He remembers going to a Birmingham City v Leeds United game, when it seemed as if the police outnumbered the 2000 away fans.

> *We were herded off trains and escorted to the ground. We were surrounded the whole time in the match and kept waiting after the match before we were let out. It was like being in a war zone. Football was no longer a sport, it was a social order issue. When you think back to games like that it is easy to forgive and forget the picnic hampers you see at matches nowadays. If you were doing research on football in the 1980s, the thing people wanted research into was hooliganism and crowd behaviour.*
>
> *   I think people forget now what a different world it was in the late 1980s and early 90s because the general message that was coming out from Downing Street was that football was a pain in the arse. One newspaper wrote about it as a scum sport for scum people and the message that came out from Thatcher's government was not much different. It was a sport that was constantly shaming the*

nation; the government wasn't interested in it. It was a game for the poor with poor facilities; it was a game shot through with corruption and scandal.

At the beginning of the 1990 World Cup there was considerable Tory anxiety about what fans were going to do and how they were going to behave. By the end, though, the image of the sport was quite different. Suddenly it was theatre, it was opera. This was Nessun Dorma. *Gradually the anxiety and focus on fans gave way to Cabinet Ministers saying publicly: 'I can't stay in the house this afternoon, I've got to get away to the match.' It was very interesting on a social and cultural front what happened. There were real shifts going on and a real shakeup beginning to replace the old ways.*

During those dark days, it seemed as if following football was the love that dared not speak its name. Supporters had to stand in the rain to follow their favourite team and were often at risk from punch-ups and pitch invasions. As Williams' experience shows, travelling to some away games was like participating in a military operation, with fans herded on to public transport and shepherded to and from the ground by police. To some extent it still is. The sport was loathed at the highest level of government and was seen as an unnecessary social evil and a law-and-order issue for politicians, not a sexy, glamorous leisure pursuit.

Now flash forward to 1998. The sports minister, Tony Banks, is a mad football fan who was speaking up for the game in Parliament even when all that his colleagues saw was an easy target. His boss, Tony Blair, has leapt on the bandwagon, once persuading the Japanese Prime Minister to phone a good-luck message to 'his team' Newcastle United before a Cup Final and annoying his cabinet by banning them from taking ministerial trips to France during the World Cup (although strangely many found their way across the Channel, while promises of big screens for the public went unfulfilled). And at 1998's FA Cup Final, the game even had God on its side, or at least his representatives on earth. Dr George Carey, the Archbishop of Canterbury, is an Arsenal fan, while England's senior Catholic Cardinal Basil Hume is a Newcastle supporter. Nobody thought that they were certifiable for admitting as much and the revelation did both of the clerics some good.

The perception of the fan has changed and changed utterly. Some of the old concerns linger. Many people still worry when confronted by large crowds of supporters. Passengers on trains and public transport will cringe and cower if fans are around. Plenty of bars still display 'No colours' on the taproom door each Saturday. Yet while genuine fears about hooliganism remain, politicians and media pundits now often seem keen to take the fans' side, or at least more determined to ensure that they get a hearing.

There is still trouble associated with matches, as incidents during the 1997–8 English season showed. One weekend saw a Fulham fan die as a result of an incident outside Gillingham's ground plus pitch invasions at Everton and Barnsley. A linesman was attacked at a Portsmouth game on another weekend. Previous seasons have seen fights in the family stand at Queens Park Rangers' Loftus Road ground. Then there was the chilling reappearance of hooliganism's export-strength division during the World Cup, particularly before England's game against Tunisia in Marseilles. Yet after that, while the threat remained, the promise, thankfully, was not fulfilled. Therefore the talk today is of a lunatic fringe or a tiny minority being behind the unpleasantness, not the whole world of supporters.

So that's three cheers for the supporters, the media, the politicians and the clubs. Hooliganism has been tamed and contained, if not eradicated. People inside the game are also upbeat about the changes that have taken place to combat racism and boost female attendance. At West Ham, where there were serious problems with racist chanting in the past, managing director Peter Storrie is now reasonably relaxed:

> *You will always have a certain element of nutters who want to fight and who attach themselves to sport, be it football or cricket or whatever. But that is as much a problem for society as it is for football and really the hooligan element has gone now.*

The FA Premier League's recent fan survey found just 5 per cent of people who thought that hooliganism was on the rise. Just 19 per cent had witnessed fighting and only 6 per cent had seen missile throwing.

Local councils and politicians once more look on their football club as a source of civic pride. Towns fight to keep their club, since the football team is seen as a major part of the town or city's identity. Local people putting in their own money saved Bournemouth from football death. The consortium trying to save the club wooed the receiver who was briefly in charge of the club and the council gave free use of its facilities for mass meetings to raise money.

Areas of the country where there is no professional football are realizing that they are missing out on something. Businesspeople in Dublin have for a long time now flirted with the possibility of bringing English and Scottish professional teams to their city. Wimbledon and Clydebank from Scotland's Second Division have had serious talks about moving across the Irish Sea, mirroring the massive competition for American sports franchises among cities in the US.

John Williams says:

You couldn't do that in the 80s. People were trying to get rid of their football teams. The big story then was residential opposition to football relocation. Residential complaints. The costs of policing. The image the football club brought to the town. It wasn't universal – Liverpool didn't want rid of Liverpool Football Club – but in the main the debate was around: 'Who wants a football club because it is nothing but trouble?' Now it is all around: 'Can we keep our football club?' All Newcastle had to do was threaten to go to Gateshead and the council was terrified.

And, as Williams further points out, the value of a club can go some way beyond that in business terms. Let's say you are trying to lure some new investors to your town:

Does it have a Premier League team? Will it be fun for its executives to come and watch and will they have European football? It's not simply a commercial puff. These sorts of incentives are now very important for executives at major companies because what locations offer are so similar these days – labour market and so on – because information technology has massaged away the differences of loca-

tions – it's more important to be online than on the coast – because *of all these factors, previously marginal things such as football are interesting and important. Football wants to see itself and is seen as a major potential commercial attraction for attracting business, as a major focal point for regional development.*

You only have to look at what happened to Barnsley. Everyone's attention was focused on Barnsley for one season. When they were in the Nationwide League, nobody would have known who was in the Barnsley squad, nobody would have cared apart from the 8000 people who started watching their games in the 96–7 season. Last season everyone was interested in Barnsley. Barnsley is on the map. You can bet your life civic dignitaries are dining out on the fact that Barnsley is suddenly known to people around the country and probably to people around Europe, that Barnsley had a Premier League team who were entertaining Manchester United and Newcastle. Business will be being done on the back of that. They will be on telly and the tourism industry will have a little bit of a boost, though God knows what you would go and see in Barnsley. Malaysians will turn up in their droves to investigate the attractions of Barnsley.

So all of this supports football and its development and makes supporting football glamorous. But what about the supporters themselves, the other die-hards, the ones who used to go when the chants were in semaphore? Williams and his colleagues have identified at best some ambivalence on their part:

Supporters are schizophrenic about this. At one and the same moment supporters are complaining about the game becoming too commercial and the role of business becoming too important. At the same time they moan when their clubs are not ambitious, when they won't spend money, when they won't sign players. Supporters are beginning again to do what Italian supporters do. They are boasting about the wealth of the people who run their clubs – 'How much money has your backer got? We're a floated club, we've got loads of money.' There is a kind of seductiveness about the new finances of football clubs. There is also a sense in which the ambitions of a board are only shown by how much they are willing to spend. You literally do get supporters' organizations saying to directors: 'Look, if you are not willing to spend money, get out.' That is very new and very troubling. It speeds up the whole merry-go-round.

In the 1996–7 season at Leicester, Martin O'Neill was being roundly criticized by everybody because he had not spent any money and fans were saying Leicester would go down. Very late in the day he made a few signings and fans were still saying it was not good enough. They lost four or five games and people were calling for his head. By the end of the season he was in line for the Manager of the Year award. They had won the Coca-Cola Cup, they had stayed up. But if they get into a losing run in the future fans will want him out again. The whole timeframe has ratcheted up. The function of clubs seems no longer to be to serve up a weekly dollop of football for local people. It is to produce what is measured as success in a Premier League and particularly length of stay in the league.

However, it is not always quite that simple. There are signs of a more broad-based backlash.

New football, new problems

The shift in perception has been huge, as John Williams notes:

Now people want to be identified with a football club not because it is authentic and gritty and working class but because it is hot and sexy and people are buying into it and you have to have a connection to be authentic. Showing an interest in the game is like saying, 'I am aware of what is happening.' Football is the hot leisure and cultural pursuit to be involved in. Fans are not simply the people that come and watch. Fans are, in the truest sense of the word, consumers.

You don't have to go back very far to find examples of football teams, large football clubs that did no more than play. That's what they existed for. You would get a surprise if you went to talk to the people who ran Liverpool when they were at the height of their powers in the late 70s and early 80s and even into the late 80s when the club was still winning league championships. In 1989 at the time of the Hillsborough disaster Liverpool arguably had a team which was as strong and successful domestically as it had ever been. It was at the end of a long run of league championships, the most successful team in the history of the British game. But you couldn't buy a product connected with Liverpool FC anywhere else than in the club shop. In fact, to call it a shop was laughable. It was a hut. It had become something of a local tradition for the people behind the counter to treat you in as surly a way as possible. They had no interest in selling you anything. There were no licensed deals of any significance. Once you stepped away from the football ground you could not buy a licensed product of the football club anywhere. People could turn up on the off chance from Scandinavia. A group of Finns could turn up and say, 'I've brought my family with me, I've been a Liverpool supporter all my life, so could we just have a look at the stadium?' and the club had no interest. Its only interest was in producing the football team.

Maybe now, though, it is time to push the pause button and rewind to Williams's comment that fans are now consumers 'in the truest sense of the word', because it is over this issue that New Football's new, reinvented supporters are beginning to get angry.

Stadium tours, club shops – ranging from Chelsea's designer look to the Marks & Spencer appearance of Man United's outlets at Old Trafford and elsewhere – better catering inside better grounds, and all the other paraphernalia of New Football are not evils in themselves. The supporters even accept rises in ticket prices where there is a tangible link between the percentage increase and the return on the pitch. The problem is, however, that fans believe that they have gone from being commercially ignored to being commercially exploited in the crudest manner.

In Summer 1998, market research agency Mintel published its first report on English football for two years. It found that enthusiasm for the game had generally increased still further in that time. More than 25 per cent of fans interviewed said that they watched a lot of football at home and over 20 per cent were keen pub-based spectators. Some 20 per cent of consumers said that watching football was 'one of their main hobbies' against 15 per cent in 1996.

But for all this growing passion for the beautiful game, there was another equally important trend that Mintel picked out regarding the fan–club relationship. There are still many negative factors which consumers associate with the game. These mostly concern the commercial exploitation of their activities by clubs, with two in five consumers believing that the big clubs are 'ripping off' supporters and a similar proportion agreeing that football clothing is too expensive.

Linked to this, over a third of adults believe that professional clubs change the design of their strip too often. More worrying for clubs is the fact that there have been significant increases in agreement with these negative views in the past two years, suggesting a perception among the general public that clubs have got more rather than less greedy during this time.

Beyond this, there is the increasing sensation that commercialization is being used as a tool to force traditional working-class supporters out of the game and to gentrify football in a search for wealthier, middle-class fans with more to spend both inside and outside stadia.

The changes that have taken place in the UK population, with more people working in offices rather than in factories, rather undermine the class-based argument. People in the UK have seen incomes rise across the board and massive social shifts have taken place. People are taking up new leisure pursuits. Football crowds are nowhere near the peaks of 1948–9 when 120,000 crowds were seen at UK league games. Yet fears of exclusion gather renewed force when you speak to the fans. Many of the people who are threatening to cancel their season tickets and are ignoring all the merchandising blandishments are people who have already been through years of ever-increasing charges from their local clubs. They are not packing football in because they cannot afford it as much as because they are sick of it.

A case in point was one long-standing Chelsea season-ticket holder who attended a government Football Task Force meeting in London during Spring 1998 to protest about the latest hike enforced by his club. He said that in the last six years he had lived with the price of his seat rising almost eightfold to the fabled £1250 level and had decided to call it a day, even though the club had just had two successful seasons, winning three Cups including one in Europe:

I would not say I feel betrayed. The club has taken its decision and I have taken mine. If I would say something it is that I while I could afford to pay the new rate, I would not feel comfortable sitting there. I'd be in the stand thinking 'This is bloody stupid. I am bloody stupid' rather than watching the match. I'll still support Chelsea, but I think that the way that I and other people have been treated has certainly left us less passionate about the club.

In other words there *is* a limit, even among those who have been with a club for many years and, in this gentleman's case, endured a great deal more bad than the good of the late 1990s. Chelsea does get picked on because it charges more than anybody else does, but there are others. Bolton Wanderers, for example, had the gall to announce an 18 per cent rise in Reebok Stadium tickets immediately after it was relegated from the Premiership in May 1998. The club would be offering lower-quality football but wanted more money for it.

In most cases, a letter from the chairman will accompany the ticket-renewal form explaining that increases have been made to cover, typically, the cost of players. Chelsea certainly is a big spender – having added Pierluigi Casiraghi and Marcel Desailly to its already talent-packed squad in mid-1998 – and Bolton has to cope, like Nottingham Forest before it, with a drop to Football League income while still carrying a Premier League wage bill. However, there are signs that fans are not willing to accept quite so direct a tradeoff.

Both these are publicly quoted clubs which can be expected to continue to pay dividends to shareholders and, beyond that, they are supposed to be efficiently run so that costs are kept under control, rather than money being spent and then just passed down the line. The people of Bolton responded to the increase by pointing out to their club first that it would receive the Premier League's £1.65 million payoff to support its fall from grace and, secondly, that on relegation the club sold one of its stars, Alan Thompson, to Aston Villa for £5 million. In short, income on these deals alone would ultimately equal the loss of Premier League cash.

Often, the problem appears to come down to communication, certainly from the point of view of the Football Supporters'

Association, the fans' main pressure group, and that of the many supporters spoken to in researching this book. The most common complaints at Football Task Force meetings, all of which are recorded, have been prefaced by comments like 'Nobody asked us about...' or 'We were never consulted about...'

The FSA's own proposal to the Task Force makes some direct suggestions about controlling ticketing and merchandising prices, as well as more general issues on the FTF agenda like racism and player conduct. However, it does not, as even many directors never mind fans believe, call for mandatory supporter representation on club boards. Nor does it specifically call for the creation of a government regulator, even though the Task Force's founder Tony Banks is moving in that direction.

In both cases, the FSA's position is subtly different, so as not to interfere with a club's pursuing what it sees as a valid commercial programme.

On representation and communication, the FSA says:

> *The FSA believes that a number of arrangements may be effective at local level. We don't believe, however, that having a fan on the Board is the answer. A much more approachable and flexible idea might be a steering group made up of supporters, directors and other members of staff, working together on a voluntary basis, looking at ways in which the club can be taken forward to ensure that supporters' representation is openly considered when the decision process takes place behind the closed doors of the boardroom.* ***This would give supporters the chance to consider the options, listen to the reasoning behind particular decisions, as well as give them the opportunity to air their views on behalf of the people they represent.*** *(our bold)*

If you want to be cynical, you can still describe this as being a busy-body, but it sounds more like focus group work, something that not merely companies but now political parties regard as invaluable to their activities. Then there is the FSA's view on regulation:

> *There have also been some appalling examples of clubs being mismanaged and used for private gain. There are real fears about the*

*future and well being of clubs when the only motivation in decision
making becomes the short-term financial gain of their owners,
whether or not a club has been floated.*

*[This] ... argues for greater regulation of the industry, either
internally or externally imposed. The characteristic arguments for regulation are when an industry is vital to the well being of individuals
or communities and/or it is a monopoly supplier to its customers. Both
of these arguments apply to football clubs. They are not just like the
local Marks & Spencer because they are an important part of the history and culture of the towns and cities in which they are situated.
The game itself is an important part of our national culture.*

All of this, particularly with the option for internal regulation,
concurs with what Sir John Smith observed – and he was com-
missioned by the FA to produce his report. And again, communication, or more precisely a lack of it so far, is critical to what is
being said.

The fact is that people like the FSA love their football and want
other people to love it as well. Where things are done well these
people actually applaud the changes. They want balance, a position
with which John Williams concurs:

*The Italians have been talking for a long time about football serving
different functions for different parts of the audience. The function it
serves for the hard-line supporters – the Ultras in Italy – is a function of identification, passion, locality and place. The function for
the people who watch in the £120 seats on the halfway line is to be
seen to be at the match, to have an interest and to be where the
movers and the shakers are.*

*There is a sense in which you see that higher-end stuff happen-
ing at some of the big clubs here. This is the way some clubs have
been selling what they do – that football is a good place to do business at. Leeds United had an advertising campaign a couple of years
ago saying that 30 per cent of the business that is done in Yorkshire
is done at Elland Road.*

However, getting it right involves cutting across more markets
than the Club Class spectators in suits.

Williams has noted how football and the way it relates to its fans have changed at his local team, Leicester City, which is recognized as one of the more commercially sharp operations making genuine efforts to market the game. One notable success was the boosting of attendances at reserve games. In the past, Leicester's second team played in front of 700-odd die-hards who would watch virtually any sort of game involving people wearing Leicester City shirts. Now, the reserve matches regularly attract crowds of 5000. One match against Man United reserves pulled in 17,000 – a crowd in front of which some Premiership first teams would not be at all ashamed to perform.

Williams comments:

> *People aren't coming to watch the reserve games, they are coming to be part of the event, they are coming so their kids can have their faces painted, they're coming to see the dancers and to be part of the ra-ra event. They don't care if it's Grimsby they have come to see or if Grimsby are the ones in the striped shirts, whoever they are. They are coming for a night or a day out.*

The community is being reached – but who are the people who are now watching football?

The New Fan

People in the game certainly agree that football and fans have changed. The jokes about new fans being middle-class families with a picnic hamper wondering why nobody picks the ball up and runs with it, or women who are just there to ogle the sexy bodies on show, or even corporate hospitality suits too blind drunk to spot the ball are all a bit stale now. But then again...

The Sir Norman Chester Centre tracks who the supporters of the sport are through its annual surveys. Its work illustrates the changing attitudes, and also where the game needs to rebalance its approach.

Research done by the centre is carried out for the Premier League and focuses partly on season-ticket holders and partly on people without season tickets. All clubs in the Premiership with the exception of two provide names and addresses of season-ticket holders to researchers. The *refuseniks* are Liverpool and Manchester United. United did not want to give away commercially sensitive information, even though it was for an obviously non-profit-making organization, and Liverpool could not come up with an address list. In other words, United is too mean and Liverpool too dozy, which sums up something about English football depending on your prejudices.

Quibbles aside, the picture that emerges from the research shows fans as wealthier, better educated and more footloose in their support than they used to be. Gentrification has taken place. Supporters are most likely to be men aged between 21 and 40. Nearly half the average Premiership crowd is made up of males between these ages. Almost a third have some form of higher education. Wimbledon has the highest proportion of graduates among its fans at nearly 40 per cent, followed by Manchester United and Leeds. Coventry City and West Ham attract fewer graduates, with about a quarter of their fans boasting higher education qualifications.

Three-quarters of all supporters are in full-time employment, while the rest of the crowd is made up of students and the retired, with the unemployed constituting a tiny 5 per cent. Nearly a fifth of the crowd, however, earn more than £30,000 a year, which is hardly representative of the population as a whole where average male wages are around £19,000. The clubs with the best-paid fans tend to be in the south of England, with Wimbledon, Spurs and Chelsea topping the league. One club which breaks the mould by being based in the north of England and having well-paid fans is, of course, Man United. The worst-paid fans tend to be at other northern clubs such as Everton, Sheffield Wednesday and Newcastle United.

The New Fans are less drawn to their local side. In order to qualify as a local fan, a supporter had to have been born within 20 miles of their club's ground, according to researchers. The prejudiced will have to eat their words, because incredibly enough Man United managed to notch up 80 per cent on that score. Obviously the Taunton Reds did not return their questionnaires, but it does mean that United still draws most of its support from its home community. The clubs with the biggest proportion of local support were sides such as Newcastle and Blackburn Rovers, with near 90 per cent local backing. The clubs with the lowest proportion of local support were the London sides such as Arsenal, Chelsea and Spurs and, more surprisingly, Leeds and Southampton, although both those two are in areas where fans are likely to commute because of the regional geography.

For fans as a whole, 73 per cent of season-ticket holders were born near to their football club. Figures also show that 30 per cent of supporters do not go to the Premiership ground nearest to where they live now, although the influence of the London clubs, where fans will go to a ground further away from home to support their team, probably explains most of that result.

It virtually goes without saying that ethnic minority support for football is still a very small minority. Nearly 99 per cent of the fans surveyed were white, compared with the 5 per cent of the UK population reckoned to be non-white. Arsenal and Manchester United are the clubs with the highest proportion of non-white fans, although even at these clubs the figures are only 2.8 and 2 per cent respectively. Newcastle has the lowest proportion of non-white fans at just 0.3 per cent. Sunderland, when it was in the Premiership, had no ethnic minority fans. And all the talk of a growing female support for the game does not quite add up. Only around an eighth of the crowd at an average Premiership match is female and this is reckoned to be an all-time high.

When groups such as the FSA talk about fans being attracted to the game who might not stick through it with their club, the figures tend to bear out this assessment. Whatever Mintel says about growing general enthusiasm, the support of fans for their team is not all-consuming. The Eat Football, Sleep Football attitude promoted by advertisers is not entirely the case. Around a fifth of season-ticket holders do not go to all their club's home games. A third of people who don't own season tickets go to five or fewer games in a season. Women and fans who are counted as being born locally are more loyal supporters, according to the research. High-earning fans are more likely to have season tickets but less likely to attend every home game. More than three-quarters of fans earning less than £10,000 go to all home matches and nearly 11 per cent of them go to 16 or more away games. Just over half the supporters on more than £30,000 attend all the home games and only 8 per cent of them go to 16 or more away matches. Being able to get tickets makes a big difference at the bigger clubs, but research shows that Chelsea and West Ham fans are the most loyal followers away from home.

The report also shows that there has been a definite change in support since the Premier League started. More than half the people with season tickets surveyed have been going to games at their club for more than 20 years. The proportion falls to a third when the question is put to those without season tickets. But this also shows that plenty of new fans are coming into the game. Nearly one in eight season-ticket holders have only been going to games for five years – roughly since the start of the Premiership. And among people who don't buy season tickets, the figure is nearly a third. For female fans the figures are more striking. A third of women spectators have only been going to their club for the past five years, compared with a sixth of male fans.

Researchers have looked at the fans who are coming home to football, finding unsurprisingly that the recently promoted clubs and the less well supported were the most successful in bringing back fans. Wimbledon has pulled in more fans as it has become more successful, as have Bolton and even Queens Park Rangers and Middlesbrough when they were in the Premiership. Around a sixth of the fans coming back to the game had supported another side before. At Wimbledon, half the current season-ticket holders were previously fans of another team – anathema to the traditional fan who inherited his support from his family. The new fans are the better off, with more than a third earning £25,000 or more. Children of supporters are also likely to back another team, with a quarter, unsurprisingly, supporting Man United. At Wimbledon, for instance, a quarter of fans with school-age children admitted that their kids supported someone else.

The reasons they are coming home are the inevitable ones of watching world-class foreign players in improved stadia. Comments quoted by researchers include a scriptwriter in his 40s from London: 'It's entertainment now, as opposed to tribal war.'

Another was a fan in his 50s: 'Fans are treated like guests now, not sheep like the old days.' The following was from a female in her 20s: 'Never realized how exciting watching live football can be and to be able to see all the country's top players is a bonus.' And a fan from the north east said: 'To be able to relax and enjoy the football due to good crowd control instead of looking over one's shoulder to see where the next missile was coming from.'

As all the positive comments show, football support retains a committed hard core. More than a third of fans regard their club as being more important now that it was five years ago. Nearly 60 per cent of supporters rank football as either one of the most important things in their life or very important. Among people without season tickets, there is a sizeable minority who are perhaps not as committed, with a fifth ranking football as 'just one of the things that I do'. However, the passion shines through in the comments collected by researchers.

A bank manager in his 30s: 'It gives me a common interest following my separation.' A postman in his 40s: 'It gives me something to share with my son.' Another divorced dad: 'I get a lot of pleasure with my daughter at this club.' And the fanatical fan shines through in comments from a manager in his 20s: 'Nearly all my most emotional experiences have come watching this club. The agony and the ecstasy, it's fair to say it dictates my life.' Ah, Albert Camus would have been proud of you, son. Another fan characterizes his football support thus: 'It's something that gets into your blood: it's like a love affair.'

So what do they think?

There is some unease among the fans quizzed about the changes to football, ranging from concerns about match-day presentations to fears that their club is concentrating too much on business. The survey found that 46.2 per cent of Manchester United season-ticket holders think that there is too much emphasis on business activities at their club, some way ahead of second-placed Leeds on 32.2 per cent, with Spurs, Chelsea and Newcastle making up the rest of the top places. All of these clubs are stock-market quoted and rich. At poorer clubs such as Wimbledon only 3.3 per cent thought there was too much emphasis on business, notwithstanding rumours about a move to Dublin. Coventry and Southampton fans take a similarly relaxed view, but Southampton is, of course, also stock-market quoted.

This is a small point but it helps illustrate the dichotomy for fans. They want their team to do well, they want a massive, expensive stadium with tremendous facilities, they want foreign superstars and they do not want hooliganism or an air of menace. They also do not want the game to be too commercial. But if they are supporters of weaker, less wealthy sides, they realize that they need money to compete.

John Williams has worked through the data and takes the view that it is difficult to be dogmatic:

> There is now a resistance movement among supporters who say the game is too commercial, it's too global, we need to be local, we need to serve our local communities, it's wrong that people who live in Reading or Torquay are Manchester United fans, they should all come from Manchester. There's plenty of that going on as a resistance movement to the forces of globalization. But there's also not far behind a celebration of the decline of the intimacies and parochialism of local support. Global exposure is everything now.

Quite frankly, so what?

For all the talk of the glories of the Premiership and the new fans coming into the sport and the economic benefits of the game to its localities, there is a pervasive air of discontent among fans. The UK government's Football Task Force is just one manifestation of this. It taps into worries about racism, merchandising ripoffs, soaring ticket prices and concerns about the City and stock-market involvement in the game. Its brief is to examine all of these matters and come up with ideas to make the game more responsive to its local communities.

At the launch of the initiative, Sports Minister Tony Banks said:

The game of football has changed dramatically over the last decade. Following the Hillsborough tragedy it was essential for football to think afresh about the safety and comfort of the spectators coming to watch our national game. The depth of top quality stadia in this country shows that we are well on the way to meeting that challenge.

But we should not assume that this is the only challenge facing the sport. That is why the Government has decided to establish a Football Task Force to ensure that those in a position of power have an opportunity to hear the views and suggestions from all quarters of the game. Many clubs are taking action to stamp out racism but more needs to be done. There are questions, not just of access for minority groups like the disabled, but how clubs can avoid alienating the less well off from the sport that they love. Let's really make football Britain's family game. There are many ways that clubs can achieve this and I hope that the group will highlight some of the good things already going on within the game.

The FSA supports this view wholeheartedly, but there is a private concern as to whether other members of the Task Force are similarly well inclined or merely keeping an eye out for their own interests. It has several battles that it will not be able to win because it simply cannot count on Banks's support.

The FSA wants an end to all-seater stadia in the Premier and First Divisions in England, arguing that the policy has made the game too expensive. It wants changes to the law on ticket touting so that fans do not fall foul of laws designed to trap profiteers when they sell on a ticket at face value. It wants more games shown on terrestrial television so that supporters do not have to fill Sky's coffers if they want to watch TV games. More important games such as the Coca-Cola Cup Final and European matches involving British teams should be included on the list of sporting events that cannot be sold to satellite broadcasters, the FSA believes. It would like more money from TV to go to lower-division teams and has won some support for this idea from MPs, although a private member's bill to this end failed to win government support. It wants National Lottery cash given to the Football Trust and better public transport to grounds now that many clubs are abandoning old city-centre stadiums for out-of-town sites which are harder to reach.

Outside observers have backed the concerns of the fans. Think tank Case Associates has highlighted ticket prices' rising trend. In the Premiership and old First Division they rose 222 per cent on average between 1985 and 1995, at a time when inflation climbed by 52 per cent. Cinema ticket prices rose 51 per cent during the same period and the price of a pint of lager went up by 99 per cent. And ticket inflation is not confined to the Premiership. Lower divisions have seen similar though not as stratospheric rises. In the First Division the rise is 169 per cent in 10 years, in the Second it is 151 per cent and even in the Third, where there are definitely no foreign superstars and expensive stadia, it is 145 per cent. And yet somebody is buying the tickets, because attendances continue to rise.

Similarly, fans seem perfectly happy to spend money on merchandising. Just 9 per cent disapprove of merchandising and the figure falls to below 5 per cent if people are asked if they actually oppose merchandising. The average fan spends £109 a season on merchandising compared to £85 two seasons ago, with Newcastle fans the biggest spenders on £159, although the figures were compiled before former chairman Freddie Shepherd and vice-chairman Douglas Hall expressed their views of fans' willingness to spend on replica kits. Newcastle leads the field for sales of shirts. Not for nothing is St James' Park described as looking like a barcode, as 73 per cent of season-ticket holders have bought a shirt. Just 5 per cent of the Toon Army do not own a single item of merchandise. In contrast, just 38 per cent of the restrained people of Southampton own replica kits and the fans who spend the least on merchandising are Southampton and Wimbledon supporters, who shell out a mere £64 and £69 a season. More than half of all people surveyed had bought replica kits during the season, with club videos, magazines, hats, scarves and badges also big sellers.

Little acorns

Amid all these tales of willing-to-spend adults, it is not that surprising that many club executives still adopt an attitude of: 'Crisis? What crisis?' As ever, football's short-sightedness, born of the euphoria that still surrounds its apparently ever-increasing earnings, has blinded it to a few home truths. Foremost among these is the issue of where its patient, season-ticket-desiring fans will come from, not so much in two, three or four years' time but across the next decade.

Football's big fan problem is that its Generation Next could prove to be a generation lost. City analysts have noted the fact that football could alienate its fans by milking them too vigorously, but of greater concern is the extent to which this could effect parents' responses to the game, even if they themselves continue to attend. Nigel Hawkins of Williams de Broe comments:

> *Support and attendance at matches has historically been generational: an adult supports a team because his father did and he used to take his children to the ground. Some of us are wondering if that is still the case however, considering the rise in prices and the cost in bringing kids as well.*

TV commentator Des Lynam takes a similar view of the role of television and the cost of Sky. He told one trade magazine:

> *Children who live in homes without Sky do not see much football and we have contributed to that. Match of the Day first goes out so late, we often finish after midnight. ITV's league package also seems to always go out very late, sometimes in the early hours of the morning. With our audience, youngsters are in bed, you might get some teenagers, but the older ones are out on the town. There is now the 7am repeat on Sundays and that was something I and others pushed for but it's still hardly peak children's viewing. The scheduling does not do football many favours, to be honest.*

Ominously for the people who fear the loss of young fans, just 27 per cent of people surveyed by the Sir Norman Chester Centre attended matches with children. The vast majority went with friends, while 9 per cent always walked alone when they went to games. The loneliest fans appear to be Chelsea supporters with 17 per cent of season-ticket holders going to games by themselves – presumably because they can't find a friend rich enough to buy a season ticket. Or maybe it's a case of two friends clubbing together and only being able to afford one ticket. Or maybe Chelsea fans have no friends.

As noted earlier, Sir John Hall, one of the supposed dons of Financial Football, has voiced his concern about the little acorns but, for all the fine words, many clubs seem unwilling or unable to do anything about it. At Newcastle, bringing in the children will supposedly be achieved by raising the capacity of St James' Park from 35,000 to around 50,000. But the cost of this programme will almost certainly not be offset on the most profitable timetable if the majority of seats are to be lower-priced family stand capacity. In that case, the club's institutional shareholders may – ironically – cry foul.

Among the most popular sides, the same problem arises again and again. Whatever Arsenal does to raise its capacity at Highbury or by a move to a greenfield site, the costs involved will again tend to militate against attempts to offer the kind of cheaper seats that will attract parents and children.

The bottom line for football is that at the base level it is too expensive to get into to justify its position as a national game for much longer, and young fans are being excluded by ticket pricing and TV.

Sports minister Tony Banks sees the problem this way:

Do you know what the fastest growing sport in Britain is? It's basketball. Now without trying to put off the kids who play, I find that strange. You have to be bloody tall to play basketball even at a pretty low level. But it isn't that strange when you consider that the sport is accessible as well as being well marketed. Watching a game is affordable for a whole family, so the kids are going along there and they are getting hooked. So what will football do if it loses those people when they are in their 20s and have money to spend? Football never did much for them beforehand, so why should they be interested?

The greatest irony here is that in the US, admission to basketball at its top level is already ludicrously expensive. You don't have to be a season-ticket holder of a few decades' standing to get a front-row seat for the LA Lakers, for example – you have to be Jack Nicholson. And yet, the NBA has counterbalanced this by attractive marketing for lower-league, particularly college games, so that access is still available to a desirable product. This stands in stark contrast to the way in which football leagues are progressively breaking up in Europe, with the consequent suggestion that clubs outside the elite are not worth watching or supporting.

In some respects, it all comes down to dialogue – or a lack of it. The people who realize that the bubble could still burst tend to be the supporters. The problem is that while fans have legitimate concerns, they are also awkward buggers and they are also often plain wrong. It is hard, for instance, to find a Man United fan who will now admit that he or she joined in the late 1980s chants of 'Fergie out', but given the noise they made, even Old Trafford cannot have recycled that much of its support. Either way, everyone apart from a few very honest types now say that they always thought that Mr Ferguson would give them the finest team in the land.

The emphasis that the FSA puts on the communication issue may therefore be the key to resolving all these problems. Such a dialogue might be the best way of waking clubs up to the fact that they are genuinely pricing out loyal customers, to replace them with others who are not necessarily buying into a team, but into success. However, the FSA does also want regulation, with some economic justification, and given these and other developments in the game, particularly the emerging troop of new owners, the creation of new lawgivers needs to be considered as an issue in itself.

CHAPTER 10

OFFSIDE: BLOWING THE WHISTLE ON FOOTBALL

I am coming round to the view that football needs to be more tightly regulated because of the money in the game today and the influence it is having.

Tony Banks, minister for sport, *The People*, April 1998

FOOTBALL HAS TO CHANGE. IT IS ALREADY MOVING TOWARDS some form of regulation despite opposition at various levels of the game. British sports minister Tony Banks has made it clear that he expects the game to clean up its act or face government intervention. Sir John Smith's FA-commissioned report also proposes a regulator to promote a code of conduct covering football's sporting and financial aspects. The European Union has used its existing regulations, specifically competition and employment law, to pass judgement on football, and its competition commissioner Karel van Miert has said that there is more to come. The Bosman ruling and decisions that TV rights should be taken away from leagues and given to clubs have been the two most significant legal developments facing football in recent times, and both emanated to some degree from Brussels. The EU also took a central role in the dispute over ticketing for the 1998 World Cup.

Fans, of course, have been looking for something like this for several years. Patterns of ownership also make the demand pressing as they potentially change to admit conglomerates and others who see football as a media business. Even if this is yet to happen, a system fit not just for today but for the immediate future is required.

The big issue concerns the form and scale of the change that any or all of these interventions will cause. Banks's current thinking tends to suggest that the UK regulator may be no more than an ombudsman, an independent arbiter of supporters' complaints over pricing policies and other consumer-protection issues. Sir John Smith wants an internal policing system that goes further to look at clubs' financial probity, and his proposal borrows from existing systems for corporate governance, including the Cadbury Code for UK business, and for conduct in public life, such as Lord Nolan's recommendations for UK politicians. The EU's strategy, meanwhile, is more difficult to judge, being based presently on the application of existing rules and regulations as and when cases are brought – although Van Miert promises more action, he is yet to make the Brussels position fully clear.

Football has changed more in the last decade than at any time in its history. Its finances, in particular, are gearing up for the twenty-first century, but within an administrative structure that has undergone little change since the late nineteenth and early twentieth centuries.

Old farts

Any founders of the Football Association magically brought back to life from a cryogenic deep freeze would not be too lost if they saw the game today.

They would be pleased to find that the game they started and nurtured had continued to grow and attract huge numbers of fans. The massive stadia dotted around the country and the vastly improved facilities for players would impress them. If they went into a ground the experience would not be too disconcerting. The rules on the pitch are roughly the same and they would recognize the names of most of the clubs, although they might be surprised at how far some of the mighty had fallen.

The shorts are a bit shorter, the shirts a bit different and the balls a lot lighter. The FA founders might want to see a bit more hand shaking and gentlemanly behaviour on the pitch. The goal celebrations would probably disgust them, as would the absence of tackling from behind, but otherwise they would not worry too much.

The essential structure of the game they bequeathed has not changed too much on the pitch despite all the years. Even off the pitch, the way it is organized is not radically different. There is still a Football Association presiding over the game and while the First Division is now called the Premier League, it still looks like the same game. A visit to a FA Council meeting might not be too different from previous experiences. The same organizations are still members – the Armed Forces and the universities, for instance, continue to play their part. There might even be some of the same people there if the ages of some of the game's politicians are anything to go by.

However, a visit to a Premier League meeting would be something different. The issues there and the sums of money talked about would be alien. Pay-per-view, veiled talk about European Super Leagues, wage inflation, the BSkyB contract, sponsorship, commercial income, merchandising, foreign players and their contracts, Bosman, the ending of the transfer system, player valuations – these would be far from familiar. In those meetings the idea would come over that while the game remains the same, everything else has totally changed. They would see that football had changed off the pitch from a sport that tolerated a bit of business for funding badly paid professional players into one that was essentially a business and a massive international multibillion-pound business at that.

The recently defrosted mind of a FA founder would have difficulty coping immediately with what had happened to the game. And he would not be alone, because most of us who have lived through the changes also have extreme difficulty in coping with what has happened.

What the frozen FA man would not immediately grasp was that, of course, the transformation into a multinational industrial giant had happened only relatively recently. He would not know that he was looking at a business in the throes of radical reform. He would probably not be told that the changes were the result of happy accident rather than a cunning plan translated from blue-print into stunning reality. He would not know that ownership of many clubs had passed from local benevolent or malevolent dictators to companies quoted on the stock market. He would not guess that the change in the method of ownership meant that other, even more remote owners could come into the game, not just UK and European financial institutions, but US media groups and even Arab investment trusts. He would not know that live football was shown on television but only in a quarter of homes, which paid to see a selection of games. He would of course be unaware that there were plans to show all games live on television and charge for each individually. He would not know that football fans were complaining that the working man's ballet was now as about as expensive as the Royal Ballet. He would find it hard to believe that fans wore the same shirts in the pub as did players on the pitch and he would find the prices even harder to believe.

Still, even someone whose mind was encased in permafrost would see that football faces some pressing problems that have the potential to overwhelm it and make the beautiful game ugly. The basic problems are its soaring costs, mainly due to wage inflation, and the ways in which the game is trying to meet its bills. These include increasing ticket prices, flirting with pay-per-view television, developing merchandising and other revenue from catering and conferences, and thinking about a European Super League.

The frozen FA man would see that these financial pressures were translating into sporting pressures. He would think that a top league that made it difficult for outsiders to come up and compete, effectively because they could not afford to, was in danger. He might also reckon that a game that failed to renew itself by allowing new competitors to emerge was in peril, and he might further conclude that sporting competition was being replaced by financial competition which, while fascinating to some, was entirely different and did not draw the crowds quite as effectively.

He would immediately realize that some of the structures he had been involved in setting up were no longer appropriate to the new football world. Originally, football clubs were not supposed to be money-making ventures, although they were supposed to be financially self-supporting. Regulations still exist from the old days which limit the dividends that shareholders can extract and which set down principles of serving the community – particularly in terms of the game's current relationships with its supporters, these appear to have been mothballed. He might also ponder the fact that an FA he had helped to found to unite all the clubs in the country now seemed more concerned with its own separate commercial activities and promoting the growth of a mere 20 out of Britain's 43,000 officially recognized professional and amateur teams. In short, he would realize that the rulebook needed a very thorough overhaul.

Common ground

All football associations and all the leagues were founded on the basis of different groups coming together around a common cause. The financial revolution of the past 10 years has vastly expanded the number of interested parties which need to participate in taking the sport forward. Teams, team owners, fans, investors and sponsors all now require a say in how things should develop. This is radically different from the game's long-held and official view that only its immediate participants matter, with the national side at the top of the hierarchy. Even that has long been under pressure because of the club-versus-country tension, but the sheer scale of investment today ratchets up the tension.

The debate going on about the future of football now involves more than realizing that it has a common cause. The game has to redefine its common cause and accept that it has to be more inclusive. It is facing challenges to its authority from governments at one level and customers at another.

Where is football's common cause at the moment? Why did the English Premiership and Scottish Premier League break away if not to demonstrate that the common cause meant very little to them? Why, they asked, should they hand out the money that they earned to their lesser rivals? What is the common cause of an English Third Division side and Man United? What is the common cause of a struggling Premiership side and Man United, for that matter? There is apparently little incentive for clubs to build a common cause and seemingly no tangible benefit from it. Would it really cripple the big clubs if they lost the magic of the FA Cup, with its irritating threats of playing at non-league grounds and getting beaten? And do small clubs actually worry about the logistics of pay-per-view unless it affects their gates?

Nevertheless, building a common cause and persuading clubs to unite around it is still crucial to the future of the sport. Achieving it is difficult, which means that the case for a regulator of the football industry builds all the time. The game faces a huge raft of problems, ranging from the relatively simple but grim ones of high prices to more complex issues of how to control the ambitions of clubs and players who are becoming richer and richer and less interested in the future of rivals in the same game.

The common cause starts with the acceptance that football is an interdependent economy, revolving around businesses that are not businesses in the traditional form. Simply expressed, the top clubs need the small clubs in order to survive. The traditions of the sport are based on the ability of clubs to climb the leagues or plummet. Success certainly has to be rewarded, but failure has to be punished.

There are those who will argue – particularly in an English game with 92 clubs or even a Scottish one with 40 – that there are so many clubs that at a certain level success and failure become unimportant. Only 20 or 30 or 40 teams really matter, or so the economics go. However, season after season, the Football League's main calendar finishes with fans as interested in who wins a division as they are with the club that ends up 92nd and faces expulsion to the Vauxhall Conference. Similarly, over 1997 and 1998, many supporters followed the progress of Macclesfield, the Cheshire team that entered the League in 1996 and has been promoted after successive seasons. What matters is that those who follow such events are not necessarily supporters of the clubs involved.

When Brighton & Hove Albion faced financial extinction and seemed likely to occupy the Third Division's graveyard slot, its Fans United campaign drew supporters from virtually every British club and even a sizeable number from the Continent. These fans were making their belief in the value of football's plurality more explicit than ever before. Even the FA's own investigator accepted this point. Sir John Smith states:

> *Football cannot be treated purely as a business. There are two reasons for this. First football clubs represent considerably more in emotional terms to their supporters (customers) than the average business. Secondly football clubs are not characteristic of businesses generally. An efficient commercial company will always attempt to maximise its market share, and in an ideal world will want to become a monopoly supplier of whatever it produces, however difficult this aim may be in practice.*
>
> *Football as an industry cannot operate in those terms. It is natural for every club to want to be the most successful, but achieving a total monopoly of trophies would lead to the extinction of spectator interest. There must be some degree of competition, or there would be no reason for having a football club. In football the attraction of success must always be balanced by the risk of failure.*
>
> *That is why leagues exist. A league, as the name suggests, is a cartel, but one that exists to promote and ensure competition.*

Leading sides may not see plurality as their common ground. Fair enough, the chances of a Man United, Arsenal or Chelsea being relegated are remote, but not as remote as they may think. Ask a Spurs, Everton or Newcastle United fan. However, apart from exclusion threatening to diminish the value of competition, it also challenges the football brand. Those who follow the game would feel that it was attractive on fewer levels were the lower divisions told to shuffle off and die. This, it can be fairly assumed, would have an effect on their passion for their own teams and their willingness to spend the hundreds if not thousands of pounds now being demanded. The consequences would therefore be felt at both the top and the bottom.

Whatever clubs may say of their duties to their shareholders, they need to remember their similar responsibilities to their stakeholders, including, most prominently, the supporters. These two spheres of influence are not and never have been contradictory. Managing the stakeholder side of the business should deliver profits, dividends and commercial success. If clubs are unwilling to recognize this economic reality, then the argument that some external force should oblige them to consider a world beyond shareholders and directors becomes more powerful. Furthermore, club directors have a custodial role whether they like it or not. This raises a further important question.

Who guards the guards?

Electricity, gas and water companies in the UK have rapidly become used to the idea of a central regulator for their industries after the way they were organized changed dramatically after privatization. Each industry now has its own Office for Regulation, for instance OFFER running electricity, OFGAS in charge of gas and OFWAT controlling water. Even the British National Lottery has its own regulator in OFLOT, which does not seem to do an awful lot but is there nevertheless.

On that basis, British football's regulator would just have to be called OFFSIDE. The appointment of a watchdog with wide powers over the game would be a culture shock for a sport which has not been keen on outside intervention. Self-regulation has always been the name of the game, a point re-emphasized by Sir John Smith.

The former policeman, in his report on the game, specifically ruled out the appointment of an outside body to look at English football's financial probity. The game resisted government intervention in the case of the identity card scheme proposed by the Thatcher government in the 1980s, and it only grudgingly conceded to the conditions set down for stadia after the Taylor report.

But only a regulator would have the powers to knock heads together and persuade and pacify. Only a regulator would have the power to impose solutions if all else failed. Only a regulator would be able to examine proposals for changes in the way the game was run and look at them purely in terms of the good of the game, not the good of just one club. A regulator would be able to take the side of fans when they were in a dispute with clubs, but equally could give an unbiased assessment when the supporters were wrong. The regulator would be independent of the clubs and not reliant on their support in the future to do his or her job. A regulator would be able to look at the possibility of price controls for match tickets. He or she could work on disabled access to grounds and look at public transport facilities. He or she could take action on racism and tackle the problem of corruption, laying down codes of conduct for managers and players. The regulator could look at the whole issue of television and football and the merits and demerits of the relationship. He or she could examine the potential for pay-per-view television and the problems inherent in the move. He or she could work on merchandising and could stop clubs and the English national side changing strips every 10 minutes. The regulator would be a very busy person with a large staff if they were to take on the whole raft of issues that there are to consider in British football.

And yet providing him or her with the regulatory framework within which to cover so much ground effectively would not be easy. The US has provided a great deal of the inspiration for the new business ideas of British football and is seen in some quarters as providing a model for managing the game's commercial side. After all, American sport has grappled with many of the problems already thrown up by the changes in the business of sport. Yet while it does have stronger regulatory structures in place, many of the financial problems facing UK games seem even greater in the US.

The big earners in basketball, baseball and gridiron would sneer at the supposedly massive money our footballers receive. Fans have grown used to ticket price inflation and merchandising. They have long been the celebrity supporters bragging about their attachment to the games and the fashionable teams that pull in huge crowds when they are winning but struggle for spectators when they are losing or no longer have the superstar of the moment. The US has seen how far star power can go, with basketball's Michael Jordan at the Chicago Bulls just one of the most recent examples of a player being bigger than a team. Americans have had to contend with the problems caused by superstars for much longer. Admittedly they have never had a hooligan problem, but they have always worked carefully to ensure that the games are family sports and the experience for spectators is a pleasant one.

On one level, there are ways in which several more avaricious club owners in the UK would like to see the US form of regulation in operation across the Atlantic. But they do tend to pick on the little things that most supporters would reject out of hand.

Foremost among those is the inability of American sports to recognize concepts such as history and tradition. This is most clearly expressed in the idea of 'franchising'. Since 1980, 14 baseball, gridiron and ice hockey teams have moved from hometowns because another city has made their owners a better financial offer. Such mobility has not been merely a case of crossing a river, as was the case with the original Woolwich Arsenal, or moving a few miles west like Newton Heath which is today's Manchester United. Teams in the US have been moved across state borders and, in some instances, all the way across the country from the East to the West Coast and vice versa.

European owners would like to do the same, as is evinced by Sam Hammam's ongoing battle to move from Wimbledon in south-west London, where his local council, Merton, seems to block his every attempt to build a stadium, to football-starved Dublin, where some of Ireland's richest businesspeople await him and his team with open arms and wallets. In Scotland, the owners of Clydebank are attempting to pull off the same trick by relocating a Scottish Second Division team without a ground to Dublin. True fans of any club, however, can have little respect for such a proposal, even if it would cause barely a ripple across the Atlantic. Vesting so much power in a club's shareholders to a point where they can ignore supporters so completely is just not – excuse the metaphor – cricket. British football still respects some of its traditions and the idea that loyalty is portable has not quite caught on.

The second undesirable aspect of US sports regulation is the acceptance of exclusivity. There is no relegation or promotion in the National Football League, National Basketball Association or Major League Baseball. Teams must apply for so-called pathfinder franchises, which await a reshuffling of the various conference and regional structures before they can be admitted; a system that has little to do with valued principles such as sporting success and competition on the field. In British sport, so far, losers go down and winners go up. A Premiership club, if it is very bad or unlucky or Man City, can tumble down the leagues. A lower-league club can fight its way to the Premiership. An American team can do neither, although it can be moved from city to city. Given British football's existing structures, what would such an exclusive approach mean for teams like Barnsley, Swansea City or Northampton Town, all of which have enjoyed some time in the top flight during their histories? Even mighty Aston Villa spent part of the 1970s in the old Third Division before rising to its current position of power.

Going further, pathfinder franchises are strictly rationed. No NFL team, for example, can ever face the threat of a neighbour bidding for its fans unless that neighbour is based at least 250 miles away. Some duplications do exist, but these are a historical consequence of the competition's creation from two rival leagues in the 1950s. Apply this to the UK or Europe, even on a more limited geographic scale, and imagine how Liverpool and Everton, Arsenal and Spurs, Real Madrid and Atletico Madrid, AC Milan and Internazionale would feel.

If this is the unacceptable face of the US sporting structure, the problem is that those aspects that are more popular also tend to have become unworkable in the real world.

Smaller British football clubs like the US idea of the salary cap, which has also caught on in rugby league and rugby union. However, it is doubtful that this could work in soccer. The NFL and MLB operate salary caps to try to ensure that squads are evenly balanced. The advent of free agency in US sports in 1987 – an almost identical situation to that created by the Bosman case in Europe – has severely hampered the efficiency of this measure.

Free agency not only guarantees freedom of movement for out-of-contract players but also, by law, allows them to negotiate their own salary packages. This has inevitably led to wage inflation and a consequent need to raise the salary cap almost continuously to accommodate it. Cuba Gooding Jr in the movie *Jerry Maguire* shouting 'Show me the money' is a more plausible face of US sport than the hair shirt of the salary cap. In other words, the threshold has kept on rising to a point where some of the poorer teams now believe that the cap is on the brink of collapse.

Then there are the natures of the different markets for playing talent. US sporting owners claim that the cap fits them and can work because their game is effectively and hermetically sealed. The best players in any of their major sports almost always come through the north American system, because only in that continent do these games have a sufficient level of popularity to support the infrastructure that will develop the talent. But, as is the case with football, if the talent marketplace were global, imposing a domestic US salary cap would not work because teams from, say, Mexican, Japanese or even Spanish leagues could steal away the top stars by the simple device of not controlling the wage structure. This is therefore a system which is struggling to work in the US, and is probably unworkable in any sport that crosses a significant number of national boundaries. Football salary caps are simply unthinkable. The English Premiership could certainly impose wage restraints on its finest and then wave them off at airports as they trek round the world finding someone willing and able to pay them more.

Arming the guards

The Americans do not have it all right, but they do not have it all wrong either. Where they have succeeded is in the administration of the centralized aspects of their sports. Some clubs are richer than others but the income gap is not as glaring. They have ensured in particular a more fairly graduated – although still not entirely equitable – distribution of income. Both the NFL and the NBA operate centralized TV rights packaging, merchandising and marketing programmes, from which each member team receives an equal share of the income regardless of which gets the most broadcast coverage or sells the most souvenirs, replica kits or even perimeter advertising.

The one respect in which teams can operate individually is in relation to their gates, hence US owners' pioneering work in corporate hospitality and other approaches to growing stadium revenues. Nevertheless, these are not in themselves enough to give one team a financial advantage over other league members to a point where it dominates a competition.

The Dallas Cowboys, America's team and the Man United of the US, has tried to break the centralized sharing of the spoils with the controversial merchandising concept of 'identity rights'. But, again, its recent sporting form suggests that it still cannot claim preeminence. The most conspicuously successful NFL team in the 1990s after the Cowboys is the Green Bay Packers, which is always there or thereabouts come the SuperBowl. It has one of the smallest grounds with a capacity of 35,000 and operates a community ownership scheme, rather than depending on a rich benefactor-cum-investor like the Cowboys.

US sports also seem better equipped to control not merely how money is shared but also how it is spent on transfers, if not wages. Gridiron, baseball and basketball all operate draft systems which give teams finishing in the lowest league positions first choice of the new college- or minor league-developed talent, while the most successful teams take those considered of a lesser quality. The responsibility for developing little acorns is therefore taken away from the big sides and put into the hands of the outsiders, guaranteeing them a role and a future in the game.

US sportspeople must, in essence, serve an apprenticeship at a level that keeps minor league competitions interesting because fans can catch up with tomorrow's superstars. The concept is not totally alien to the UK experience, as it is merely an extension of the loan system already in place at teams in the UK. Clubs can loan a fringe player to a lower-league side with the aim of ensuring that he gets first-team action. No less a player than David Beckham has been on loan, playing a part in the success of Preston North End.

A variant on the US draft system based on young players being exclusively fed through lower-league clubs could begin to make matches in football's supposed doldrums a more attractive proposition for fans. These would be games where fans saw nascent talent in a real league environment rather than being forced to seek out relatively meaningless reserve team games. Surely this would be preferable to the creation of nursery sides owned by the bigger, Premiership clubs that would have total control over the talent delivered and that would make a local team subordinate to their requirements? In a nursery club world, the lower-league club would have little incentive to be successful, since the higher up the hierarchy it rose, the more potential there would be for a conflict of interest with its parent. However, applying US successes such as the draft in Europe depends on there being sufficient political will.

Employing the guards

Politics and sport have long been closer than most people would like to admit, but the direct intervention of politicians or political appointees dependent on legislated powers is a recipe for disaster. Sport is only ever likely to find itself high on a parliamentary agenda in the nastiest kind of dictatorial regime where it is exploited for propaganda purposes. In a democratic society, the people's representatives have far more important things to deal with.

The t-shirt might say 'Football is life, the rest is just details', but does anybody really believe that? As a result, a politically based body would not be able to keep up with the rapid changes now taking place, because it would be necessary for it to get new laws expanding or modifying its powers almost every month. Any minister of sport, no matter how much of a fan of the game he or she is, remains a political appointee subject to the whims and reshuffles of government. Similarly, the current regulatory bodies such as the Football Association are too enmeshed in the present problems of the game to be able to step back and take on another role.

Consequently, what a game like football needs is an independent organization which nevertheless has strong links to government, but which is more importantly rooted in the game and freer to adapt to changing conditions. For example, the current problem perceived to be facing football is the activities of owners who control independent companies and who are thought to be seeking excessive profits. However, one near future revealed in this book would be of football clubs subsumed within conglomerates with very different definitions of how they would extract value from the team.

The US has its fair share of similar bureaucracies, but in sport applies a different approach. Each of its leading games has a broad administrative structure, but at their peaks sits one individual, a commissioner, with a remit to be dynamic, interventionist and, when required, downright ornery in dealing with owners.

He enjoys the power to do this because he is both part of the commercial structure and outside it. Commissioners are paid and employed by the different sporting bodies, but they are chosen and their appointments are confirmed by the US Congress. They can only be sacked with the approval of Congress. This does concentrate a frightening amount of power in the hands of one individual, although his responsibility to both sporting and political masters is intended to secure the system with checks and balances.

The landscape also gives the administrator a responsibility both to the pure business side of the game and to the fans/stakeholders in that sport. The example of franchising in the US proves that this power has not always been exercised well, but the principle is perhaps more important. And because of the commissioner's links to government, he can get results. When US sport faced a similar situation over competition law and sales of TV rights in the 1960s to that now confronting European clubs, it was the commissioners who secured various exemptions for leagues from US antitrust legislation by arguing that the only and disproportionate beneficiaries of breaking up a league-negotiated licensing structure would be the biggest sides. European competition commissioner Karel van Miert would do well to note that point.

So what does Europe offer as a possible variation on this theme? David Mellor may cast himself as the fan's champion because of his role as chairman of the UK's Football Task Force. But the organization itself suffers from serious limitations. It can make observations and recommendations but these have no legal force and, unlike a full formal government inquiry or commission, there is no suggestion that any such force will be given to them later through legislation. Many club owners already regard Mellor's Task Force with thinly disguised contempt. When he suggested that the directors of Bradford City might have sacked its black manager, Chris Kamara, on racial grounds, football boardrooms were united in condemnation. So these men will back him and his Task Force to the hilt if it seeks ways to combat overt racism and hooliganism or improve access for the disabled – how could they do otherwise? – but if it trespasses into commercial areas, the hue and cry will be loud, long and probably final.

However, were the broad church of interests represented on the Task Force – supporters' associations, players, clubs, managers, administrators, media and even referees – to be reconstituted and given more formal powers, it could promote the creation of a common ground and some common values more effectively. Within itself it would also function as an important conduit to overcome the obvious communication difficulties now damaging the football business.

The Football Association could argue that this is its own role, but the broadening of football's community of interest militates against this view. The FA has come to represent only a part of the game, not the whole. As such, its proposals for self-regulation could still go forward, but the need remains for a body above and beyond that.

Guarding the future

Regulation in major industries tends to be based on two principles: first, that the industry is a monopoly; and second, that the industry provides an important public service. Football scores on both of these criteria and therefore any regulatory organization would require a broad range of powers to deal with the scale of the task.

The game is obviously a monopoly in whichever country it is played, because there can only be one league champion and one major cup winner and only one national team that feeds off the football played. In addition, a company or collection of individuals cannot simply set up a football club and, for instance, join the Premiership. That is a restraint of trade in commercial terms and yet to allow anything else to happen would destroy the fundamental nature of the game.

Football also provides a public service. Its administrators admit as much when they talk publicly about the sport's ability to unite the nation. They also talk about the game's role in bringing together communities and reaching out to often-excluded sections of society. Politicians acknowledge the game's power by their current eagerness to be associated with success and failure on the football field. Businesses are keen to back football financially and to ride on its coat-tails for commercial gain. But they will also admit that the game can boost productivity in factories when the local team is winning and hit trade when the team is losing.

In the past this combination did not need an independent regulator – the FA could perform the task. Football was a professional game and it was therefore a business, but it was very much a small-scale industry. Today, football is still some way behind traditional sectors – manufacturing need not fear just yet – but it has grown substantially and at such a rate that without control it threatens to become a classic bubble economy. Money has irrevocably changed not merely the game but its nature, and hence intervention is required.

The tensions between fans and directors are the most high-profile examples of what creates the demand for external control. Manchester United and Brighton supporters alike are beginning to sound little different to the protestors who dogged British Gas about directors' bonuses and British water companies about their overall incompetence in the face of ever-growing profits. However, we should also spare a thought for the shareholders, many of whom are also season-ticket holders and long-time supporters of their nest-egg teams.

In most cases, the publicly quoted football clubs are still controlled by one individual or family that holds either a majority stake or controlling interest. Only Leicester City, Leeds United, Spurs and Manchester United could, arguably, put themselves outside this corral, while Newcastle United, as one example, remains largely under the influence of the Hall and Shepherd families. At Aston Villa, Doug Ellis has a controlling interest; Mike McDonald might have quit as chairman of Sheffield United but remains the largest shareholder. The list goes on and on.

For the sake of football's long-term relationship with the City of London – and after a rapid courtship and nuptials it has, for better or worse, embarked on an Irish-style, no-divorce relationship – an external regulator is also required to restore confidence. City firms and other investors do have their doubts that the game is poorly run or, at least, prevaricates over its true intentions and strategy.

So, even for good, sound business reasons, some form of regulator is required. The question is where his or her responsibilities should start and end.

Securing the objective

On one level, communication between clubs and those who invest in them as either shareholders or stakeholders (or both) needs to be encouraged and, if that doesn't work, forced. A regulator must oblige clubs to explain their decisions where they directly affect the consumer. Exploitation is occurring, but it is equally true that what sometimes looks like the grossest capitalism can be for the good of the team.

An excellent example here might be Nottingham Forest's decision to continue to charge Premier League entrance fees when it was relegated to the First Division. The extra money was sought to maintain its wage bill and to add to the squad so that the team could return to the top flight as soon as possible. It worked, but most supporters made noisy protests and suggested boycotts. How do they feel now?

A regulator could still set rates that clubs would be expected to charge according to their league and their ambitions. A club that declares that it is heading for the Premiership could therefore argue that its prices should be high, but would also be setting a more transparent target that its fans would expect it to hit or do its damnedest to hit even if it failed. Further forms of benchmarking could include pricing of merchandising and pricing of pay-TV subscriptions where one company held exclusive rights to a competition. The regulator could also set down terms for access to live TV coverage and highlights that would not take the game away from those on low incomes or from children who cannot watch late-night programming.

With a specific remit to consider the overall football economy, while the FA retained control of the game, a regulator could also apply pressure and establish conditions that would ensure a fairer distribution of income throughout the sport, rather than allowing an elite to apply Darwin's law at its most brutal.

There are certain issues, however, that would remain outside a regulator's control. Foremost among these would be salaries. Salary caps are unworkable, particularly given the game's global economy, but even on domestic levels because of inflationary pressures. Controlling individual salaries would be equally perverse, as it happens in no other industry – government found itself incapable of acting against the utilities' so-called fat cats, for example. Even if such powers were proposed, they would never stand the test of the courts.

A regulator would also have no right to intervene in transfers, as these are the most confidential commercial transactions most clubs are engaged in and, typically, need to be performed in private because of the vast sums involved. Business is business.

Finally, the regulator would also find that EU activity was outside his or her remit. However, while the EU seems surprisingly reluctant to state what its explicit football policy is, a regulator would be the UK game's advocate and representative. He or she could start by asking a few questions that remain unanswered about Brussels' future intentions.

Football, though, is more than just a business. It is a public resource. It is the one thing that Britain gave the world that the rest of the planet is relatively pleased with. It is the Copacabana beach, a tin can on a street in Heckmondwyke, and a table for Posh Spice and David Beckham at Le Gavroche. It all boils down to a question of balance and, unfortunately, there seems little chance that the game as it is currently constituted can provide that itself.

To date, the most sophisticated analysis of the game, its importance and its economy all in one is reckoned to have been Lord Justice Taylor's report on the Hillsborough disaster, the document that ironically began the financial revolution. Nevertheless, his astute observations about the relationship between fans and owners, the obsession with profit and an atmosphere of neglect presaging catastrophe still hold much force. Those who have read all of Taylor's observations say that they came about because he was an outsider. A regulator at the head of a community of football interests but with a dispassionate view of the current situation could, perhaps, take the game closer to stability.

CHAPTER ELEVEN

THE NUMBERS GAME

There is no reason why any football club should not be profitable.
Gerry Boon, doyen of football consultancy and
Deloitte & Touche partner, September 1997

ANY DISCUSSION OF FOOTBALL COMES DOWN TO STATISTICS AT
some point. The ones that should matter are those like games won
and lost, goals scored and conceded, and numbers of bookings. And
yet in the sport's new world, turnover, profits and income from
various activities are just as important. The ongoing sporting success of big teams like Manchester United is underlined by any
analysis of how the money flows in today's game. Pitch and profit
are fundamentally and inextricably linked. However, the story that
football's financials tell today is even blunter, highlighting the
growing gap between the haves and have-nots.

What follows is an analysis of the market performance of 20 of
the 21 British football clubs quoted on either the main London Stock
Exchange or the smaller Alternative Investment Market. These clubs
have been chosen because they operate to stricter financial reporting
requirements than non-quoted clubs and because those regulations
mean that they issue more contemporaneous figures – Deloitte &
Touche recognizes in its comprehensive survey of all UK clubs'
accounts that the posting of reports at Companies House lags at least
one year behind the season most recently completed.

The 20 clubs featured here are shown in Table 1 (in order of
their market capitalization as of July 1998).

Table 1   Quoted UK football clubs ranked by market capitalization

	Club	Market cap. July 1998 (£m)	Competition 1997–8
1	Manchester United	433	FA Premier League
2	Chelsea (Chelsea Village)	117	FA Premier League
3	Newcastle United	104	FA Premier League
4	Tottenham Hotspur	67.5	FA Premier League
5	Celtic	62.4	SFL Premier Division
6	Aston Villa	54.4	FA Premier League
7	Leeds United (Leeds Sporting)	48.3	FA Premier League
8	Sunderland	32.4	FL Division One
9	Bolton Wanderers (Burnden Leisure)	22.2	FA Premier League
10	Nottingham Forest	21.4	FL Division One
11	Southampton (Southampton Leisure Holdings)	18.8	FA Premier League
12	Charlton Athletic	17.0	FL Division One
13	Birmingham City	16.8	FL Division One
14	Leicester City	14.3	FA Premier League
15	Sheffield United	13.6	FL Division One
16	West Bromwich Albion	9.8	FL Division One
17	Heart of Midlothian	9.8	SFL Premier Division
18	Preston North End	9.0	FL Division Two
19	Queens Park Rangers (Loftus Road)	7.4	FL Division One
20	Swansea City (Silver Shield)	2.4	FL Division Three

In each case, the analysis is based on the most recent publication of half-year (or interim) rather than full-year results as of July 1998, with the exception of the section on salaries. Interims have been used because they represent the most recent statistics published by all these clubs and also because one club – Nottingham Forest – has not yet been quoted for a sufficient period to produce full-year figures as a plc. One club, Millwall, has been excluded. Millwall's most recent figures cover a 14-month period, following the club's forced move into administration and subsequent rescue by a consortium under Theo Paphitis, owner of the Ryman stationers operation. As such, it does not offer an opportunity to compare like with like.

Several other caveats should be added because of the use of interim figures. Most of the statistics quoted will show slight differences in gate receipts, TV income and some other data because of variations in accounting periods and the frequent case that a club may well have played more or less than half of its home games by the mid-point of the season due to vagaries in the fixture lists. Moreover, TV money cited in half-year figures does not include merit awards, which are dependent on a club's position at the end of the season. Similarly, interim figures are typically unaudited and so some minor corrections may occur when final-year figures are released.

It is also important to bear in mind that the figures relate to the leagues in which these clubs were competing during the 1997–8 season. At its conclusion, one of the 20 clubs, Bolton Wanderers, was relegated to Football League Division One, while two others, Nottingham Forest and Charlton Athletic, were promoted to the FA Premier League. Of the 20 clubs, nine were in the English Premiership, seven were in English Division One, two were in the Scottish Premier Division (which has since broken away to form the Scottish Premier League), and there is one each from English Divisions Two and Three.

Taking an overview, therefore, these results offer an opportunity to assess the state of and trends in football generally, rather than giving absolutely precise pictures of the situation facing any particular club (although some specific conclusions can and will still be drawn).

The results analysis splits into several key sections:

○ Turnover
○ Profitability
○ Performance of selected divisions
○ Gate receipts
○ Merchandising
○ Television
○ Salaries

The final part details share performance according to the theoretical investment of £1000 in each club as of Friday 8 August 1997 cashed in as of Tuesday 26 May 1998, corresponding to trading immediately before and after the first and last days of the 1997–8 season.

Turnover

Table 2   *British quoted football clubs ranked by turnover*

	Club	Interim turnover 1997–8 (£m)	Interim turnover 1996–7 (£m)	Share of total (%)
1	Manchester Utd	51.6	50.1	20.8
2	Chelsea	36.6	10.4	14.7
3	Newcastle Utd	31.0	24.6	12.5
4	Tottenham Hotspur	19.6	17.1	7.9
5	Celtic	15.5	12.5	6.2
6	Leeds Utd	13.7	11.7	5.5
7	Leicester City	12.0	n/a	4.8
8	Aston Villa	11.9	9.4	4.8
9	Bolton Wanderers	8.5	5.4	3.4
10	Sunderland	8.0	5.2	3.2
11	Southampton	6.4	n/a	2.6
12	Sheffield Utd	5.5	4.4	2.2
13	Nottingham Forest	5.1	n/a	2.1
14	Birmingham City	4.7	4.6	1.9
15	Queens Park Rangers	4.3	3.1	1.8
16	West Bromwich Albion	4.2	3.4	1.7
17	Swansea City	3.3	1.4	1.4
18	Charlton Athletic	2.5	2.1	1.0
19	Preston North End	2.2	2.4	0.9
20	Hearts	1.8	2.4	0.7
	Total	248.4		
	Averages			
	(including Man Utd)	12.4		
	(excluding Man Utd)	10.4		

The first conclusion to be drawn from any analysis of turnover is the extent to which Manchester United is so far ahead of any other rival club. This has been demonstrated most notably by Deloitte &

Touche, in the consultants' analysis of all league accounts, but the fact that United maintains its preeminence here is even more striking because the clubs to which it is being compared are those that are also thought to be at the cutting edge of football's financial revolution, the other fully quoted plcs.

The Old Trafford club has a total turnover that accounts for more than 20 per cent of all the cash generated by all the listed sides, it is £15 million ahead of its nearest plc rival, and more than four times the sector average. United's dominance is such that the industry average drops by £2 million – a greater turnover than Hearts has in total – if it is factored out of the analysis.

However, the average also tells a story. Of the 20 clubs, 13 are below average if United is taken into account, and this drops to only 12 if that club is put aside as a special case. Share of turnover also tells a chilling tale for smaller clubs. The top three clubs in this ranking account for almost 50 per cent of all the sales made by quoted sides, and the FA Premier League's total share is 77 per cent, even though as a simple number of clubs it represents less than half of the sample.

Gulfs within the Premiership itself also start to become clear. The league member with the lowest turnover in this analysis is Southampton at £6.4 million, less than one-eighth of what Man United earns in a half season.

The clubs at the top of the list all have similar qualities. They are big brand-name clubs and each has had some success – even though Newcastle United's 1997–8 season was poor in the league, the side did make the FA Cup Final. They have also been big spenders in more ways than one. For all the money that Chelsea, for example, might spend on acquiring new players like Pierluigi Casiraghi and Marcel Desailly, it has also invested heavily in its ground, building new stands at Stamford Bridge alongside a hotel and leisure complex. As this complex has begun to open up, it has translated into the club's results by making a significant contribution to a £25 million-plus rise in turnover.

Interestingly, the results for some of those clubs below the absolute summit also tend to include mention of not merely team investment, but also property development. Bolton's parent, Burnden Leisure, commented in its figures that revenues from its new state-of-the-art Reebok Stadium were yet to pass fully through to the bottom line, because elements such as an exhibition centre were still to open. Aston Villa mentioned its acquisition of land and securing of planning permission for developing the Villa Park site. Even Man United appeared to be following for once when it announced that it was to participate in a hotel development near its ground as a minority shareholder, although in terms of redeveloping its stadium and opening themed restaurants and megastores at the ground it is already ahead of the game.

Diversification to boost the bottom line is a growing theme, although supporters may worry that this will lead directors to take their eyes off what is happening on the pitch, which remains the main definition of financial success.

Two other factors appear from these figures. First is the obvious financial difficulty which Scottish clubs have faced in contrast to their English rivals. Heart of Midlothian – which competed for the Scottish championship almost until the end of the season in 1997–8 – has a lower half-year turnover even than Preston North End. To some extent, this is accounted for by a restructuring that the club undertook during the 1997–8 financial year, but even using the figure from before this – the previous half year's £2.2 million – it would still find itself towards the bottom of the ranking. Celtic, meanwhile, is a widely and passionately supported side, yet its fifth position will undoubtedly surprise many observers. Like Manchester United it is a global brand, but it achieves less than a third of its rival's sales.

The second factor to note is the number of clubs with small turnovers – something that once might have been considered £10 million, but is now judged nearer £25 million – and which will therefore have difficulty in attracting attention from City investors. As author Alex Fynn has pointed out, many football clubs turn over about the same and sometimes even less than the £5 million seen at larger supermarkets over a full year. Indeed, if one doubles the figures above to get a rough idea of annualized performance, this can be said of 11 of the 20 quoted sides, those at the £2.6 million level and below. Having entered the City league, these clubs have an absolute need to build their income if they are to be taken seriously.

Profitability

Table 3   British quoted football clubs ranked by profits

Club		Interim profit 1997–8 (£m)	Interim profit 1996–7 (£m)
1	Manchester Utd	14.9	19.5
2	Newcastle Utd	11.6	6.4
3	Celtic	7.7	5.2
4	Tottenham Hotspur	4.0	6.0
5	Aston Villa	2.2	(3.7)
6	Leicester City	1.5	0.1
7	Sunderland	0.52	1.1
8	West Bromwich Albion	0.44	0.3
9	Chelsea	0.19	(0.40)
10	Swansea City	(0.2)	0.08
11	Preston North End	(0.42)	0.002
12	Southampton	(0.54)	(0.08)
13	Charlton Athletic	(0.59)	(1.46)
14	Leeds Utd	(1.1)	(2.3)
15	Hearts	(1.3)	(0.9)
16	Nottingham Forest	(2.4)	n/a
17	Birmingham City	(2.6)	2.7
18	Sheffield Utd	(3.1)	(1.3)
19	Queens Park Rangers	(5.7)	(4.4)
20	Bolton Wanderers	(10.3)	(4.0)

Averages
    (including Man Utd)   0.74
    (excluding Man Utd)   0.05

There are no prizes for guessing which is Britain's most profitable football team, nor for being able to explain why it holds this position. But what do these figures have to offer in more general terms? The first key observation is that even when clubs go to the various stock markets, they do not automatically start to make profits or, indeed, pay dividends to directors and shareholders. Some 11 of the 20 clubs reported a loss in their last half-year figures.

Average club performance is also modest. The mean quoted club made a half-year profit of £740,000, although 14 clubs were below this measure. Pulling the same trick as with turnover and taking Manchester United out of this analysis cuts the average drastically to a mere £50,000. Go one stage further by taking out the other eight-figure performer, Newcastle, and the average performance becomes a £650,000 loss.

In many cases there are mitigating circumstances. Bolton (Burnden Leisure) reported the biggest loss at £10.3 million, although this was largely against costs involved in building its new ground. Similarly, Leeds United (Leeds Sporting) was in the middle of an expansion programme to create new facilities including an arena at Elland Road, while Preston North End was upgrading its Deepdale ground to include, among other things, England's Football Museum.

However, some of the losses must be seen as a result of betting on future success in a very uncertain market. Only two of the Football League clubs reported a profit, and of those that made a loss some of the heaviest figures were suffered by clubs that were trying to secure promotion from the First Division, such as Nottingham Forest (out £2.4 million), Birmingham City (£2.6 million), Sheffield United (£3.1 million) and Queens Park Rangers (Loftus Road, £5.7 million).

In each case, hefty wage bills and other costs involved in trying to secure one of the First Division's promotion spots were cited in part as explanations for the figures. Yet, as the results at the end of the season showed, only certain clubs could ultimately go up – in 1997–8 quoted Forest and Charlton were accompanied by Middlesbrough – leaving the rest arguably to face equally tough levels of expenditure the following season.

Profits outside the Premiership are hard to achieve, although to give credit where it is due Sunderland did well, largely because of its massive and frequently underestimated bedrock support. Of the other First Division teams, West Bromwich Albion did achieve a modest profit, but was coming under attack towards the end of the season from fans for not showing enough ambition. That club had been one of the early pacesetters in the First Division, but its philosophy of prudent financial bookkeeping was seen as translating into a failure to invest sufficiently in the squad during the latter half of the competition. WBA also lost its manager, Ray Harford, to rivals QPR around the season's mid-point.

Among analysts, QPR's holding company Loftus Road was seen at this point as perhaps the most problematic of the quoted First Division sides. Investment in the squad did not translate into results on the pitch and, rather than bidding for even a play-off place, the club ended 1997–8 in the relegation dogfight. QPR's difficulties were compounded by the fact that the holding company also includes the Wasps rugby union side, which carried a wage bill even more in disproportion to the revenues that its sport was generating following a transition from amateur to professional status.

In the longer term, the benefits intended to underpin the Loftus Road business plan – combined administration for two professional sides, ground sharing, economies of scale for marketing and merchandising – may begin to pay off, but it could be a long haul. The wages vs income problem that exists in both rugby and football was still some way from being resolved as this book was being written. TV money for rugby, in particular, is proving hard to come by and in 1997 the UK's professional clubs took the almost unprecedented step of essentially paying a broadcaster, Channel Five, to carry a highlights programme alongside BSkyB's exclusive live coverage. The clubs came to believe that they needed exposure on free-to-air television to market their game as it took its first steps into true professionalism. What was happening during 1997 and 1998 at Loftus Road was therefore taken as something of a cautionary tale for those who talk about the multisports enterprise, incorporating holdings in a number of different markets to maximize revenues.

A final point to make about profitability is that this ranking does see Celtic begin to rise towards the top of the financial table, a more appropriate place for a club of this size.

Performance in selected areas

'Income streams' is a mantra in football's late-twentieth-century boardrooms. Existing ones must be grown, new ones must be found. Most of the prospectuses for clubs that floated during 1995 and 1996 included references not just to broadcast and sponsorship income, but also to such strange and wonderful things as 'pouring rights' (in plain English, the right to serve beers within a ground).

What follows is an analysis of three different areas which clubs now present to the City as evidence of their ability to tap into the supporters' pockets. These are television, merchandising and, the most traditional rivulet of all, ticket sales.

Television

Table 4   Television income earned by selected quoted clubs over half-year 1997–8

	Club	Interim income (£m)	Share of interim turnover (%)
1	Manchester United	7.9	15.3
2	Newcastle United	6.9	22.3
3	Tottenham Hotspur	4.7	24.0
4	Leicester City	4.3	35.8
5	Leeds United	2.4	17.5
6	Southampton	2.0	31.2
7	Celtic	1.8	11.6
8	Queens Park Rangers	1.5	34.8
9	Sunderland	1.4	17.5

We are often told that the idiot box has been a smart move for football. Table 4 shows the money earned by the nine clubs in the sample that broke down their TV income in their interim results and how that could be converted into a percentage of their interim turnovers.

In five instances, broadcaster cash accounted for more than 20 per cent of turnover and in three cases that proportion exceeded 30 per cent. That the higher percentages were achieved at what are considered small to medium-sized clubs tends to reemphasize the point that at that level there is a developing dependency culture on what television can deliver financially. In this respect, it should also be noted that the sums gathered by Sunderland and QPR would have greatly exceeded those for other First Division clubs, as both include a sizeable proportion made up from so-called parachute payments by BSkyB. These are given to relegated Premier League clubs in the first two years after their departure from the top flight. Such sizeable contributors to overall turnover will be sorely missed by these clubs if they cannot return to the Premiership before the payments run out, and show why clubs that do fall badly soon find financial hardship at their shoulder.

A second important aspect that needs to be noted for small and medium-sized clubs is that the proportions from TV by the end of the full year/season would be higher. Payments received at the interim point do not include merit awards – roughly 25 per cent of the BSkyB pot – which cannot be allocated until a club's final league position is known. An interim share of, say, 30 per cent could therefore be annualized to something closer to 35–40 per cent once that final element is added.

Such economics show why City analysts treat clubs in the lower half of the Premier League as well as those in the First Division with caution. Time and again, there is a demonstrable use of TV cash as virtually the only foundation in the accounts. This immediately raises the question as to what a club will do not just to deliver profits, but also to meet its costs if the really big bucks from the Premier League are taken away.

By contrast, two of the strongest commercial clubs – Manchester United and Celtic – do not appear proportionately to be so dependent on the broadcasters. The United result for this period included the first fruits of the club's participation in the UEFA Champions' League in addition to what it received for coverage of domestic fixtures. Nevertheless, TV only accounted for 15.3 per cent of interim turnover. Celtic, meanwhile, received very little from the old Scottish Football League deal in comparison, but the figure was boosted by BBC money for its UEFA Cup against Liverpool. Its 11.6 per cent result can therefore be seen as both an example of why the big Scottish teams have railed against their commercial treatment in TV deals and of the broader base of Celtic's revenue performance as a big side.

So just how smart is TV? The answer has to be that a club cannot treat it as the be-all and end-all, even though access to BSkyB revenues was one of the main selling points for many of the wave of flotations in 1995 and 1996. That football prices have almost universally declined since that time is, in part, down to growing scepticism about those clubs regarded as having placed too much emphasis on this single income stream. Diversification, almost in a defensive manner, does matter.

Merchandising

In its initial stages, such diversification was primarily seen in terms of merchandising. Compared to building hotels, conference centres and other stadium upgrades, boosting this side of a club's commercial activities is less demanding of capital investment. Bricks and mortar cost pounds, shillings and pence; setting up a slicker souvenir and replica kit operation, by contrast, would still involve some expenditure, but much of the cost would be underwritten by a clothing manufacturer which would pay the club for the right to produce the products.

Table 5   Merchandising income earned by selected clubs over half-year 1997–8

	Club	Interim income (£m)	Share of interim turnover (%)
1	Manchester United	15.6	30.2
2	Newcastle United	5.5	17.7
3	Chelsea	3.7	10.1
4	Celtic	2.7	17.4
5	Tottenham Hotspur	2.3	11.7
6	Leeds United	2.1	15.3
7	Aston Villa	1.8	15.1
8	Queens Park Rangers	1.1	25.5
9	Sunderland	1.1	13.7
10	Leicester City	0.9	7.5

According to the proportional measure applied to TV money, it looks here as though Manchester United is too dependent on merchandising, with its 30.2 per cent performance. And yet such accusations have a hollow ring when one considers just how far ahead of its quoted rivals the club is. The United brand is – with due respect to Ronaldo – a phenomenon, and the club exploits this fact with ruthless professionalism. Even though, horror of horrors, the 1997–8 interim figure for merchandising is actually 11.4 per cent down on that for the same period of the year before (£17.6 million), the club still earns three times as much as Newcastle United, which has an equally devoted, if not quite so global, following.

Old Trafford's performance, therefore, is the benchmark. Even if other clubs acknowledge that they do not have the same kind of history to draw on, they all realize that they need to get closer to those kinds of divisional turnover. But if that is the financial wisdom, then the response to be drawn from these figures is that clubs still have a lot to do. All the figures quoted above were increases on the comparable period of the season before, albeit some modest ones, but United's merchandising income alone is greater than the entire interim turnovers of 16 of the quoted sides.

If there is a sense in which the other teams have maybe missed the point, it is in that they may be too dependent on replica kits as the lead items in their range. Chelsea, which only had its Stamford Bridge megastore open for a small part of the reporting period, certainly is thinking along new lines and trying to broaden the range and appeal of what it stocks. The reality, though, is that football is still merely part of the way along this particular learning curve.

The fact that United's sales did fall is significant. It shows that the football as fashion problem is there even at the very summit, and that clubs do not merely need to show more imagination in their basic activities, but also have to look continually for ways to reinvent their approach. Merchandising is a volatile marketplace where participants often find that they have to run just to stand still. It is not something that will, as has been assumed in some quarters, just continue to grow and grow.

What is more, fans as consumers are beginning to resist the more outrageous attempts by clubs to tap into their disposable income. Therefore, the market may still appear to be increasing in size but, critically, it is doing so from a very low base in many cases, so that the depressing effect of customers' resistance (and, in some cases, distaste) may have been seriously underestimated.

Gate receipts

Table 6   Gate receipts earned by selected clubs over half-year 1997–8

	Club	Interim income (£m)	Share of interim turnover (%)
1	Manchester United	19.0	36.8
2	Newcastle United	13.7	44.2
3	Tottenham Hotspur	8.8	44.9
4	Celtic	7.0	45.1
5	Leeds United	4.1	29.9
6	Aston Villa	3.7	31.1
7	Leicester City	3.5	56.5
7	Sunderland	3.5	43.7
9	Nottingham Forest	2.1	41.2
10	Southampton	1.9	29.7
11	Queens Park Rangers	1.5	34.9
12	Hearts	1.2	66.7

Before making any other comment, it should be said that half-year figures for gate receipts are both revealing and deceptive for very much the same reason: season-ticket sales.

Renewals obviously flood in during the summer and therefore the extent to which any club with a large regular following can build on the kind of numbers seen above by the year end is limited. Newcastle United and Southampton, as two examples, are virtually sold out in their home supporters' stands from the first game because of limited capacity compared to demand. The final proportions are therefore certain to drop somewhat from the apparently high levels seen above.

At the same time, these high proportions do show that season-ticket sales are generally healthy and, as Aston Villa chairman Doug Ellis has pointed out, this is of great value to a club in terms of cashflow for its development activities across the remainder of the season. It is also a good sign across Premier League football, at least, that there is a continued willingness among the punters to buy into New Football.

In this context, some caution should be attached to occasional comments about gate receipts mattering less and less and a day coming when clubs will pay 'rent-a-mob' for supporters to keep things looking good for TV cameras.

From a cultural point of view, in fact, the reverse is true. The strongest across-the-board growth in ticket income is now being delivered by setting aside parts of a ground where 'fans' will pay more. Manchester United chairman Professor Sir Roland Smith said, on unveiling the club's results, that 'improved revenue derived from a lower number of matches [at Old Trafford in the reporting period] reflects *the benefits of price rises and a further 1,000 executive seats being available this season*' (our italics).

In plain English, traditional supporters are being priced out to deliver the kinds of performance that City investors demand from this Cinderella part of the football economy. Executive boxes are only the beginning when, as the good professor observed, 1000 seats can now attract premium prices. Many of those in this bracket at the Old Trafford stand, irony of ironies, are slap bang in the middle of what used to be known and feared as the Stretford End. And United is not alone. Chelsea now has a basic £1025 season ticket and some Newcastle fans acknowledge that the only way to hope of seeing their team is to put on a suit and pay through the nose. Aston Villa, meanwhile, turns over its themed restaurant, the Corner Flag, to corporate hospitality on match days.

The problem is that, in business terms, the squeeze on ticket prices has made absolute sense. The figures add up and are stronger than merchandising and, for much of the season, even television. Some traditions do not die, but they can get a lot more expensive. The question mark that remains is how much clubs can charge and, as the 1998–9 season saw prices leap again, there were the first signs that some long-term supporters are prepared to say 'no'.

Salaries

Having seen the money go into football, there is only one place to look to see it going straight back out again. Players' wages are the current financial curse on the game, as they rise beyond any apparent control.

This section differs from the rest of the financial analysis in that it uses figures extracted from the Annual Reports of the quoted clubs, essentially the only time that companies can provide a completely accurate view on the topic. It should be remembered, then, that these numbers cover the 1997 financial year, and that all the clubs surveyed have said in statements that further substantial rises are also likely to appear in their final 1998 statistics.

The first big number to keep in mind here is £19,750. According to the Office for National Statistics, that was the UK average salary in 1997. Another useful benchmark is 3.5 per cent. That was the average wage increase during the same year. Averages have been used as indicators because football clubs do not break down what playing staff earn as opposed to other employees – although if they were to do so in future, it might shame some of the Premier League's overpaid talent into behaving a tad more responsibly.

One view of the figures in Table 7 would be to suggest that there must be an awful lot of very well-paid stewards out there. The reality, though, is that the averages are inflated to such high levels because of the six- and seven-figure wage packets earned not just by superstars but throughout football teams. In contrast, many of the backroom staff at clubs will, anecdotal evidence suggests, be lucky if they are picking up the national average. Some will be working on minimum wage.

The fact remains that clubs, particularly in English football, are being forced into paying top dollar. Again, it is a strange state of affairs to see a club the size of Celtic not just below FA Premiership teams, but even a clutch of First Division sides such as West Brom and the recently promoted Charlton. These figures simply ram home the point made, we admit repeatedly, in this book about football's chronic inability to control its costs.

Table 7   Selected quoted clubs ranked by average salary

	Staff costs 1997 (£m)	Staff employed	Average salary	Increase in wage bill 97/96 (%)
Chelsea Village	14.9	125	£119,200	61.6
Tottenham Hotspur	12.1	165	£73,333	5.2
Aston Villa	10.1	178	£56,742	32.0
Leeds United	10.8	191	£56,544	n/a
Newcastle United	17.1	311	£54,984	−12.3
Manchester United	21.8	405	£53,827	70.3
Birmingham City	4.9	95	£51,579	2.5
Queens Park Rangers	6.7	145	£46,207	n/a
Southampton	2.8	61	£45,902	n/a
Nottingham Forest	8.0	179	£44,693	31.0
Charlton Athletic	3.0	84	£35,238	17.0
West Bromwich Albion	3.1	88	£35,000	12.8
Celtic	8.7	320	£27,187	25.7
Hearts	2.8	98	£28,571	24.0
Sheffield United	3.6	126	£28,254	n/a
Leicester City	1.2	77	£15,584	n/a
Preston North End	2.1	142	£14,788	51.1

Even clubs that preach wage restraint, such as Spurs and Man United, were carrying frightening staff averages in 1997, and both acknowledged that their salary outgoings had leapt again in 1998.

There is very little to say, except to stare at Table 7 in shock and horror (and possibly wish that God had blessed you with super-naturally good sporting skills). The situation is, quite simply, insane. But what should also be clear to the clubs is the trickle-down effect. West Brom is a club that tries to control costs and operate prudently, but the data makes it clear that it has been sucked into a situation where a cash-rich Premiership has set a dangerously high benchmark at the summit that is inflating costs at every step down the leagues.

The costs of staying in the Premiership, of trying to join the elite, but even of just trying to develop a team that is in equitable relationship to those around it – these are damaging football. These levels of expenditure are not sustainable in the longer term, and the majority of senior football executives recognize that. Yet when all the 1998 annual reports are in, it will be clear that little has so far been done to stem the tide.

In this environment, City analysts have been quick to cool on football. Frankly, who can blame them?

Football and the stock market

The typical minimum investment in any quoted company is about £1000. So what would have happened if you had put some of your savings on any of these clubs during the 1997–8 season? The figures have been calculated against the different clubs' share prices at the close of trading on 8 August 1997 (the Friday before the English season kicked off) and 26 May 1998 (the Tuesday after the Spring Bank Holiday brought the curtain back down).

Table 8   Season-end value of £1000 invested in selected quoted clubs throughout 1997–8

Club	Value of stake	% change
Charlton Athletic	1320.75	32.1
Sunderland	1204.82	20.5
Nottingham Forest	951.61	−4.8
Manchester United	910.77	−8.9
Hearts	877.27	−12.3
Leeds United	826.09	−17.4
Celtic	818.18	−18.1
Southampton	801.14	−19.9
Preston North End	796.30	−20.4
Swansea City	750.00	−25.0
Birmingham City	729.16	−27.1
Newcastle United	683.79	−31.6
Tottenham Hotspur	683.42	−31.7
Chelsea	652.36	−34.8
West Bromwich Albion	647.06	−35.3
Aston Villa	581.81	−41.8
Sheffield United	556.52	−44.4
Leicester City	509.26	−49.1
Bolton Wanderers	454.54	−54.6
Queens Park Rangers	350.00	−65.0

The overriding message from this last ranking is that investors are not impressed. Some of the steeper falls can be explained in simple terms of performance, both on the pitch and in the boardroom. Bolton paid the price for being relegated from the Premiership, while QPR was blasted for its flirtation with removal from Division One. The antics of Newcastle directors Douglas Hall and Freddie Shepherd, by contrast, only added to serious City doubts about the way in which the club is run. But, such exceptions aside, it is clear that the markets view British football with a fair degree of scepticism.

Only two teams would have earned you money. Charlton was, to be honest, nobody's tip for promotion from the First Division when the season kicked off, so its growth in value came from a low base. Sunderland, the team Charlton beat in a playoff, was another special case, as its share price was hammered down to a low level during the pre-season period after its relegation from the Premier League in May 1997. By the time the following season kicked off, it had plenty of room to grow back to a more natural level. Needless to say, you would have been wise to sell on 26 May because its Wembley defeat did see a slide resume.

By contrast, Manchester United, which is supposedly a 'blue-chip' stock valued over and above its connection to football, saw nearly 10 per cent clipped off its market value. Again, this was partly its punishment for having one of those rare seasons where the club seemed incapable of winning anything. All the same, this remains proof, as if any were needed, that no club is immune from the critical atmosphere. Indeed, Chelsea found that it could open its leisure development, win the Coca-Cola Cup and then go on to take the European Cup Winners' Cup and still find that investors gave it a harder time than Spurs, which spent the whole season fighting off relegation and what at times seemed like the threat of total meltdown.

This book has attempted to question the business case underpinning football's so-called development, although a pretty clear message along the same lines is already coming out of the merchant banks and institutions. The game must get itself sorted out, clarify its tactics and reinvigorate its battle plan. It is an irony of the entire situation that fans and the financial men in suits they so frequently berate seem to be saying the same thing, and yet the clubs still will not listen.

But take a look at the numbers and ask yourselves what is going wrong. It is only half-time, but there is still a lot to do in the second half.

SOURCES AND BIBLIOGRAPHY

Primary sources

Direct reference has been made in this book to the content of the following books and reports:

Boon, G. (ed.) (1998) *Deloitte & Touche Annual Review of Football Finance*, Deloitte Touche Tohmatsu

Butcher, C. (ed.) (1998) *The Football Business*, Mintel

Fynn, A. and Davidson, H. (1996) *Dream On*, Simon & Schuster

Gorman, J. and Calhoun, K. (1994) *The Name of the Game: The Business of Sports*, John Wiley & Sons

Graham, G. and Giller, N. (1995) *The Glory and the Grief*, Andre Deutsch

Inquiry by the Rt Hon Lord Justice Taylor (1989) *The Hillsborough Stadium Disaster: Interim Report*, Cm765, HMSO

Inquiry by the Rt Hon Lord Justice Taylor (1990) *The Hillsborough Stadium Disaster: Final Report*, Cm962, HMSO

Keegan, K. (1997) *My Autobiography*, Little Brown

LeGrand, J. and New, B. (1998) *Fair Game? Tackling Monopoly in Sports Broadcasting*, DEMOS

Malam, C. (1997) *The Magnificent Obsession*, Bloomsbury

Nichols, P. and Sharp, M. (1997) *BBC Radio 5 Live Sports Yearbook 1998*, Oddball

Rottenberg, S. (1956) The Baseball Players Labour Market, *The Journal of Political Economy*, vol 64

Sharp, M., Burnett, A. and Tracey, P. (1997) *Here We Go (Again)*, Charterhouse Tilney Equity Research

Sharpe, G. (1997) *Gambling on Goals*, Mainstream

Smith, Sir John and LeJune, M. (1998) *Football: Its Values, Finances and Reputation*, The Football Association

Sugar, B. (ed.) (1997) *I Hate the Dallas Cowboys*, St Martin's Griffin

Sugden, J. and Tomlinson, A. (1998) *FIFA and the Contest for World Football*, Polity Press

Williams, J. (ed.) (1998) *FA Premier League Supporters Survey*, FA Premier League

The following publications were used as direct references for material in this book:

The Mirror, As, The Daily Express, The Daily Mail, The Daily Telegraph, El Mundo Deportivo, L'Equipe, The Economist, The Financial Times, France Football, The Guardian, The Independent, FourFourTwo, Goal, Investors Chronicle, Kicker, Marca, Match of the Day Magazine, The Observer, Soccer Investor, Sport First, Sunday Business, The Sun, The Sunday Telegraph, The Sunday Times, The Times, Total Football, Total Sport, When Saturday Comes, World Soccer.

The following television programmes also provided background information:

Panorama (BBC/Ray Fitzwalter Associates – adaptation of David Conn's *The Football Business*), *Premier Passions* (BBC), *Hold the Back Page* (BSkyB, various editions), *The Footballers Football Show* (BSkyB, various editions). Substantial recourse was also made to programmes across the entire output of BBC Radio 5 Live.

Some share prices and other financial material were drawn from information published via the Internet-based ESI share information service (http://www.esi.co.uk). Other major Internet resources included Soccernet (http://www.soccernet.com), Yahoo UK news (http://www.yahoo.co.uk) and Infoseek news (www.infoseek.com).

Secondary sources

The following books and reports were used in research for this book:
Allan, D. and Bevington, A. (1996) *Doom to Boom*, Mainstream
Bassett, D. and Bale, B. (1997) *Harry's Game*, Breedon
Boon, G. (ed.) (1997) *Deloitte & Touche Annual Review of Football Finance*, Deloitte Touche Tohmatsu International
Bose, M. (1996) *False Messiah*, Andre Deutsch
Burns, J. (1996) *The Hand of God*, Bloomsbury
Calleja, B. (1997) *La Guerra 'Incivil' del Futbol*, Plaza & Janes
Carder, T. and Harris, R. (1993) *Seagulls! The Story of Brighton & Hove Albion F.C.*, Goldstone
Cheeseman, D., Lyons, A. and Tichler, M. (eds) (1997) *Power Corruption and Pies*, Two Heads
Claridge, S. (1997) *Tales from the Boot Camps*, Victor Gallancz
Conn, D. (1997) *The Football Business*, Mainstream
Cooke, A. (1994) *The Economics of Leisure and Sport*, International Thomson Business Press
Cresswell, P. and Evans, S. (1997) *European Football: A Fans' Handbook*, Rough Guide/Penguin
Crick, M. and Smith, D. (1989) *The Betrayal of a Legend*, Pelham
Dalglish, K. and Winter, H. (1996) *Dalglish: My Autobiography*, Headline
Davies, H. (1972/1992) *The Glory Game*, Mainstream
Davies, P. (ed.) (1996) *From Fergie Out! to the Double Double*, A&C
Ferguson, A. and Meek, D. (1997) *A Will to Win*, Andre Deutsch
Fynn, A. and Guest, L. (1991) *Heroes and Villains*, Penguin
Fynn, A. and Guest, L. (1994) *Out of Time*, Simon & Schuster
Fynn, A., Guest, L. and Law, P. (1989) *The Secret Life of Football*, Queen Anne Press
Glanvill, R. (1994) *Sir Matt Busby: A Tribute*, Virgin
Hammond, M. (ed.) (1996) *The European Football Yearbook 96/97*, Sports Projects
Hammond, M. (ed.) (1997) *The European Football Yearbook 97/98*, Sports Projects
Harding, J. (1991) *For the Good of the Game*, Robson
Harte, C. (1997) *A Sportwriter's Year*, London Sports Reporting Agency

Horton, E. (1997) *Moving the Goalposts*, Mainstream
Inglis, S. (1996) *Football Grounds of Britain*, CollinsWillow
Inglis, S. (1997) *Villa Park 100 Years*, Sports Projects
Jenkins, D. and Holly, J. (1996) *Survival of the Fattest 2*, Red Card
Jenkins, D. and Holly, J. (1997) *Survival of the Fattest 3*, Red Card
Johnson, A. (1994) *The Battle for Manchester City*, Mainstream
Kelly, S.F. (1992) *A Game of 2 Halves*, Kingswood
Kelly, S.F. (1996) *The Pick of the Season 1995–96*, Mainstream
Kelly, S.F. (1997) *The Pick of the Season 1996–97*, Mainstream
Kuper, S. (1994) *Football Against the Enemy*, Orion
Kuper, S. (ed.) (1997) *Perfect Pitch: Home Ground*, Headline
Kuper, S. (ed.) (1998) *Perfect Pitch: Foreign Field*, Headline
Lambert, C. (1995) *The Boss*, Pride of Place
Llaurado, J. (1994) *El Barça D'un Club, D'un Pais*, Columna
McClair, B. and Wooldridge, J. (1997) *Odd Man Out*, Andre Deutsch
Morgan, J. (1997) *Glory for Sale*, Bancroft Press
Murray, B. (1998) *The Old Firm in the New Age*, Mainstream
Nelson, G. and Fowles, A. (1995) *Left Foot Forward*, Headline
Nelson, G. and Fowles, A. (1997) *Left Foot in the Grave*, CollinsWillow
Nieto, M.A. (1996) *Negocio Redondo*, Temas de Hoy
North, S. and Hodson, P. (1997) *Build a Bonfire*, Mainstream
Redhead, S. (1997) *Post-Fandom and the Millennial Blues*, Routledge
Rollin, G. (ed.) (1996) *Rothmans Football Yearbook 1996–97*,
    Rothmans/Headline
Rollin, G. (ed.) (1997) *Rothmans Football Yearbook 1997–98*,
    Rothmans/Headline
Rollin, G. (ed.) (1998) *Rothmans Football Yearbook 1998–99*,
    Rothmans/Headline
Royle, N.J. (ed.) (1996) *A Book of Two Halves*, Victor Gollancz
Scully, G.W. (1995) *The Market Structure of Sports*, University of
    Chicago
Sik, G. (1996) *I Think I'll Manage*, Headline
Stride, S. and Bishop, R. (1997) *Stride Inside the Villa*, Sports Projects
Taylor, R. and Ward, A. (1995) *Kicking and Screaming*, Robson
Vuori, I., Fentem, P., Svoboda, B., Patriksson, G., Andreff, W. and
    Weber, W. (1995) *The Significance of Sport for Society*, Council of
    Europe

INDEX